CRITICAL ACCLAIM FOR
The Best Travel Writing Series

"*The Best Travel Writing*: Here are intimate revelations, mind-changing pilgrimages, and body-challenging peregrinations. And there's enough to keep one happily reading until the next edition."
—*San Francisco Chronicle*

"*The Best Travel Writing* is a globetrotter's dream. Some tales are inspiring, some disturbing or disheartening; many sobering. But at the heart of each one lies the most crucial element—a cracking good story told with style, wit, and grace."
—*WorldTrekker*

"There is no danger of tourist brochure writing in this collection. The story subjects themselves are refreshingly odd . . . For any budding writer looking for good models or any experienced writer looking for ideas on where the form can go, *The Best Travel Writing* is an inspiration."
—*Transitions Abroad*

"Travelers' Tales, a publisher which has taken the travel piece back into the public mind as a serious category, has a volume out titled *The Best Travel Writing 2005* which wipes out its best-of competitors completely."
—*The Courier-Gazette*

"*The Best Travelers' Tales 2004* will grace my bedside for years to come. For this volume now formally joins the pantheon: one of a series of good books by good people, valid and valuable for far longer than its authors and editors ever imagined. It is, specifically, an ideal antidote to the gloom with which other writers, and the daily and nightly news, have tried hard to persuade us the world is truly invested. Those other writers are in my view quite wrong in their take on the planet: this book is a vivid and delightful testament to just why the world is in essence a wondrously pleasing place, how its people are an inseparable part of its countless pleasures, and how travel is not so much hard work as wondrous *fun*."
—*Simon Winchester*

THE BEST TRAVEL WRITING

Volume 9

TRUE STORIES
FROM AROUND THE WORLD

THE BEST
TRAVEL WRITING
Volume 9

TRUE STORIES
FROM AROUND THE WORLD

Edited by
JAMES O'REILLY, LARRY HABEGGER,
AND SEAN O'REILLY
INTRODUCTION BY TIM CAHILL

Travelers' Tales
an imprint of Solas House, Inc.
Palo Alto

Travelers' Tales and *Travelers' Tales Guides* are trademarks of
Solas House, Inc.

Credits and copyright notices for the individual articles in this collection
are given starting on page 319.

Art direction: Kimberly Nelson
Cover photograph: © 2012 Ralph Lee Hopkins, Kayakers observe Adélie
Penguins (Pygoscelis adeliae) on iceberg, Weddell Sea, Antarctica
Page layout: Scribe Inc., using the fonts Granjon and Nicholas Cochin
Interior design: Scribe Inc.
Production Director: Natalie Baszile

ISBN 13: 978-160952057-1
ISSN 1548-0224

First Edition
Printed in the United States
10 9 8 7 6 5 4 3 2 1

Discretion rebelled against the folly of my plans, but as usual met a crushing defeat at the hands of curiosity.
—RICHARD HALLIBURTON, *THE ROYAL ROAD TO ROMANCE*

Table of Contents

Publisher's Preface

"Indeed there exists something like a contagion of travel,
and the disease is essentially incurable."
—Ryszard Kapuściński, *Travels with Herodotus*

Ryszard Kapuściński was one of the most remarkable travelers of the twentieth century, a Polish
journalist whose work straddled not only the globe, but
the east-west chasm of the Cold War. While there are those
who question the veracity of some stories told in his books,
he's the kind of traveler I admire most, one with endless
curiosity about place, the people and events swirling about
him, even in the most hellish situations (he covered many a
war and revolution). He doesn't dwell overly on his emotions, just enough to make you know he's not indifferent
to suffering, fear, illness, and loneliness. He finds beauty
in humanity and nature everywhere, but seems perpetually
aware of the shadow a human being—or a mob—can cast
at a moment's notice. But (and this, shall we say, is what
sets apart the enlightened traveler from the dilettante) he is
a hugely informed wanderer, one who reads and questions
constantly, one for whom Herodotus, and history, was a
lifelong inspiration and passion. *Travels with Herodotus* is a
beautiful last literary voyage—Kapuściński died in 2007—
from someone in the same twentieth century league as H.V.
Morton, Chiang Yee, Patrick Leigh Fermor, Wilfred The-
siger, Norman Lewis, Nicolas Bouvier—and the very much

still alive Jan Morris, Jonathan Raban, Paul Theroux, Pico Iyer, and William Dalrymple, to name but a few who never fail to inspire me with their fusion of place, history, and personal experience.

One thing these writer-explorers have in common is that they are big readers: wanderer-scholars with outsize curiosity and the hearts of poets, much like the writers in the book you have in hand. The culture of the wanderer is alive and well, and no doubt you yourself cherish being part of it, inveterate traveler or timid pilgrim, or you wouldn't be reading this. That stranger coming to town, that vector of change and magic, that catalyst of romance and curiosity, might well have been you on a past journey, might well be you on the next.

Why not seek to be the best guest or visitor you can be when you roam, the prepared stranger that Kapuściński endeavored to be? Why not encourage others, young and old, to do the same? Thus when you indulge your travel "disease," your contribution will be all the richer for those who encounter you, and you in turn will be rewarded, for while it has become cliché, it is still true that "chance favors only the prepared mind" (Louis Pasteur).

Choreographer Martha Graham said something that applies to you, the traveler-pilgrim, as much as it does to the dancer and artist:

> There is a vitality, a life force, a quickening that is translated through you into action, and there is only one of you in all time, this expression is unique, and if you block it, it will never exist through any other medium; and be lost. The world will not have it. It is not your business to determine how good it is, nor how it compares with other expression. It is your business to keep it yours clearly and directly, to keep the channel open . . .

You bring something special to the places and people you visit, even if your passage is like morning fog on a lake—so be prepared. Read until your eyes droop, every night. Set aside electronic tethers. Listen to the foreign sounds, study the maps, read strange prayers. Take what you learn with you, but be prepared to abandon it as sawdust when the sun rises over your day far away, and a new world is born.

JAMES O'REILLY
Palo Alto, California

Introduction

It Lives

TIM CAHILL

We live in age in which we are blessed with a plethora of information about destinations of interest; an era of travelers eager to share knowledge and photos and experience. When I started writing about travel, especially to remote and—at the time—little known areas, research took place in a library. Information was often difficult to obtain. My trips were planned in the broadest of outlines. I'd heard rumors, for instance, that the salt mines of the Sahara desert were still operating. Could that be true? The words "salt mine" were the proverbial description of a joyless and exhausting job. Just so.

Travel writers tend to have a network of friends knowledgeable about various areas. Back in the day, you made a few phone calls. Information came from trusted sources. And you took precautions: geez, what if a publishing concern paid you to go find the salt mines and you discovered that they no longer existed. And hadn't for centuries.

Now it is my contention that failure is as good a story as success. Sadly, many editors do not share this perception. So it was always necessary, on these dodgy sorts of stories, to find something else in the area—something known to exist— that might make a good narrative. Well, research suggested that to get to the salt mines, it would be necessary to travel up through Dogon Country. The Dogon are an ethnic group, largely animist, known for their masked dances, which, even years ago, were very often done for tourists.

The journey proceeded apace, and it turned out that the salt mines did, in fact, exist, just as they had since 1000 A.D. Great slabs of salt, mined from the desert floor, were hung off the sides of camels like saddle bags, the clear mineral glittering in the bright desert sun as the long line of camels made its way over the ridges of sand dunes and back to Timbuktu on the Niger River. It was a story.

But I'd already covered my bases and seen a bit of the Dogon. The culture was both impressive and fascinating. One of my traveling companions also impressed me with his eye for the sacred. The Italian gentleman was a longtime desert rat who had searched for the mines before (and failed). He also knew the Dogon and collected some of their masks. It wasn't a business. ("I am very good at buying and very poor at selling.") No, he felt some connection to the people and their beliefs, so when masks were laid out for us to examine and perhaps purchase, he invariably chose the one that was "not for sale." I learned that some of the masks were, in fact, consecrated and used in actual ceremonies. And no, it wasn't a negotiation technique: certain masks were not for sale at any price.

How, I wondered, could my friend pick out the sacred masks every time?

"You can't see it?" he asked me.

"No."

He explained. "It is as if you are looking at a picture of a man. In one picture he is alive. In another, he is dead. You can see that. For me, it is the same with the masks."

In time I believe I could begin to see which masks were alive. When I saw that Life—and knew I'd seen it—something inside me soared.

But I already had an overlong story about the salt mines that included menacing warlords, a would-be kidnapping, and a bad sand storm. It was enough. I never wrote about the

Dogon. But I do have a mask hanging in my office. It was, I was told when I bought it, to have been retired from the dance. It looked alive to me. Still does. I don't always feel its dry desert breath, especially in the mornings when I stumble to my desk with a cup of coffee sloshing in my hand. But sometimes, in odd moments when the work is going well, I feel that sacred mask watching me. I have that feeling now, as I write.

And that is what we have here, in *The Best Travel Writing, Volume 9*. These true stories from around the world are alive, and you may feel their breath in your heart. To the degree they breathe, they are sacred, as all our stories are sacred. Yes, even the ones that make us laugh aloud.

As I've said, information is an invaluable commodity, but to a writer it is only the inanimate raw material that is used to create a living breathing thing. We call that "thing" a story. Stories are the construct we use to organize our thoughts about the world; they are the lenses we use to make sense of the chaos of information that bombards us daily.

Story is the essence of literate travel writing. Bewildering situations arise as a matter of course, and it is story that lends comprehension to the case. Baffled, perhaps bewitched, the writer stumbles onto one key that unlocks the mystery. That key is called the "story."

Story is generous about the forms it embraces. Young writers in most advanced fiction courses will be told that "character is story." So it may be in travel writing. David Farley's impressions of Minsk are a jolting introduction to the character of the city: it's an often inebriated place of ambiguous political opinion and no little sophistication. Peter Wortsman's character study of Vienna is very nearly one of psychoanalysis. Vienna! How appropriate.

In many pieces here, the story is about how decisions were made—or had to be made—in the face of changing circumstance. John Flinn is presented with a life or death decision. John Calderazzo handles the same sort of dilemma in a remarkable story that combines elements of Buddhist thought and history with his own concepts of conservation and mortality. Marcia DeSanctis considers a moral over the course of twenty years.

Colette O'Connor's delicious piece about the sort of underwear favored by French women involves a new personal choice. Tom Miller's short memoir amuses while Erin Byrne's dreamlike meditation on the Celtic poet's soul gives us both a physical and meta-physical way to think about travel.

It's all here, and various stories will appeal to various sensibilities. What is alive and sacred to one reader may not be the story another can hear breathing. But all these writers here have been to the proverbial salt mines. They've dug up raw knowledge and watched it glitter in the unblinking sun. And they've discovered, in a collision of events, that precious arrangement we call story. Like the most sacred of the Dogon masks, a well-told story is animate; a sacred thing that, at its best, can send the soul soaring.

There's a lot of that here. Enjoy.

❧ ❧ ❧

Tim Cahill has been laboring in the salt mines of travel writing for more than forty years. He is the author of nine books and the winner of many awards, including The National Magazine Award and several Lowell Thomas Awards from the Society of American Travel Writers Foundation. The co-author of three IMAX screen plays (two of which were nominated for Academy Awards), Cahill lives in Montana and still travels for a living.

≈ ≈ ≈

The Offer that Refused Me

Business is business.

Once, a man I will call Sam wanted to buy me. Actually, he wanted to purchase my occasional services, on retainer. He proposed securing an apartment for our assignations, which would take place whenever he desired, however rarely or frequently he came to Paris, which is where I was living at the time. In French, they referred to such a place by the word *garçonnière*, which in English meant, roughly, "fuck pad." I could decorate it however I chose, and enlist the services of some Parisian decorator, with whom I could wade through oceans of silk swatches. I tried to imagine an existence that would be parallel and invisible to the one I was leading. In that life, my artist boyfriend and I lived in a dank apartment which was rendered more so by dog-brown wallpaper that the landlord, Monsieur Ballou, would not allow me to steam off. I combed the weekend flea markets for bargains, gathering—candlestick by candlestick, mirror by mirror— the narrative for my future with the man I loved and would marry in six months.

There I was, back in the UAE. On the flight there, the
pilot pointed out the oilfields that burned black, thick, and
everywhere as our plane flew high over Kuwait, a few months
after President George H.W. Bush had declared victory over
Saddam Hussein. I was on my way to the same hotel in the
same country where I had been stationed before the war, but
this time I was not going with an American television network, but as a freelance producer researching a documentary. I had seven days in which to find the right person to
"play"—news-speak for getting someone to agree to participate in a story. Within the first day, my first choice had fallen
through, and shortly after that, my second. All of my journalist friends and colleagues had long since gone home, or
headed for new adventures in Riyadh or Baghdad. I only had
a handful of local contacts, one of whom suggested Sam for
our segment. So I began to pursue him. It became the focus
of the next couple of days and nights: how to get Sam to meet
me so I could bring my request to him personally, to get him
to appear on camera.

For three days, I waited by the phone in my room at the
Hyatt. Order after order of hummus came to my door—laced
with cumin, a stream of dark green olive oil running over the
top. I had grown addicted to it when I had been there during
the war. I missed my friends, how we woke up and hopped
an airplane to Qatar or Dhahran, and came home at the end
of the day, swapped stories and got blissfully hammered by
the rooftop pool. I could not leave the room, so I smoked and
watched CNN. And sat.

At last, the call came in. Sam's assistant had arranged
a meeting. Within an hour, the driver I hired for $25 a day
delivered me to a glass tower which sprang from the desert. I
could see it from a distance, a megalith surrounded by miles
of brown dust. The region would soon transform from primitive backwater to billionaire playpen, but the boom was a
couple of years away yet, and the scattering of Jetson-inspired

skyscrapers that erupted from the landscape looked freakish and random. Inside, the air conditioning was so cold the skin beneath my fingernails turned violet.

Sam was in his late forties, and wore thick glasses and a dishdasha, the long white robe that is the traditional male dress in the region. His office was empty except for a waiter who padded in and out silently, due to his cloth slippers. I fell all over myself thanking him for his service, and he responded with a brisk up-down twitch of the head. Ringing phones tinkled somewhere in the background, so I assumed there was employee life elsewhere on the floor. Sam and I sat across from each other on leather couches with a table between us, in a sprawling space strewn with carpets. Outside, beyond the glass panes, there was only sky and heat—120 degrees worth.

The visit was cordial enough, but Sam barely acknowledged my interview request. I talked, flattered and flattered him some more while the waiter brought more tea and switched up the delectables tray, from which I sampled cakes and dried fruit.

"We would be remiss if you were not included in our piece," I said as I reached for a dried date, and held it between my thumb and forefinger, an inch from my lips. "You are too important for us to do the story without you." I popped the fruit into my mouth.

Sam alternated a nibble of his sugar cube with a sip of tea, and repeated this gesture throughout. At last he thanked me, declared the meeting over, and invited me the following day to his beach club for lunch.

Sam knew how much I needed him for my story, and right then he began to lay out the terms of his deal, the price of poker.

I slipped into the elevator, grinning calmly in spite of the caffeine that made me feel edgy and strange. "You have a bikini?" he asked. My smile melted down my face.

"I do hope you will seriously consider my request," I said.

"I will see you at the beach," he repeated, as the doors shut, cutting him off from my bewildered expression.

The next day I suited up in my room at the Hyatt, deliberately flouting the country's strict laws, which I presumed were neutralized at resorts filled largely with expats. I had packed an old blue bikini, faded from the neighborhood pool in Paris, where I regularly repaired to swim my way—back and forth, lap after lap—out of anxiety about work and money. My sandals had higher heels than were necessary, and I looked in the mirror and saw the unmistakable contrivance, the beauty contest sleaziness of pairing dressy sandals with a bathing suit. It felt like an episode of Charlie's Angels, where Jaclyn Smith attempts to coax a villain with her charms.

Hastily, I fastened my linen shirtdress, and as I did, felt the discomfort of crossing a line, the twin surge of panic and fear one feels when drifting on purpose into a risky neighborhood after dark.

I wore it all to meet Sam—a careful stain of crimson mouth, a dress unbuttoned just enough, and underneath, the abdomen-baring attire he requested. I hoped that he would be pleased enough to agree to an interview. As a freelancer, I could not bear the thought of calling my boss to tell him I'd failed. I needed the seven hundred bucks a week. So if a little degradation could get me hired on another project, I could live with it, as well as the accompanying nausea that was bubbling up inside of me.

Sam did not invite me to join him at lunch, so I sat and read distractedly on the beach, getting more ticked off and disgusted with myself each minute at the progress of this twisted pursuit. The heat was thick, so I dipped into the waveless Persian Gulf waters, and strolled along the white sand. At last, he summoned me to his table and as I approached the patio, I fastened a wrap around my hips.

"We need to fatten you up," Sam said and howled at his joke.

"Then I need to eat," I said firmly. It was day four. "Are you considering doing our story, because if not, I need to find someone else, quickly."

"Of course," he said.

"Of course, what?" I asked.

"Of course I am considering it." He shrugged.

With his right hand, he scraped the corner of a sugar cube on his lower teeth. His left hand held the tea glass.

"Meet me for dinner tonight," he said.

"I have a fiancé," I said.

"Dinner!" he said. "Don't worry. You are not my type. I will pick you up at seven at your hotel."

At dinner that night, Sam got very revved up about lobster. The menu arrived and without opening it, he ordered for me.

"I'm from Boston," I protested. "I only like Maine lobster."

In fact, I did not then or now like lobster.

He held forth grandly. "The best in the world is from Oman. Caught off the island of Masirah. In the South Arabian Sea." I would witness the expression that ensued many times—an attempt at desirable, the rake manque. Poor guy. Poor me. What the hell was I doing?

"No way," I demurred, shaking my head. "Maine lobster or no lobster."

But I dutifully ate his Omani offerings, and ripped off the claws the same way I would at a summer clambake in Gloucester, Massachusetts. The flesh was not white, but deep orange, almost red.

That night, he dropped me off at the hotel and as he did, he said, "You are very sweet. I like you."

"I like you too," I said. I meant it. I hated myself right then, but Sam was pleasant enough company.

"I will do your interview next week. You must arrange it with my office. But you must have another lobster with me tomorrow night."

I kissed him on the cheek. "Thank you," I said. "But I really don't like it."

Sam busted up again at that one, and then spoke. "You will find in life that you end up liking some things that you think you don't like."

"I'm happy you're doing the interview," I said. "I'll have to hire a local stringer, because I have to go back to Paris in a few days." Sam frowned, and I swung my legs out of the car. "G'nite."

Back in my room, I ran a bath and as I began to undress, I heard a knock.

"Miss DeSanctis?" I opened the door to see the concierge, who handed me a bag.

Inside was a square jewelry box. Though I was alone, I instinctively looked around before I opened it. It wasn't exactly a watch; it was more like a cathedral in a box—diamonds, gold, a choir of angels.

I stared at it, no longer hearing the rush of the bathwater, or the chattering anchormen on CNN. And then, with no idea of what else to do, I put it in the room safe with my passport and cash, watching the red lights blink as I shut the door.

The next night, over dinner, Sam was unusually forthcoming. We discussed his country, whose hotels crawled with mercenaries and U.S. government contractors since the war had ended. If there was a wife, she never came up. I told him about my artist fiancé, and the hopes for my career.

"I don't know what to say about your gift," I finally said. "Thank you. It's beautiful."

"Why didn't you wear it?" he asked, grinning broadly. "I am very insulted."

I stumbled through an answer. And then came the proposal.

"I would like to take care of you," he said, in so many words. "You will be available to me, although I am rarely in Paris. It will be mutually beneficial." He knew how to hook me: between the lines, the promise blinked in neon, *Think of your artist*. Moreover, it was a subject that seemed to invite little debate, suggesting that he had made such arrangements before, and for him this was just a simple transaction, a contract that required my signature. Money never came up, but the generosity was implicit.

I lived in Paris, so the concept of "mistress" was hardly taboo; I just never thought it would be me. I will never forget his question when I balked.

"Why ever not?" he asked.

Indeed, why ever not? I wasn't prudish, but I was traditional. Sex usually came with love, or else with unbearably close friendship for one secret night. I had been in love several times, but it was only with my fiancé that the constant need to find the next one seemed to end for good. I was done with dabbling and discovery. I knew I wanted to marry him. And now I was debating a massive betrayal so I could comfortably afford our road ahead? I felt despicable, and I confess, intrigued. The temptation was in the freedom the offer paradoxically represented—an antidote to the difficult path I was already, willingly, on.

My destiny was choosing me, and it was not shaping up to be cushy. Life as a journalist would never be secure and would probably not make me rich. I suspected I lacked both the political will and the steel spine that might be required to soldier up through the ranks to television moguldom. My dream job at the network had fallen through, and in Paris, I was too far from the mother ship to matter. So I took freelance jobs, and had a few loyal friends in New York who hired me regularly. But I wanted to stay in Paris and I was in love with an artist who might never be secure or rich either. I had already seen frequent and undeserved humiliations at his expense. I was not sure I could stomach the vicissitudes of the art market, or bear fickle collectors, rich enough to dare strike bargains with the artists they claimed to support. But giving him up was unthinkable, even though we already seemed perched on a precipice of financial uncertainty. And then, there was our apartment, dank and boggy, filled with greasy cooking fumes from the neighbor who skinned her own rabbits for dinner. Monsieur Ballou stopped by whenever he pleased to remind us of the incredibly low rent he charged which for us, nevertheless, was no bargain.

In short, Sam would make the life I wanted possible; the poverty vow now seemed not even to pertain to me. He did not seem pressed for an answer when he dropped me off after dinner. Because I was slightly flattered, and too stunned to be properly humiliated, I thanked him for his offer. After saying, "Good night" at the hotel entrance, I went upstairs to stare at my watch. I slipped it on my wrist and studied the ungroomed nails on my same old hands, one of whose fingers held my engagement ring that I had worn for all of three months.

The next morning, I ordered a giant breakfast as if I was already on somebody's expense account. Cappuccino, eggs, sliced mango, waffles—sixty dollars worth of food arrived on a tray, complete with a vase of yellow roses. Then, I called the concierge and rented one of the hotel cars. The highway was almost devoid of traffic. With no speed limit, I barely noticed when my black Toyota crossed the border into Oman. The frontier guard was perplexed by my entering his country without reason, so with a menacing wave of his American-made weapon, he sent me back in the same direction I'd come from. I drove aimlessly, accompanied by pirated cassettes I had bought at the souk, the familiar music—Tom Petty, Bonnie Raitt, the Black Crowes—that usually filled up my Paris apartment. I stopped to swim at a wadi I knew from the year before, and sunned myself in the white heat.

My boyfriend, soon to be my husband, would never need to know if I let Sam buy a tiny share of me. And I trusted Sam to keep his side of the bargain: not to interfere, ever, in my life. I tried to imagine lying beneath him on a mattress, wondered what fantasy I would need to conjure up to try to sidestep guilt and shame. I wondered if I would even be able to entertain this plot against my Catholic-girl nature. I was no virgin, of course, but so far, I had never been much of a cheater, either.

After dinner that last night, Sam and I were in his car, and I braved a kiss with him. We were in the parking lot of the hotel. I had drunk too much wine but felt none of the stir-rings shellfish were supposed to induce. I accepted his lips, felt his rough moustache and the strange odor of an unknown mouth. I closed my eyes and attempted to push my brain out of the way. I was aghast from my hope that I might feel some-thing, and even more ashamed at my disappointment that I did not.

I would be boarding a plane home in the morning.

"I'm still considering your offer, Sam," I said. He stroked my hair, pushed it behind my ears. "But I'm pretty sure I can't do it."

"I am an optimistic man but unfortunately, not a very patient one," he said brightly.

Nor—given his excellent mood—did he seem like a heart-broken one.

"I'm so sorry, Sam," I stammered, "I'm so flattered . . ." I grabbed his hands.

"My dear," he said flatly. "Business is business."

I felt no relief, only stung. I had mistaken his attention for attraction. I drew a breath and leaned in to kiss him, flat and square, on his mouth—a consolation prize, an invitation back.

But Sam didn't want me anymore. The deal was off. He had already moved on. Sam would not have let someone he might sleep with once in a while get the best of him. He was a busy man.

We said goodbye, he tousled my hair and we teased each other, probably about crustaceans, Maine vs. Oman, a truly exhausted joke. Inside the hotel, I saw a friend from the war, and we drank Stoli and tonic at the bar, one after the other, squeezing hunks of lime. Chris was a photographer and old Gulf hand, who landed in his old bailiwick to sniff out the next big story. Mercenaries. Terrorists. The construction boom. He would be there if and when it all began to blow. We talked about mutual friends, and the fun we had craning our necks out of airplanes, getting shots of aircraft carriers that cruised the Gulf waters. He had lost his purpose, was desperate for another conflict. After more vodka than I needed, he offered to take me to the airport the next day.

Upstairs, I clambered onto the bed, and lay drunk and still with the lights out, aware of the mildew smell I had encountered too frequently the year before. I slipped under the blankets, and swished my feet to generate some heat. The room was chilly, an enclosed chamber never penetrated by the soft desert air. Beyond my window, there were a few twinkles in the distance—cars, planes, the lights of an adolescent city. Voices passed my room in the corridor, followed by a trace of cigarette smoke that drifted through the crack below my door. Then, I picked up the phone to call my boss to tell him I had struck out. Lame, cowardly, pathetic—whatever I was, I did not have the power to do what was necessary, so I resolved to end the game right then. For a nice girl from suburban Boston, these waters were too deep.

After checking out in the morning, I met my friend for coffee. His red hair was tousled, and I could tell that he had stayed too long at the cocktail lounge.

"I almost fucked a guy for a story," I said.

"Please," he said. "Happens every day."

He shrugged, and I shrugged back. "Anyway, I wasted a whole week."

"Can you stay one more day? I'll find someone for you," he offered.

"Would you?" I said. "God where've you been."

"Sure," he said. "I know the perfect guy. He'll do it in a heartbeat. Are you sure you can't stay?"

"I'm done," I said. "But could you do me a huge favor?" I held forth the bag with the watch inside, along with a sheet of paper with the address of Sam's office tower. I had also enclosed a letter. I asked my friend to lock the package in his room safe, and drop it off when he could.

A week later back in Paris, Sam called.

"Is your artist selling any sculptures?" he asked.

"He is," I replied. "Why don't you buy some?"

"Your friend came by today," he said.

"I'm glad I could trust him with such a treasure," I said.

"It was yours, dear."

"It was very generous of you," I said.

"You were not really my type," he added.

"So you said," I said.

"But you are very sweet," he finished. "And hard working. I will be happy to do your interview, any time. I do mean that. I always keep my word."

"I believe you," I said. "Thank you, though. We've sorted it out."

We had, in fact, found a great character for our film, with no conditions.

"Why did you include your phone number in your little note?" he asked.

"You tell me," I answered.

It got to me, I suppose, that what he desired was not me. He wanted guaranteed sex with a practical New England girl. That's easy to explain, the part of the story I laughed about for a while with my fiancé, now my husband of twenty years. As if I never debated it on the highway to Oman. As if I didn't feel that in this warped scenario, I had somehow failed. I'm thankful that the combination of chemistry and morality swooped in to save me from a certain, regrettable prison. But I wish I'd kept the watch. Right about now, I would sell it.

Marcia DeSanctis is a writer whose work has appeared in many publications, including Vogue, The New York Times Maga-zine, *and* Town & Country.

JOHN CALDERAZZO

❧ ❧ ❧

Rabies

Deep in the mountains of Bhutan, an awakening.

The bite came out of nowhere—came when I was thinking of other things or maybe nothing at all, jet-lagged and exhausted as I was in the thin Himalayan air, chasing my breath at 10,000 feet. Maybe I was distracted by the ranks of snow peaks standing unbelievably high in the north. Or maybe, because it was my first full day in Bhutan, I'd been coaxed into a kind of trance by the sheer unreality of the place, the gorgeous mountain valleys and then this twisting mountain path crowded by giant, dusty-pink rhododendrons. At any rate, I wasn't at all ready for the attack.

A couple of hours earlier, my wife SueEllen and some Colorado friends and I had been talking and laughing as we started up the path, climbing through blue pines to Tiger's Nest monastery. The forest was dripping wet, luxuriant with shadows, tangy with sap. Over the years, I'd seen more than my share of ecological destruction around the world, I'd hiked through too many places that once were, so I felt thrilled to be in a country that had preserved so many of its trees, a fruitful darkness of original forest that covers 70 percent of its land. What other place in Asia—or anywhere on earth—can say that?

As the forest gradually began to thin out, we came to a small tower of whitewashed stones, cemented foursquare over a stream. It was a lovely thing, dappled with sunlight and standing alone, a stupa of some kind, though in travels I'd made through Thailand and the Tibetan plateau I'd never seen one that straddled tumbling water as this one did. When I drew close, I noticed a small wooden ladder designed to let someone peer through a screened window, so of course I climbed it. Inside, in dim, wet light, rumbled a barrel-shaped prayer wheel carved and painted with Sanskrit syllables. It was the kind of wheel I'd often seen monks and pilgrims turning with their hand as they walked clockwise, mumbling or chanting, around and around the outside of a temple.

But this wheel, aside from being hidden away, was mounted on a baffle powered by flowing stream water. This meant that gravity, in concert with the high, melting snows to the north, was the engine that kept everything going. The rumble was deep, and it seemed to me as if the earth itself was praying. I loved the sound of it.

The wheel, I knew, embodied a Buddhist chant of compassion for all living things. Thanks to the push of the water, the mantra was being flung out endlessly into the impermanent world of even Earth's highest mountains. Or maybe especially these mountains, since the Himalayas are also the fastest growing range on the planet.

Beneath the wheel's rumble, I began to make out something else—the tinging of a bell. When I leaned in closer, I saw that the bell was being struck by a stick, or possibly the thin leg bone of a deer, which was attached to the slowly turning wheel.

After a while, SueEllen and the others lost interest and moved on up the trail. I stayed. Closing my eyes, I stood a short distance from the stupa. The sound of the bell above the churning melt-water was beautiful and mesmerizing, the whole world breathing, and soon I was breathing with it. Though I was alone now, I didn't really feel alone, and I began to think about people I knew who needed good thoughts. Acquaintances with cancer. My mother and her years of bone-gnarling arthritis. A recent student staggering under the blackest of depressions. A close friend whose heart was cracking from the kind of forces that tear continents apart.

Why, I wondered, couldn't I slow down more often on my own, back in Colorado, and allow this door to compassion to open a little bit more often? I also wondered why, in some more personal matters—to gain some relief from the routine snarls of job, marriage, politics, not to mention my uncertain place in the grand scheme of things—I needed to travel so far from home to find this kind of solace. If there's something about mountains themselves that encourage calm mindfulness, why couldn't I find it in the Rockies, whose foothills rise, after all, right out of my own back yard?

After a while, I opened my eyes and rejoined the path to the monastery. As I zigzagged up through crumbling rhododendrons, the rice fields of the Paro Valley below me swung into and out of view. In the high, now cloud-hidden north, the snow peaks roared up and out like the expanding edge of the universe. I was sure of this even though I could no longer see them.

And then I felt a strange restlessness begin to drop over me. A sky fever, maybe, or a kind of mountain-peak virus, urging me suddenly to hike faster. This was odd, given how tranquil I had felt just minutes before, and considering my jet-lagged exhaustion. I'd been unable to catch much sleep on the plane to Asia, or nap on the metal benches of the Bangkok airport or even in the hotel the night before in Paro.

So I began to stretch out my legs and swing my arms. Step by springy step, I soon caught up to the others. I passed our cheerful guide, Pema, then SueEllen, who half-smiled and rolled her eyes at me as I shouldered by in a delirium of hurrying up the path.

Maybe I was following some bodily imperative. Six months earlier, on Thanksgiving Day, I'd attempted to summit the ice-bound Mexican volcano Pico de Orizaba, which stood almost a mile higher than most Colorado peaks. To reach that 18,500-foot level, and to keep up with my roped team of decades-younger fellow climbers, I had trained intensely for six months. But it was a joyful kind of intensity, I came to discover, because I grew to love the single-minded physical nature of the challenge, as I turned dozens of laps in a pool or charged miles uphill every other day with forty pounds of rocks in my pack, my body changing by the week. At the same time, I was being pushed by fear and a drive to avoid humiliation, to not hold back the team that was trusting me, the old guy, to stay with them on those 35-and 40-degree snow slopes.

And after an eleven-hour slog, I made it! We made it—the whole team of nine. Many of us cried as we stood on the summit and looked out over 100 miles of countryside, the curve of our beautiful planet actually visible, I could have sworn. I felt I had accomplished one of the best things in my life.

But the feeling didn't last, and after I'd gotten safely home, I found myself suddenly thrown back into my ordinary, domestic, earthbound existence, and much to my distress, my euphoria drained. Within a month or two I felt lost, denatured, diminished by a lack of danger in my life. I grew bored, gained weight, and though my work life of teaching and writing seemed as rich and busy as ever, I kept casting around for new things to do. When I couldn't find them, I felt a gloom settle over me, and I drank more than I should have.

So maybe it was that now, back in mountains and bracing air that made the world feel whole and new, I was making some small attempt, in my sky fever, to recapture that almost erotic thrill.

Within an hour, gasping and far ahead of the others, I broke alone from the forest into sunlight and tremendous views, into gigantic vaults of air, a world of sheer cliffs and abysses. It was like an ancient Chinese poem come to life. Thin waterfalls dropped a thousand feet or more, and narrow steps carved into the cracked, almost vertical rock walls forced me to slow down. To grow dizzy here might be to slip and die.

From a cliff wall opposite hung our destination, Tiger's Nest monastery, unreal and beautiful.

Its golden-roofed temples, I'd read, celebrated a monk who found his breath and a measure of peace by meditating for three months in a cave. Then he flew up here on the back of his consort, a female tiger, to conquer a local demon. He's credited with having brought Buddhism to Bhutan.

SueEllen and the others were far behind. After another half-hour of up and down walking, sometimes hugging the mossy cliff walls where no handrails were present, I approached the outskirts of the temple complex. Just off the path was a hut where monks had hung newly-washed robes the color of blood. Because I was so tired, or because my head was swirling with stories of magic tigers, or because the views were so spectacular, I paid little mind to a dog lying on a mat in front of the hut. Up close, he looked thick-bodied but drowsy, tired, arthritic, old.

I thought I might peek around the back of the hut to catch a glimpse of monkish life. Living in the cold shadows of these mountains, at this altitude, could not be easy. But when I left the path and tried to sidestep past the dog, he lunged up at me with no sound at all. Just like that, he was standing on his hind legs right in front of me, pitching forward, his front paws flailing for balance, and then he clamped his jaws down—hard—on my upraised forearm.

Time went a little bit crazy. Probably, his vice grip lasted no longer than a second or two before he let go and dropped back down again into a simulation of sleep. Then he sighed, as though nothing more remarkable than life itself had tried to slip by him in its cloud of want.

I didn't feel any pain at first. I wasn't even sure what had happened.

When I re-gathered my wits and pushed up the sleeves of my shirt and fleece top, I saw that the skin on my forearm, though reddening slightly, looked unbroken. I examined it a pore at a time, my heart pounding. Soon enough, my friends, having seen what happened from a distance, caught up and helped me check further. No skin breaks. A miracle!

But then I noticed a throbbing on my left side. So I rolled up my clothes, and somebody said, slowly, "Oh, my." Bite or probably claw marks were already pooling red. Could a microbe of saliva, transferred from mouth to paw, have somehow traveled through my clothes?

Damn, damn, damn!

But maybe they were just pressure wounds. SueEllen helped me look for tear or puncture marks in my clothes. "Listen," she said finally. "Nothing got through. You're fine."

Easy for you to say, I thought, not very generously. Because really, who could say for sure?

I'm usually a calm and undramatic person, especially when I'm outdoors. But I was aware now that my logical mind had morphed into one of the clouds drifting about these airy heights—insubstantial and easily torn. My chest grew tight, and I noticed that my breathing had become shallow, high up in my lungs. Several times I tried to concentrate on the far-off snow peaks hidden in the clouds, but a roar I kept hearing made me think of blood rushing to my head—and rabies.

I did know that the rabies virus, if not killed off by shots taken within days, can migrate undetected through the bloodstream to the brain, and then, weeks or months later, can snarl up suddenly, sparking a strange agitation. After the agitation come seizures, a coma, and certain death. I also knew, after I riffled through my guidebook as my friends looked on, that rabies is endemic in Bhutan. But getting shots would mean flying all the way back to Thailand—now—meaning my expensive trip would be over before it had really started. It was that or take my chances.

While SueEllen daubed my wounds, my friends seemed to be studying me gravely. I had the feeling that they were already practicing their goodbyes, even as they reveled in their own good fortune. That's what my voice of panic was whispering to me, even as I realized that I was beating up myself with worry.

Then a monk was at my side, hand on my shoulder, telling me through Pema's translation that he'd never seen this dog act sick. Still, he promised to observe it for a week. He dug into his robes and pulled out . . . a cell phone! As Pema jotted down his number, I wanted to laugh, but couldn't: I was deep in these mountains, deep in demons, and though the eyes of this man, who looked about my age, were very kind, I could feel my blood pushing on through my veins, and I had no tiger to fly me home.

In other words, I was already suffering from rabies of a spiritual kind.

"Alone," I said softly, to everyone. "I'd like to sit alone for a while, if you don't mind."

So I moved a little bit away from the group and sat very still on a boulder, the hut and the golden-roofed temples behind me. I tried to calm myself by looking off across the heights at the gigantic, cracked-rock walls and the tracery of the carved steps below, which looked insubstantial now in the distance.

After a while, I found myself staring at a slender cascade hundreds of yards away that was breaking in mid-air into mist. God, it was pretty. With my binoculars, I watched drops of moisture spin free for a few moments in solitary glory, turning into private diamonds of sunlight in their brief, falling life, or at least this particular life. Then, down among the boulders at the cliff bottom, the drops rejoined the others, losing their individual natures in the ongoing crush and foam of creek water.

This was my life, too, I suddenly realized. This mist, unlocked and blazing with light, floating so briefly between the before and after of tumbling stream-water . . .

I looked down several thousand feet at the green, unbroken forest hiding the world I'd hiked up from. All those braided roots and branches and treetops, and streams gurgling through.

Compassion for all living things, I remembered, includes the self.

The self—myself, me.

I think it was then that I felt my shoulders begin to relax. My chest un-tightened. I closed my eyes, took in ordinary air, and began to breathe in rhythm with the distant, faint tinging of a bell.

≈≈ ≈≈ ≈≈

John Calderazzo teaches creative writing at Colorado State University, where he has won a Best CSU Teacher and other awards. His essays, poems, and short stories have appeared in Audubon, Georgia Review, Los Angeles Review, Orion, North American Review, Writer's Digest, *and many other journals and anthologies. His writing awards include The Carolina Quarterly fiction prize and a Colorado Arts Council Literary Fellowship. His books include* Writing from Scratch: Freelancing, 101 Questions about Volcanoes (for children), *and* Rising Fire: Volcanoes & Our Inner Lives, *a collection of essays about volcanoes and culture. He recently finished a book of poems,* At the Night Window. *He is also co-founder of an innovative climate change initiative that you can see at www .changingclimates.colostate.edu.*

❧ ❧ ❧

Vanishing Vienna

"There was a third man . . . I didn't see his face."
—Graham Greene

When last I visited Vienna the natives were busy launching a hot air balloon to combat nuclear arms. The mood was very gay, very *gemütlich*, very Viennese. Three portly aerialists were to rise in a wicker basket, proclaiming world peace. Actually only one was portly with a long beard and wild curly locks that took up additional space; his companions, a man and a woman, both blond, trim, and elegantly outfitted in a blue and a red jump suit respectively, though colorful, were subsumed by the ballast of his being, fluttering like scarves round his neck.

Trouble was the ton of multi-colored nylon refused to fill. Undaunted by the resistance of the material and cheered on by the crowd, the three took turns climbing out of the basket to blast flames from the mouth of a compact mechanical dragon into the massive bladder on the lawn. And when at last the slumbering giant stirred, a score of sympathizers had to hold it down long enough for the fat man and his friends to clamber aboard, deliver a few fitting words on disarmament, smash a champagne bottle, and soar into the firmament waving, disappearing through a gap in the clouds.

Baroque by temperament, restrained by Catholic creed, Vienna's personality—if a city can be said to have one—is curiously split between a compulsive exhibitionism and an equally powerful bent toward concealment.

Take the proper gentleman I spotted in a pedestrian underpass, peering intently at the ground, peeking up every now and then to meet the eye of a passerby to test the effect of his attire, or lack thereof—his clothing folded neatly in a heap beside him, he wore nothing but a pair of orange briefs and black nylon hose, and no one seemed to bat a lash. It may well be that people simply didn't see him, that by standing perfectly still, not imposing his presence but silently posing, this latter day Albrecht Dürer in drag could flash for a selected audience without overstepping the threshold of respectability. In a civic sense, he succeeded in becoming invisible. Or perhaps like President Waldheim, he wore his emperor's new clothes well. The Viennese have a keen sense of propriety combined with a wondrous talent for overlooking extraneous details, a talent that they put to good use a few decades ago when sudden disappearances were all the rage.

Vienna is a city from which people seem to be forever fleeing.

My father, for instance, did it in the sidecar of a motorcycle huddling to hide his prominent nose and other suspect features.

My uncle left disguised as a child prodigy due to debut in London pictured in the passport of an accommodating friend.

An aunt of mine married an Egyptian and reenacted Exodus in reverse.

Cousins twice removed shipped off to Shanghai, Uruguay, New Guinea, and other picturesque places.

And my paternal grandfather, a respected engineer who had a hand in the construction or repair—I'm not sure which—of the *Riesenrad*, the colossal Ferris wheel (slow spinning insignia of Viennese escapism), and who proudly served his Kaiser as an officer in World War I, left his war medals on prominent display lined up atop his commode with a note: "You know where you can put these!" the day he stripped and swam across the river to Czechoslovakia.

Escape is still a popular pastime in Vienna today.

Consider the conversation I had with an attractive young woman at a cocktail party.

"What do you do?" I asked.

"Oh nothing really, nothing at all," she smiled a strangely absent smile, "I'm married, you see." Which response would have perfectly sufficed anywhere else, but being Viennese, she felt the need to elaborate. "When I was a child," she said, "my mother took me away on a vacation, I can't remember where. And I liked it so much I decided that that was all I ever wanted to do, to be on a permanent vacation."

Restraint skewed the same tendency in another young woman, turning her escape hatch inwards.

She was seated stiffly erect a few rows in front of me on the No. 71 Streetcar to the Central Cemetery, a novice nun in stern black habit without the slightest worldly allure. I was on my way to visit my deceased grandmother, the only member of the family who still maintains a local address. I looked up to check for my stop and a stray hair caught my eye, a chestnut brown strand that broke out of the prison of the young nun's hood fluttering in the wind of a half open window, sparkling in the Sunday morning sunlight. There was something so seductive about that one wild hair dancing about lewdly in contrast to the sobriety of the cloth that I felt a sudden overwhelming desire to see her face.

Eagerly I pushed my way forward through the crowd, convinced that I was about to discover a rare bird whose plumage the common world had never noticed. All else was a blur to me except for that single hair and the mystery it betokened.

And when at last I arrived at my destination and turned to look, she turned her face away.

Did she sense that someone was watching her? Did her piety compel her to try to hide?

The sunlight served me well, and in the streaked reflection in the glass I saw it—Dear God!—a horseshoe of repressed passion nailed to her brow, clutching in its vice grip any flicker of illicit feeling, any crude diversion from the sacred path.

Though I admit I am a mere novice escape artist, hardly a Houdini, still my experience may, nevertheless, shed light on the general phenomenon. Is Vienna's elusive heritage not buried in my heart?

I was standing waiting for a tram at the southeast edge of the *Burggarten*, on the *Ringstrasse* (Vienna's grand boulevard), a corner dominated by the seated statue of the poet Goethe exhibiting himself with magisterial disdain, his bronze impassive gaze oblivious to the petty concerns of the slaves of time.

(I had passed him once before, my mind on other matters ostensibly gathering material for a play, noticing nothing but the pigeons perched on his tarnished head. Thus I was somewhat surprised, to say the least, to be roused in my sleep by the hotel telephone and to find that it was Goethe on the line, the monument not the man—I'm quite sure of this, since the voice had a hollow metallic tone common to statues and operators and the operator had no cause to call me. The poet introduced himself, said he'd known my mother as a young woman, and might he be of some assistance to her son? It was true, my mother had adored him, having taken all his words to heart, many of which she could recall on cue and recite with little prompting; she had carried his collected works with her into exile from Vienna to London to New York.)

Standing face to face with her idol, I smiled at the comedy of dreams, and a curious thing happened.

There was a certain woman I had been avoiding, a painter pushing sixty who clung desperately to the images of her

unhappy youth. We had met at her opening: macabre charcoal sketches, shrunken faces with bulging eyes, not very
cheery stuff. We got to talking. I reminded her, she said, of
a boy she'd known in Budapest before the War who'd disappeared in a transport. Would I, she asked, pose for a pietà in
his memory in the buff? Politely, firmly, repelled by the idea,
I declined, but the painter kept calling to press me to change
my mind until finally I changed my number.

I spotted her now on the *Ringstrasse* advancing toward me
from the opera among the matinée mob. She hadn't yet seen
me but the angle of her gaze was set such that it was bound to
meet mine in a matter of seconds.

No streetcar in sight, no kiosk to duck behind, no news-
paper to cover my face. I wanted to run but my feet froze
beneath me. I wanted to turn my head away but the muscles
in my neck tightened, locking my chin in place.

No way to deflect the inevitable.

And then it happened. The poet came to my rescue by
sheer example.

Unable to escape, I had no other recourse but to stand my
ground and become a statue. Every joint and muscle in my
body stiffened, the blood congealed in my veins and for an
instant, the time it took her to pass, I am convinced that my
heart stopped beating. And I became an effigy of myself, as
still and invisible as a monument and vanished in contemporary disregard.

Other family members have found themselves immortal-
ized in like manner. I think of the salt pillars of the Bible, how
seeing too much can turn a body to stone.

"What do you think of it?" a woman asked my opinion
of the memorial to the victims of the War recently erected
on a prominent site just behind the opera. Its centerpiece is
a bearded old man on hands and knees obliged to scrub the
sidewalk (a posture adopted by my maternal great uncle
shortly before his disappearance). "It's a shame!" the woman

said, not waiting for my response. "What's done is done," she shook her head, "and such things happened, of course. Put up a monument if you must, but must you put it *here*? Why not put it someplace else where it's less visible?"

Monuments capture the nostalgic spirit of the city. The Viennese have learned to transcend the flux of time by simply standing still and looking backwards.

Stalwart ancients pose in imitation of their beloved emperor Franz Joseph, sporting his famous white mutton chop whiskers.

Indomitable widows permanently occupy streetcar positions clutching their precious poodles in the seat beside them: snarling blinders, bulwarks against age.

Even Viennese punks have something static, ever so faintly *Fin de Siècle* about them, as if the leather of their impeccably tattered jackets came from an ancestor's recycled Lederhosen and their safety pin earrings were filched from an aging dowager's pincushion.

Everyone, young and old, hovers in a somnambulist trance, like photographs escaped from an album.

The effect can be unsettling.

A sleeping beauty perfectly preserved in her century long repose, Vienna waits for prince charming to come and wake her, only the prince is long since dead, the monarchy itself has fallen, the beloved emperor with his mutton chop whiskers has been replaced by a scowling corporal with a toothbrush mustache and, thereafter, by clean shaven civilians given to selective memory loss, while beauty lies resplendent, a silent movie queen in her outmoded finery, oblivious to time, puckering her lips in anticipation of a kiss.

How rude it would be to wake her!

I was just getting settled in a new apartment (a cold water flat in a pre-War building). Having not as yet had any guests, I did not know the sound of my doorbell.

And so it was that I awoke one night in near total darkness to a persistent ringing and reached automatically for my alarm clock. The glowing hour hand pointed to a phosphorescent number three, but the clock itself was silent. Must be the church bells, I thought, and pressed the pillow over my ears—Vienna has almost as many sanctuaries per square inch as Rome. Then I became aware of a pounding at my door and a muffled command: "*Aufmachen! Polizei!*"

Adrenal terror flooded my veins. I threw off the blanket, jumped into my pants and shuffled barefoot to the door, trembling with historical recall.

"Open up! We know you're home!"

I did as I was told.

My visitors, two faceless men in trench coats, did not wait to be invited in.

The one inspected my belongings, the clothes and books I hadn't yet gotten around to unpacking. The other approached my table that doubled as a desk, sat himself down and examined the scattered pages of a work in progress. Then he rolled a sheet of clean white bond into my Olivetti portable and typed as he talked.

"Name?"

"Peter W."

"Nationality?"

"American."

"Occupation?"

"Writer." I shivered, feeling naked without a pen in hand and minus my shirt and shoes.

"Now then, Peter W," he inquired, "where is Peter R?"

"Don't know," I said, "I just sublet the place from him, I've never met him."

"Where do you send your rent check?"

"To a numbered bank account."

"A curious coincidence, wouldn't you say, that you and he should share the same first name!?"

"A coincidence, yes. Peter is a popular name."

"It seems," said the man at my typewriter, "that Peter R has disappeared."

A silent pause.

"What are you doing in Vienna, Mr. W?"

"Researching a play."

"What kind of play?"

"An hysterical—uh, historical play."

"Let me give you a word of advice," he said, fingering my manuscript pages.

I listened intently, curling my icy toes. Every writer dreads the verdict of critics.

"Never" he said, "mix fact and fiction!"

I nodded, wondering if anyone will believe that this really happened.

"That will be all," he said, tearing the sheet out of my typewriter, rising from my chair, waving his colleague to the door. "We wish you a pleasant stay in Vienna!"

It was just a mistake, I later learned, an administrative mix-up at the local precinct. Still, word of my nocturnal visitors spread. The widow next door, whom I had often helped with her groceries, refused to talk to me after that. The super and his wife, whom I'd tipped well at Christmas, likewise shunned me. My entrances and exits were henceforth accompanied by a chorus of creaking doors pulled open and slammed shut. My actual departure several months later must have seemed redundant to my neighbors for whom I had in any case long since ceased to exist.

≈ ≈ ≈

Peter Wortsman's restless musings have appeared in The New York Times, Los Angeles Times, *the* Boston Globe, *the* Washington Post, *the German newspapers* The Atlantic Times, Die Welt, and Die Zeit, *and the popular website* World

Hum, *among other print and electronic outlets, and in the last five volumes of* The Best Travel Writing. *He is the author of a book of short fiction*, A Modern Way to Die; *two plays,* The Tattooed Man Tells All, *and* Burning Words; *and the travelogue/memoir* Ghost Dance in Berlin: A Rhapsody in Gray, Travelers' Tales. *His numerous translations from the German (a verbal form of border crossing) include the German travel classic* Travel Pictures, *by Heinrich Heine*; Tales of the German Imagination, *from* The Brothers Grim *to* Ingeborg Bachmann, *and* Selected Tales of the Brothers Grim.

BRUCE BERGER

≈ ≈ ≈

Mysterious Fast Mumble

The search for the Tower of Babel leads
unexpectedly to Baja California.

A plunge into Spanish at its worst proved, in retrospect, an odd stroke of luck. The year was 1965 and I arrived in Spain ignorant of the language, though fluent in French from six years of study. It was the beginning of Generalísimo Franco's last decade as dictator as well as the beginning of an adulthood I didn't know what to do with, and while passing through Andalucia I wound up taking a job as a nightclub pianist. One gig led to another, I moved in with the drummer of a band I played with and, in a glorious cacophony, I was swamped by new sounds.

One wouldn't choose to learn Spanish from Andalusians any more than one would choose to learn English from Cockneys, Mississippians or Valley Girls. Though Spanish is spoken from the front of the mouth, Andalusians speak it half-gutterally from the back of the throat. They don't pronounce the endings of most words, their singulars and plurals sound alike, their *l*'s sometimes come out like *r*'s, and they spray these sounds as if from an AK-47. To make sense of what I was hearing, I bought the only grammar book in all of Cádiz, a second-year primer for English speakers. I don't know what I missed in year one, for the book had the basics I needed, including the declensions of the infamous Spanish verb. I studied and talked, trying to correlate the two, often visualizing the spelling of the words my friends didn't finish. French only helped by freeing me from English word order. When Andalusians eventually told me I spoke "better" than they did, I didn't take it for a compliment, for I knew what they meant: I pronounced words entire because I imagined them in print, and I was structurally incapable of speaking simultaneously from the front of my mouth and the back of my throat. I spoke "correct" Spanish because it was so much easier than Andalusian, whose distortions I would never master.

In my failure to sound like my friends, what I didn't appreciate was that three years of immersion in Andalucia paid off, for it enabled me to penetrate the language in its wildest distortions. Andalusian was not a dialect, merely a regional variant, and I couldn't—and still can't—make sense of such actual dialects as Galician and Catalán. On the other hand, through similarities among Romance languages, I am able to hold conversations with speakers of Italian and Portuguese as long as they, minding the gap, speak clearly and correctly— just as they can grasp my all-purpose Castillian. This linguistic baggage was put to the test when I left Spain in 1967 and made my first trip to Baja California, my verbal first step in Mexico, the following year.

Anxiety vanished with the first exchanges, for the speech was quite comprehensible. There was no *th* lisp on the *z*'s and soft *c*'s but the sounds were otherwise familiar, and the unexpected difference was in the vocabulary. Eyeglasses were *lentes*, not *gafas*; luggage racks were *parrillas*, not *bacas*—changes learned one at a time, easy to incorporate. The shocker was to be told to stop saying *coger*. I couldn't understand it. *Coger* simply meant "to take" or "to hold", and it was used in dozens of expressions—to turn right or left, to find someone at home, to catch a cold: it was one of the commonest, most nondescript and useful connectors in the language. But it turned out that in Mexico it meant only one thing. It meant fuck. It was not semi-respectable, like copulate; it was the f-word itself. So built was *coger* into my every second sentence that I had to learn dozens of dodges, a different substitute for each occasion. I told people that Mexican Spanish was in-*coger*-ent, pronouncing it "incoherent" while rolling the *r*, but no one in either language ever got it.

As I spent more time in Baja California Sur, making a social transition from American travel companions to local friends, I found there was a regional speech called *choyero*, after cholla, the most common and annoying local cactus, also spelled *choya*. Unlike the engulfing verbal universe that was Andalusian, *choyero* was a set of slang words and country pronunciations made fun of in the city: *muncho* for *mucho*, *noshi* for *noche*, *'orrasho* for *borracho* (a drunken slurring of "drunk"). After a couple of decades of exploring the state, traveling into the mountains by burro and mule, skimming the coasts with fishermen, socializing with various strata in La Paz, I thought that I had experienced the verbal gamut. It wasn't until 1990, twenty-two years after I had first set foot in the peninsula, that I started spending time in a mountain range called La Giganta, and there I heard something new.

I was attracted to La Giganta because it contained the peninsula's last unroaded coast, over one hundred kilometers of soaring volcanics, secret recesses, isolated fishing communities and sporadic oases, a stronghold that fended off vehicles with an escarpment that fell, in many stretches, straight from the sky to the sea. Behind the continuous eight hundred meter cliff were isolated drainages peopled by a scattering of ranches accessible from the interior by an hour of careening on crumbling back roads. It was in La Giganta that I became

friends with a rancher I called by his nickname, Lico, and I
spent increasing time in a pair of ranches founded by his family, one on the coast and one up top, beyond the escarpment.
Life led Lico from one ranch to the other, and at the ranch of
the moment I got to know his extended family and, up top,
his neighbors. Because these were working operations with
nonstop chores, I was not a guest to be entertained but a com-
panion and observer of what would have been the same without me. When the word "embedded" was used for reporters
who lived with the troops in Iraq, it occurred to me that I was
embedded with La Giganta ranchers.

What I heard were two kinds of speech, one of them
ordinary *choyero*. The other, delivered only at close range,
was nasal, higher in pitch, nearly lacking in consonants, and
might be described as a "fast mumble." I was, to be sure,
never addressed in this manner myself, but others spoke it
freely around me, at mealtime, around the campfire, when
they crossed paths at close quarters. When Lico and I took off
to visit other ranches, or to camp and explore in La Giganta,
I noticed that people who knew each other well sometimes
spoke in this manner, while those in the area who presum-
ably knew both manners of speech but were meeting for the
first time addressed each other in *choyero*. Vertical terrain cut
off contact by cellphone, but when Lico called accessible relatives from my apartment during visits to La Paz, he stuck to
choyero because of the cellphoner's incessant need to *project*.

I had thought that an ear trained to penetrate Spanish at its
most twisted, flexible enough to pry meaning out of other languages, would not be balked by a variant in a pocket between
La Paz and Loreto, but such was not the case. I let the sounds
flood the whorls of my inner ear, wielded my Andalusian
chops—and did, in fact, pick up occasional Spanish words
and even topics of conversation, if not what was actually being
said. As an experiment, when I felt that I understood enough

to suggest that they were discussing, say, where the cattle had wandered, I would remark in an equally soft voice that I had seen three cows in arroyo San Felipe—mainly to see if it startled anyone that I had caught the thread. Such interjections, no doubt irrelevant, were ignored. Year after year I fought for purchase, my ears on point, but never made headway. None of my outside friends were familiar with the area, and I didn't ask Lico himself about it so as not to seem intrusive, or make him self-conscious about how he spoke, or scare his family off from speaking normally in my presence.

I hardly expected so remote a mystery to turn a corner in my hometown of Aspen, Colorado, but it was there, during dinner with physicist Murray Gell-Mann, that a new factor surfaced. Known to the outside world for quark theory, Murray is also a virtuoso linguist fluent in some three dozen languages, with knowledge of scores more. Having traveled with him in mainland Mexico and Spain, I can vouch for the perfection of his Spanish, though he modestly says his French is better. What most bonds us, I think, is a mutual obsession with words, for analyzing our words as we communicate with them, for speculating about others, and most of all for playing with them without shame in the process. When I told him that Mexican Spanish was in-*coger*-ent, he instantly issued its overdue laugh. In Baja California he had only been as far south as Guerrero Negro, but even about the town's name he had a theory. "It is well known that Guerrero Negro is the translation of an American boat shipwrecked there, named *Black Warrior*. My own belief is that the boat was built in Tuscaloosa, for Tuscaloosa is Choctaw for 'black warrior.' The name 'Guerrero Negro' has its ultimate origin in Choctaw."

"Tuscaloosa is pretty far inland for boat-building," I said, "and that theory strikes me as naval gazing. But there *is* a curious phenomenon further south." I described, in full, the phenomenon in La Giganta.

"Well," stated Murray, leaning back in pre-lecture mode, forgetting about food. "There were three indigenous languages in the southern part of Baja California. Pericú and Guaycura were independent languages, not much is known about them, and they're gone. But the northernmost language, Cochimí, was part of the Yuman family of languages, some of which are still spoken in southern Arizona and California. If Cochimí was cut off for centuries and perhaps millenia from its Yuman origins, it would have gone its own way, but if enough of its words survive, linguists might be able to trace the degree of transformation from Yuman that remained in Arizona. Rate of change is a measure of when speakers of a language separated, and if Cochimí's degree of change from other Yuman languages can be established, it might be possible to fix an approximate date for the Cochimí migration to Baja Califonria. Since the speech you're talking about is between Loreto and La Paz, any words that survived would have been Cochimí."

I had no further information of my own to supply. Murray resumed eating and the conversation changed course, but I left the meal with my mind racing. Was I unable to penetrate the fast mumble because it was laced with Cochimí? Was there enough language left that linguists could determine when the Cochimí migrated to the peninsula, speaking a branch of Yuman that would have evolved at a rate measurable by linguists? The area of Cochimí speakers coincided with that of the great cave paintings, whose makers remained unknown. If it could be determined linguistically that the Cochimí arrived as far back as the first images, could it be determined that the Cochimí, in fact, were the mysterious painters? Soon after dinner with Murray I encountered an article on the lost indigenous languages of Baja California, authored by a team of linguists and posted on a La Paz website, which mentioned as a long-established fact that Cochimí indeed belonged to the

Yuman family of languages. Murray might have been wing-
ing it about Choctaw, but about the origins of Cochimí in
Yuman he was on solid ground.

In March of 2009 I was asked by a La Paz environmental
organization of which I was a board member, Niparajá, to co-
author a book with photos on La Giganta and its contiguous
mountain range to the north, Sierra Guadalupe, with the goal
of promoting biosphere reserve status for the whole cordillera.
Such a designation would complement existing biospheres El
Vizcaíno to the north and Sierra de la Laguna to the south,
extending protective measures to the state's volcanic spine.
I quickly agreed. The integrity of ranching culture was central
to the plan, and I realized the moment had arrived to bring its
speech anomaly to public attention. As part of its ranching
tradition, La Giganta boasted a linguistic phenomenon that
deserved preservation—and study. The book itself would
draw attention to the speech, and because the supervising
structure of biosphere reserves attracts grant money, somewhere down the line a linguist might actually be dispatched
to check into it.

I also realized that what I had to go on—personal observation, inability to understand, stray facts and speculation—were
less than the basis I needed to introduce a new phenomenon
to print. I needed someone with academic discipline who
might have encountered this enigma. A name leapt into my
mind: Fermín Reygadas. An anthropology professor from
the Autonomous University of Baja California Sur, Fermín
had explored the state by vehicle, foot, mule, archeological
dig and ties to living ranches, and I was sure that his apti-
tudes included speech. I had known him socially for years,
had interviewed him formally for a previous book, set up the
interview and punched the tape recorder.

I told Fermín that I had heard an alternate form of speech
in La Giganta and asked if he had encountered it. "I know

exactly what you're talking about," he declared, and as he began, I realized I didn't need to ask questions, only to listen.

When Fermín first visited La Giganta with a colleague, who was also from Mexico City, they made a list of one hundred-fifty words they did not know. There were areas of usage. When ranchers spoke of cars they used contemporary Spanish, and when they spoke of cattle, pack animals or plants they employed a vocabulary out of use elsewhere. Fermín and his friend began to investigate these words, found them to be indeed legitimately Spanish, but to represent a seventeenth century vocabulary long superseded in the rest of the peninsula. The Giganta, communities, isolated from such new influences such as mining to the south and north, spoke a language still frozen in the seventeenth century, which is to say, the language of the artisans and growers of crops that the padres recruited from the mainland, principally from Sonora.

There was indeed another influence, but it was from the area itself, for many of the bachelors from Sonora married Indian women, and the children grew up speaking with their mothers as well as their fathers. Fermín and his associate didn't identify actual Cochimí words, but the nasal sound of the alternate speech could well derive from inflections of the aboriginal tongue. "It sounds like this," said Fermín, and he suddenly abandoned his professorial bass for a nasal whine in which he squealed "*Nyeh nyeh nyeh nyeh!*" Was he demonstrating or lampooning? After multiple replayings of the tape I couldn't decide, or help laughing.

Two well-studied sources offered remnants of the lost languages of Baja California Sur, he continued. The journals of the missionary padres, above all those of the Jesuits glutted with free time after their expulsion from the Americas in 1767, were full of linguistic information about the tribes they tried to convert to Christianity. Further clues lay in La Giganta's toponyms, its place names. In the Sierra de la Laguna, for

instance, there were only a half-dozen toponyms that derived
from Pericú, and everything else was named for saints. In La
Giganta, by contrast, there were literally hundreds of place
names that derived from Cochimí, providing further data for
linguists. Through anthropological studies, the meanings of
some of those names could be determined—whether a loca-
tion was a canyon, a hill or a plain; the presence or absence
of water; the abundance of animals to hunt. Some of these
words could be correlated with versions in the records kept
by the padres, and all the language that had been converted
to European spelling and survived in written form had been
studied in minute detail. But since the twenty-year-old collection of antique words by Fermín and his colleague, study of
living speech in areas formerly occupied by the Cochimí had
been zero.

Now that I was researching a book instead of just being
nosy, I felt secure about asking Lico himself about what he
was speaking. They had two forms of speech, one of which I
couldn't understand, and I proceeded to describe my impression of it. Lico rushed to assure me that there was no wish to
exclude. It was only a kind of shorthand they used for talking
about practical matters on the ranch.

I reassured him that I hadn't been offended but was just
curious. I had been in ranches all over the state and had heard
that sound only in La Giganta. Now that I was writing about
the area, I felt I should account for it. I had interviewed a professor from the University of La Paz about it and had the tape
with me. Did he want to hear it?

We opened beers and Fermín held forth on the dining table
with a view toward the enclosing peaks. I paid close attention
to Lico's face when Fermín reached his *nyeh nyeh nyeh nyeh*.
This, I thought, might finally offend, but Lico listened with
no change of expression. Lico had little to say about Fermín's
discourse, finding it an elaboration of what I had already said.

I raised the possibility that there might be Cochimí words mixed with the Spanish. No, there were no Indian words, said Lico, just Spanish spoken another way.

Fermín and associate had found Spanish but no Cochimí, and Lico denied any non-Spanish words, but for me the case wasn't quite closed. In La Giganta, any word that survived nine generations since mestizo children grew up talking Spanish with their fathers and Cochimí with their mothers would have gained a fully Spanish pronunciation and been assimilated into the language. In English, for instance, we routinely refer to coyotes and chocolate, staples of English vocabulary, unaware that both terms derive from Nahuatl, which descends from Aztec. The same process would have transformed Cochimí originals into local *choyero*. Fermín and friend, widely knowledgeable and focused in the detail, were not finally linguists schooled in the permutations of Yuman. It was conceivable, desirable—and unlikely—that a Yuman specialist would venture into La Giganta for field work, but even a linguist with more general training might collect words that couldn't be accounted for in Spanish and send them to a Yuman specialist, wherever he or she be.

Before the book introducing the fast mumble to the public was published, a biologist friend to whom I had described the phenomenon sent me an emergency e-mail: a young man who was leaving the next day to pursue a doctorate in linguistics in Mexico City, and who would be gone for two years, could meet me that very afternoon for coffee. My friend thought it important that the doctoral candidate arrive in the capital aware that there was a local linguistic anomaly to be accounted for. I sped to the internet café.

In his early twenties, the student was intelligent and personable. My friend accompanied us for an hour, then left us for another hour to ourselves. The young man was passionate about words, and had taped *choyeros* discussing the topics of their choice so he could collect and compare accents. He had never visited the area of the fast mumble or heard of its existence, but he found it fascinating. I told him it wasn't speech they used with strangers, but I would be glad to introduce him to my friends, and once they were used to his presence he would hear all the mumbling he liked. He replied that the doctoral program required two years of book and class study before he could do field work, but his ultimate plan was to return to Baja California Sur and become one of its few resident linguists. The fast mumble would itself vary from place to place, he said, so he would need to study it across its range. As an unstudied phenomenon it might even be a possibility for a doctoral thesis, though it was far too early to tell. A turn of conversation revealed that we were both pianists dedicated to Chopin, which gave me new confidence in his ear. I left the conversation elated that a seed had been planted, however long it would take—if it did—to fructify.

As for my own inability to penetrate the fast mumble, I realized that its inclusion of 150 Spanish words so old they were new to Fermín, delivered in a slurred *sotto voce*, was enough to render their sound opaque to my foreign ears even without permutations of Cochimí. Purely my own was the notion that the Cochimí might be established as the creators of the unattributed cave paintings, simply because the degree of change in their speech from a remote mother tongue indicated that they were around when the murals were created. Such a historical bank shot was so tenuous that it was less hypothesis than personal fantasy. But, as the genre of mystery books and movies shows us, the human being delights in inventing conundrums, then solving them.

≈ ≈ ≈

Bruce Berger has published eleven books, the majority of which investigate the intersections of nature and human culture in desert environments. Among them are The Telling Distance, *winner of the Western States Book Award and the Colorado Book Award, and* Almost an Island, *an account of thirty years' experience in Baja California. His essays have appeared in* The New York Times, Orion, Outside *and many other publications. For recreation he plays benefit classical piano concerts in Mexico.*

ERIN BYRNE

~~ ~~ ~~

Spirals: Memoir of
a Celtic Soul

She explores a trip to Ireland that was a
strange kind of homecoming.

*If you do not bring the kind eye of creative expectation to
your inner world, you will never find anything there.*
—John O'Donohue, *Anam Cara*

A shell-shaped spiral emerged in my center when my
child-eyes first beheld the rugged cove outside the cottage where I was born on the west coast of Ireland. The clear
wavelets lapped over grayblue rocks and my little pink toes,
and washed into my fragile senses. This shape was all around
me as I grew—mollusca, seahorses, and *Scolelepis Squamata*
(the bristleworm, slender bluish green, which swims in spirals
when disturbed)—and I collected many to set upon my shelf.

The Gaelic tongue curled into the whirls of my ear, to
the spiral ganglion, sending the sound to my brain when
my mother called me home across fields of high grass (*gabh
isteach!*) or in my own voice raised in song (*amhrán*) or when
my grandmother (*máthair mhór*) murmured her love, saying,
"*Tá grá agam duit.*" The lonely tones of a uilleann pipe chased

the wind through mist-kissed air to rustle the leaves of the wild cherry tree I climbed.

When I was four years old, my mother held my newborn sister in her arms and I put my hand upon her small head, smoothing her silky black hair.

"See this place where God breathed life into her," my mother said. "Right here on the top of her head it was; see how her hair grows around and around the spot. It happened just the same way with you, love."

She cupped her hand on the top of my head and smiled.

My grandfather took me for long walks along leafy lanes. One autumn day he pointed to a falling leaf.

"Watch the wind waft it down in spiralesque whooshes, darling," he said. He reached down and pulled the ribbon from my head and my long hair lifted and fanned out and wrapped around my face. The sound of our laughter rose and was carried off.

He put his gnarled finger on the tip of mine and whispered that the spirals there were my very own print, with none other like it in the wide world. He told me about limitless galaxies that danced in space in the very same shape, and magnetic fields that drew objects together. He showed me rings upon a freshly chopped tree trunk, and tendrils of flower stems and vines that grew in loops.

Some days at dusk, I stood on the shore and watched for my father's boat on distant waves. He'd told me that the oceans ushered their tides in and out in a spiral motion, and I trusted the sea to return him to me in just this same way.

Smoke snaked into my nostrils from a peat fire in the hearth of our cottage, then again in another cottage, then again in another, illuminating, cooking, warming, and ever burning—smoldering overnight then blown to orangish life in the morning. The smell wound around my red-bright heart while my family slept and waked and worked and ate and stared into those licking flames; we were warmed outside *and* in.

I remember arcs of sparks leaping from fires.

A strange thing happened to me when I was fourteen, walking home late one night across a high plain in County Kerry. Across the black ink-spill of sky I saw fires on far horizons. Suddenly, my spirit flew backwards over decades, centuries, millenniums to a night halfway between the spring equinox and summer solstice. I was standing inside a circle of gigantic stones and there were fires everywhere. The warm earth pulsed under my bare feet and a restless breeze raised the hair on my arms. A heavy cloak pressed my shoulders (I knew, of course, that it was white). My raised hand held a dagger.

Bealtaine, the fire festival.

I was at the place of seventeen pillars, Drombeg, called Druid's Altar, over in County Cork, miles from my home. I knew the bonfires were the burning of winter bedding and floor coverings, and some saw witches jumping through flames in ethereal ecstasy while others performed rituals to protect people from otherworldly spirits. It was the Bronze Age. As I stood surrounded by the stones, spirals sparked from the fire and sprinkled down from shooting stars straight into me.

And just as suddenly as I'd appeared at the bonfires, I was at the gate of our cottage—my hand on the latch, my feet on the path. It was like something out of a story, it was, that apparition of myself. Even now when I think of that dagger, I am filled with fright. Have I been *gifted with a faery life*?

It sounds strange, but the spirals I felt that night remained inside me, wrapping around time and place, turning memory to experience and experience to memory, in spite of time's insistence otherwise. What is this shape that laps around and around my awareness of the real?

These ancient symbols existed before the written word. Before the pyramids emerged in Egypt, in a place called Newgrange on the eastern side of Ireland, the people sensed something quickening inside their bodies when they looked up at the swirling of the heavens. They sought to imprint this upon their stones, to show order coming out of chaos. The spiral's mystical powers were thought to repel evil spirits from entering tombs, and the stones of Newgrange were covered with these curving carvings.

Bees danced in a spiral near their hive, revealing the source of honey I collected as a young woman. It was for the making of the mead: ambrosia, honey-wine, the nectar of the gods, which promised pleasures of the palate and the flesh, and quickened the mysterious pulsings of arousal that were beginning to stir in my blood when I felt the touch of a certain young man.

My people always felt this force whisking through their beings, so they carved, painted, and drew it upon their treasures: jewelry, tools, precious metalwork, and always the stones.

What does the shape signify? The self-expanding out or the natural world reaching in? The spiritual balance between ourselves, the sun, and the cosmos? Land, sea, sky or the Holy Trinity? The constant spiraling of the soul through death, initiation and rebirth? The answer is unknown because myths and spiritual ideas in Celtic culture were passed down one generation at a time, through ritual, storytelling, music and dance, but never the written word—these secrets were too sacred.

One thing is sure: Theories and sophisticated stories were spun to explain our existence, and we Irish developed brilliant minds and unparalleled lyrical grace that remained unsullied through centuries of enslavement.

Throughout my years in Ireland, the green ribbon grew like stardust out of a magic wand, sparking in one long line that looped up and around and through my eyes, ears, skin, hair and heart, tingeing my life with magic.

Childhood passed swiftly. It seemed suddenly I was a grown woman living in America, married into a clan who kept Irish traditions by producing a never-ending stream of children, celebrating life's end with four-day-long wakes, and declaring love often with kisses on the lips and long-winded, sentimental toasts.

Now my home is Washington State where the rain keeps everything green, but I pine for patchwork farms and roads lined with wild fuchsias. I think of Ireland so often that this country intertwines with that country until both places are one.

The ring I wear has three spirals, the *tristele*, a tiny silver reminder of what winds within. This shape is, to me, *álainn*: beautiful. I chose it to decorate my home: My favorite upholstered chair is covered with gold threads of spirals, the rug beneath my feet is bordered with wavelets of them, and a print upon my wall of van Gogh's *Starry Night* has in its center an undulating starswirl in greeny white-blue—all around my house spirals pirouette. There is even a calligraphic curlicue at the top of the first letter of my own symbolic name.

I see widening gyres in my mind's eye, next to me on life's journey, gently rolling or flying forward. Through times of poisonous loneliness, stinging sorrow, or the dark grip of grief, they illuminate my path like a chain of tiny emeralds pulled across an expanse of black velvet, making visible the invisible, making brighter the divine.

These sixth-sense Irish arabesques steer clear of the English in me and skirt the Scottish, but cling to my Americanness. Their motion is ceaseless, their repetition reassuring—up and down and around and around again and again, these Celtic spirals, spinning on their predestined course. They are mine to keep; when my spirit leaves my body they will fly with me.

I came again to that Kerry coastline years later and the vortex inside me lit up like phosphorescence. As I stood on the bluff over Ventry Bay, out of the corner of my eye I saw tips of long strands that ignited and flashed from auburn to silver as the breeze again swirled my hair around my shoulders.

I returned, with my husband and sons, to fields where black and white cows lounged in front of rugged castle and cathedral ruins, to the land of the navigator whose name I gave one of my strapping sons, and the place that holds the illuminated manuscript the other son is named after. The taste of soda bread dripping with butter and honey orbited my tongue, taking me back to simple meals with many bodies wedged around a rough-hewn table inside a country cottage.

John O'Donohue, Irish poet, philosopher, and scholar, wrote that the eternal world and the mortal world are not parallel, but fused, as captured in the Gaelic phrase *fighte fuaighte*, woven into and through each other. I felt this fusion when I returned alone at night to that megalithic circle.

Drombeg sat silent and stoic upon its high plain, the stones shimmering silver in the moonlight. I had heard when the site was excavated they found the remains of an adolescent wrapped in a thick cloth inside a pot in the circle's center. I stood again inside the circle remembering the raised dagger and the hair on my arms rose: What had happened the night I crossed over?

> *When all is said and done, how do we not know but that our own unreason may be better than another's truth?*
>
> *For it has been warmed on our hearths and in our souls, and is ready for the wild bees of truth to hive in it, and make their sweet honey.*

— WILLIAM BUTLER YEATS, *THE CELTIC TWILIGHT*

I ask: Is a soul decorated only with the times and places that the body inhabits? Is not the lace we are made of more intricate and complicated than that, woven of what exists within our senses *and* what we sense from our existence? Is yours forged within the confines of reality? Mine is not.

For I was not born in Ireland, nor did I grow in many cottages there, or climb the wild cherry to the echo of the uilleann. I first set foot on Irish soil when there were slivers of silver in my reddish hair and my sons were nearly grown. But when I arrived, it was—to every cell in my body, each neuron in my brain, and all the sensors in my spirit—a homecoming, a return. The coils inside me glowed and sizzled as I *remembered*—in the truest sense of my experience of memory—a past I didn't possess.

Unreasonable to some, perhaps. But whether placed there gingerly by my ancestors—for I am surely of Irish heritage—or, stranger still, through a series of previous lives spanning thousands of years, these curls cling sweetly. I suppose there is a way to test the truth of this.

Into my soul, which has been honeycombed with golden spirals, I invite the bees.

~~ ~~ ~~

Erin Byrne is a writer whose essays have won numerous awards, including the 2012 Silver Solas Award for Best Travel Story of the Year. Erin's work has appeared in Everywhere *magazine,* World Hum, The Literary Traveler, Brave New Traveler, Best Travel Writing 2011, Crab Creek Review *and many other publications.*

DAVID FARLEY

❧ ❧ ❧

A Chip off the Old Bloc

Minsk, austere capital of Belarus and former Soviet
satellite, harbors Beatles cover bands, bookish
bohemians feasting on pig fat and vodka, and
the curious legacy of Lee Harvey Oswald.

John Lennon was late. He'll arrive in about an hour,
George Harrison told me, snapping his cell phone shut.
So, along with Ringo, sitting with a bongo drum between his
legs, and Paul McCartney, plucking away at his bass, the band
would start without him.

I had met "George Harrison," whose real name is Ivan,
the day before when a Minsk-based friend of a friend, whose
name is also Ivan, drove me out to the countryside for a
bucolic Belarusian afternoon of barbecuing and beer drinking. In the company of a half-dozen shaggy-haired hipsters
in their 20s, as large pieces of pork cooked on the grill, Ivan
and I had nursed oversize bottles of Alivaria, the local brew,
and watched water-skiers cruise by on the wide Ptich River.
That's when George Harrison had a lightbulb moment: Since
I wouldn't be in town to see the band's next gig, they should
stage a private concert for me.

And so there I was, a day later, sitting in the drab living
room of a small apartment on the outskirts of Minsk, the

capital of Belarus, a landlocked country wedged between Poland and Russia, watching a Beatles tribute band called the Apples. The L-shaped couch was crammed with the band's friends. On the coffee table, half-liter bottles of vodka framed plates of zakuski, or vodka snacks—sausage, tomato slices, cheese, black bread, and more sausage. The landscape outside the large picture window was spiked with tall gray, uniform panelky, or "commie condos," as they're sometimes irreverently called. When the band busted into "Back in the U.S.S.R.," the irony of the moment was so thick I had to sit back and close my eyes, lest I spontaneously combust.

After all, I pretty much was back in the U.S.S.R.

At least it really felt like it at times during my stay in Minsk. Much of the impression is due to the architecture: This city of nearly two million people was rebuilt from the rubble of World War II as a shining example of Stalinist city planning. In addition, it is still sculpted with grandiose neo-classic buildings, wide city-center avenues suitable for victory parades, and expansive pedestrian walkways.

Minsk is also one of the few places in Europe where the statues of Soviet heroes have not been buried. Columns topped with red Soviet stars, faded over time, still sit at the center of city plazas and squares; you can still stand on the seemingly anachronistic intersection of Marx and Engels; and pro-government slogans, in the form of large block letters stretched across rooftops, still force-feed ideology to the populace. The country even has a mustachioed strongman president, Alexander Lukashenko, who runs the place. (More on him later.)

And if that wasn't enough to send me straight to the Belarusian consulate to apply for a long-term visa, there was this bizarre nugget of historical minutiae: For two and a half years in the early 1960s, Lee Harvey Oswald—one of the most mysterious Americans of the twentieth century and the alleged assassin of John F. Kennedy—called Minsk home.

How is Oswald remembered here, I wondered, and what trace of his Cold War-era residence did he leave behind? Also, how did it come to pass that while many of Belarus's Soviet comrades have consciously broken with their past, Minsk stalled at the starting block, the capital of a country lost in time and space, still partying like it's 1959? Except for Russians who come here to lose their rubles in the city's many casinos, and the odd male Italian who explores the clubs to hit on the exceptionally beautiful Belarusian women, tourists of the world aren't exactly uniting here. There are no backpackers with dog-eared copies of Lonely Planet Belarus tucked under their arms, no fanny pack-clad vacationers wandering Minsk's broad streets.

That tourism gap is part of Belarus's appeal. We live in a world that's growing smaller, more totally connected, but also—from Perth to Prague, Bangalore to Boston—more homogenous. In coming to Belarus, I yearned to find a place that had managed to eschew twenty-first-century globalization. I wanted to say I saw Minsk before it became "the next Prague."

The day after the Apples concert, I found myself at yet another party. This time it was full of writers instead of musicians. Another friend of a friend, Siarhiej (pronounced SER-gey) Kalenda, a well-known Belarusian novelist, told me to meet him at ў, a combination bookstore, gallery, and publishing house hidden in the courtyard of an apartment complex near the center of town.

Once in a while, a full-scale after-hours bash breaks out at ў, and this was apparently one of those nights. As black-clad twenty-somethings flowed into the gallery, Kalenda, twenty-five, gave me color commentary: She's a poet. He's a writer. He's a painter. She's a graphic artist. A tall brunette delivered vodka shots to waiting hands; then came baskets of creamy, salty (and utterly delicious) salo—a pig-fat delicacy, the only delicacy worth smuggling out of the country.

But Kalenda didn't bring me here solely to eat pork products and meet a bunch of artists. After all, as he explained to me, these people weren't just poets and painters; they were individuals taking part in a simple act that would make Lukashenko's mustache hairs bristle.

I looked around. The young faces in the crowd looked like normal pig-fat-eating, vodka-shooting Belarusians to me.

"Do you understand anything they're saying?" Kalenda asked.

"No," I said, and reminded him that I don't speak Russian.

"That's it," he said, pushing his empty plastic cup into my chest. "They're not speaking Russian. They're speaking Belarusian."

Kalenda continued: "This bookstore? You won't find anything in Russian here. Just Belarusian. The publishing house?" He pointed to a small office where a group of people huddled around a computer screen watching YouTube videos. "They publish books mostly in Belarusian." Even the name, ў, was a cold slap in the Russky face. It's the only letter in the Belarusian alphabet that is not also a letter in Russian.

"So what's the big deal?" I asked. Kalenda gave me a brief history lesson.

Belarus's autonomy grew out of the breakup of the Soviet Union in 1991. For the first few years, the country was, like the rest of post-communist Europe, on a path toward free-market capitalism and democracy. But then in 1994 Alexander Lukashenko, a once obscure collective-farm manager and hockey fanatic, was elected president. He has since refused to leave office. It's true that he won reelection in 2002, 2006, and 2010 by very wide margins. But it's also true that international election-monitoring organizations ruled those elections flawed. Cementing his totalitarian reputation, Lukashenko tried reattaching the country to Russia, which my new friends told me was part of a post-Yeltsin power grab. The theory was that if Belarus officially became a province of Russia, then Lukashenko would be in a position to become leader of Belarus and Russia. It didn't work, but the president still has pro-Russian leanings, thanks in part to the country's dependence on cheap Russian natural gas.

In one of his first acts as president, Lukashenko made Russian one of the official languages of the country. Belarusian is still an official language, but since the beginning of the Soviet Union in 1917 (when Belarus was a founding constituent republic), the majority of the country has spoken Russian. No one is sure exactly why Lukashenko favors Russian over Belarusian, both of which are Slavic languages. Some say he can't speak Belarusian.

I nodded, alternating sips of vodka and bites of pig fat as I listened to my friend against the din of conversation in the bookstore party around us.

Just then a few people who'd been congregating across the room joined us. Andrei Khadanovich, a tall thirty-seven-year-old poet, the director of the Belarus PEN Center, and an advocate for the Belarusian language, and Julia Tsimafeeva, a translator, had been listening to Kalenda's history lesson and wanted to give me their two rubles' worth.

"We speak Belarusian first as an aesthetic choice," Khadanovich said when I asked him why he chose it as his main language. He became entranced by Belarusian in college and now speaks it with his wife and young daughter, something, he says, that is becoming increasingly popular. But he admits that Lukashenko's assault on the language has made speaking it a political statement. "It's us against the government. And because artists and writers and such are choosing to speak Belarusian, it has become the language of the intelligentsia."

Tsimafeeva, who works for a translation agency that specializes in the Belarusian language, said she and others are translating English-language authors such as Charles Bukowski, Ken Kesey, and Jack Kerouac into Belarusian. "By translating cool writers into Belarusian, we're hoping younger people will be more motivated to want to speak it," she said.

"The problem," Kalenda said, "is that Belarusians don't have any identity. Because we've been in the shadow of Russia for so long, and before that a part of Poland, our only identity is 'not'—not being Russian or not being Polish."

Václav Havel, the playwright, Communist-era dissident and eventual president of the Czech Republic, came up in conversation at least half a dozen times during my evening at ў. So did obscure historical Czech figures like the nineteenth-century scholar Josef Jungmann, who is credited with reviving the Czech language and identity. Which was fitting, because I felt as though I were back in Prague in the early 1980s, mingling with members of Charter 77, the Czech dissident group founded by Havel and others.

I also felt a tad paranoid. I sensed that the KGB, which, not surprisingly, still exists in Belarus, might break down the door at any second and arrest us all. I had spent the last few days wandering around Minsk with a slight sensation of fear tingling in my stomach. If it wasn't the neoclassic KGB headquarters or the ominous, boxy, and heavily patrolled presidential palace (which is strictly verboten to photograph) or the ubiquitous police presence (Belarus has one of the highest ratios of cops per capita in the world), it could have been the general Stalinist design of the city. The sprawling buildings that line the streets in the city center appear so omnipotent, so rigid and heavy—many are a block long—that they dwarf the average pedestrian, implicitly suggesting the state can, and will, crush you if necessary.

But in the carefree setting of ў, my fears were put to rest when someone refilled my cup with more vodka. "Budzma," we said: "cheers" in Belarusian. We consumed even more pig fat. Our conversation gave me hope and made me want the rest of the world to cheer for a freer Belarus.

"If only the rest of the world knew Belarus existed," Tsi-mafeeva said, inspiring snickers.

Kalenda jumped in, saying, "Whenever I travel around Europe and people ask where I'm from, I say Belarus. They say, 'Where? Belgium?' And I say, 'No, Bel-a-rus.' And they ask, 'Oh, right. That's part of Russia, yes?'"

It's partly understandable why Belarus gets lost geographically. The only international press the country gets consists of reports about Lukashenko's power-grabbing ways, from efforts to dissolve parliament to crackdowns on political opponents. In 2005, then-U.S. Secretary of State Condoleezza Rice referred to the country as Europe's last dictatorship. It's no wonder the only souvenir I could find in Minsk was a red t-shirt emblazoned with the hammer and sickle. The state image hasn't been a very good advertisement for the tourism industry. But then there's that one famous person who did find his way to Minsk, about fifty years ago: Lee Harvey Oswald. He called the Belarusian capital home from 1960 to 1962. Did Oswald's time here shape his later actions? I decided the only way to find out was to get into his apartment. Which appeared to be a long shot. How do you find the apartment of a shadowy historical figure when there are no plaques or signs or public information directing you to it? I had managed to find an address on the Internet before I arrived in Minsk. I mentioned this to Kalenda, but he doubted I had the correct information. "Everything is filtered through the government," he said. "And no one here really knows Oswald's address." Indeed, when I asked at ў if anyone knew where Oswald had lived, I received nothing but blank stares. In fact, few people even knew that Oswald had lived in Minsk at all.

Unwilling to give up, I charged my friend Ivan, the non-Apple, with the task of helping me locate the apartment. First, though, a little backstory.

In October 1959, Oswald turned up in Moscow wishing to become a citizen of the Soviet Union. The Russians said no, and Oswald attempted suicide in his hotel bathroom. Thinking he'd do it again and succeed, and fearing the United States would assume Oswald had been murdered by the Soviets, the Russians relented. Still, they suspected Oswald might be a Yankee spy, and they sent him off to Minsk, put him to work in an electronics factory called Gorizont (Horizon), and had the KGB track his every move. For a while Oswald settled down, marrying a local girl named Marina and making a few friends. After a couple of years, though, he tired of Soviet life. He applied for an exit visa for himself and Marina and immigrated back to Texas. The rest, of course, is history.

But in Minsk it's a history that still needed to be unearthed. Ivan took me to the address I'd found on the web. We approached a yellow neoclassic building, set in the center of town where Prospekt Nezavisimosti and tree-lined Komunisticheskaya Street meet the slow, snaking Svisloch River. In the leafy interior courtyard, a gray-haired pensioner sat on a bench.

Ivan asked the man if this was, in fact, Oswald's old building. The man shrugged. Then he told us that Gorizont used to own the building, so most of the people living there, himself included, are employees or former employees of the company.

"What do you want to know about Oswald?" he asked. Ivan explained that I had come from New York to see Oswald's apartment (which wasn't exactly the whole truth), and we were wondering if there was a chance we could get inside.

"It's on the fourth floor," the man said, pointing to a door across the courtyard from where we were standing, and then added: "I used to work with Oswald." He paused, then continued. "We used to go hunting together. And let me tell you, that boy could not fire a gun. We were frightened every time he tried to shoot. There's no way he could have shot Kennedy."

The man went on and on, and Ivan eventually stopped translating for me. Finally, we thanked him and wandered over to the door. We weren't sure which buzzer had been

Oswald's, so I rang all ten at once. The door swung open and we faced a sinewy septuagenarian standing in the foyer, wearing an annoyed look on his face. Ivan explained what we wanted, and the old man said a few quick words and then slammed the door shut. Apparently he said that the apartment was being renovated and we should go away.

Ivan and I had no other option but to try the door. Much to our surprise, it was unlocked, so we wandered inside and up the stairs. When we got to the fourth floor, there were two apartment doors. Ivan shrugged and knocked on one of them. It was the angry sinewy man again. "I told you: Go away!" he yelled and then slammed the door on us for the second time. I knocked on door number two. We weren't expecting much, since Mr. Friendly Neighbor had said it was being remodeled. The stairwell was silent. And then, a shuffling on the other side of the door. It opened. There stood a short, elderly man wearing a retro zip-up track jacket.

Ivan and the man began speaking. I couldn't comprehend what they were saying, but I understood when the man opened his door wider and waved us in.

The two-room apartment was crammed with bookshelves and framed photos (including several of Lukashenko). The man said his name was Edward. He was seventy-five years old. He told us he was originally from Kazakhstan and that he did not know about the Oswald connection when he bought the apartment ten years ago. He ushered us onto his balcony and told me to stand at the far end of it. I wasn't sure what he was doing, but then he handed me a black-and-white photograph of Oswald and his wife. Ivan said, "Look, they're standing in the same spot you are."

It was true. Behind them in the photo, and behind me in real life, were the pediment and columns of the ministry of defense. Then Edward took us inside, a cigarette dangling from his lips, and led us to the bathroom. "See this toilet?" he asked with more enthusiasm than I'd ever heard about a commode. He fanned his hand around it like he was trying to sell it to us. "You can see it's an old toilet because the tank is up high and connected by this pipe." We nodded. "This," he said, taking a moment to catch his breath from all the excitement, "was Oswald's toilet. Oswald sat right here!" And just in case we needed a physical exclamation mark, he pulled down on the chain hanging from the tank and gave it a flush.

Like the pensioner we met outside, Edward was convinced Oswald was no killer. He had a theory—a very long one, in fact—that suggested that Oswald was just a patsy, used by "them" because of his history of living in the U.S.S.R. Then Edward sat down at his computer and began playing a video about Oswald's role in the history-making incident. When Ivan and I looked bored by it, Edward drew our attention to a photograph on the wall, a picture of an attractive, scantily clad young brunette.

"She's nice looking," Ivan said.

"She's a fashion model. You want her phone number? Here," he said, scribbling it down on a piece of paper. Ivan looked confused for a second and then thanked him. "How do you know her?" he asked.

Edward glanced at the photo of the girl, lying on her back, her eyes looking seductively at the camera. "She's my granddaughter."

Ten minutes later, Ivan and I were sitting in a nearby pub, both giddy from the experience, me because I couldn't believe I got into Oswald's apartment, and Ivan because of the phone number in his pocket. The pub was called ID Bar. Fittingly enough for Belarus, the waiters were dressed as police officers, and the space we sat in was a replica of an interrogation room.

Despite the too-close-for-comfort atmosphere, the ID looked as though it could have been in any European capital city. And the place reminded me, yet again, that the world I'd come looking for—that stark, melancholy rot of communism—was only one facet of Minsk's personality. The city was indeed stunningly Stalinist in its own way, but it was also more sophisticated than the stereotypical images of bread lines and babushkas. Bars blared '80s heavy metal and hipper, newer artists like M.I.A. One restaurant offered sushi, served by a waiter ironically sporting a bushy Lukashenko-like mustache. At least I think he was being ironic.

Just how Belarusians managed to sustain a normal, functioning society underneath the surface of totalitarianism and to persevere through tough political times was a question I wanted to ask again and again. I did gently ask my new friends if, despite Lukashenko's seemingly endless tenure at the top of Europe's last dictatorship, they had any hope for the future. Many of the young educated people I questioned had a most surprising answer: that there was no viable opposition at the moment, so the best person to rule was—wait for it— Lukashenko. Scientific my poll was not; shocking it was.

It reminded me of Václav Havel's 1978 essay, "The Power of the Powerless," in which he argues that self-policing among ordinary people is just as important as policing. The ruled become the rulers. Belarusians might not be policing themselves in the way that Czechs did under the Soviet anti-reform policy of "normalization" in the 1970s, but their acceptance of the Lukashenko regime was, in a way, a similar act of self-preservation.

The next night in Minsk, I had dinner with my writer friend Siarhiej Kalenda. As I dug into a plate of machanka— chunks of tender pork and potatoes, with a thick gravy that diners sop up with pancakes—I told Kalenda it seemed to me that many of his fellow young Belarusians had fallen into a state of apathy. They seemed to take it for granted that there were no decent opposition figures that could challenge Lukashenko. So they accepted him as the leader of the country. Kalenda didn't disagree.

"We all know what the outcome of future elections will be," he said, telling me that he regularly protests the results and gets thrown in jail for a week or two for doing so. He did, however, harbor some long-term optimism. "Right now, it's the old generation ruling a younger and very different generation. As we get older, we'll start to take over the country and govern it the way we want."

We held up our pints of crisp Alivaria and toasted to that. We paid the bill and headed toward the door. The waiter was blocking it. "The president is driving by," he said. "No one is allowed on the street."

Kalenda and I looked at each other. He didn't seem surprised. We stood there in silence for a long minute before the waiter cracked open the door enough to peek out onto the street. Then he opened it wider and waved us out. The president's motorcade had passed, leaving the streets with a calm, empty, just-after-the-storm feeling. There was, for a moment, a sense of normalcy in this abnormal city—perhaps a brief foreshadowing of Minsk's streets when the children of Kalenda and the Ivans and the Apples will be the ages we are now. A time when "Back in the U.S.S.R." will seem less ironic and more nostalgic.

∾ ∾ ∾

David Farley is a contributing writer at AFAR *magazine, where this story originally appeared. Farley's work also appears in* The New York Times, Washington Post, Travel + Leisure, Gadling.com, *and* WorldHum.com, *among other publications. He's the author of the award-winning travel memoir/narrative history,* An Irreverent Curiosity: In Search of the Church's Strangest Relic in Italy's Oddest Town, *and co-editor of* Travelers' Tales Prague and the Czech Republic. *Farley has lived in Paris, Prague, Rome, and San Francisco, and currently makes his home in New York City where he teaches writing at New York University. Find more at www.dfarley.com.*

꙳ ꙳ ꙳

Seal Seeking

Few people succeed in getting a firsthand glimpse of the common, if controversial, practice of seal hunting.

The west coast of Greenland was rapidly fading into the distance when my bladder sounded the alarm. *You have to pee*, it said. Normally, this wouldn't be a problem. But the last hint of land was now a brown crust on the horizon, at least two hours away, and I was on a tiny fifteen-foot fishing boat, alone with three men. There was simply nowhere to go. Worse, I was in the middle of one of the most breathtakingly adventurous moments of my life—seal hunting with the Inuit amidst shimmering icebergs in the Arctic Ocean—and I was the one who had talked my way onto *their* hunting trip.

The men, of course, had been relieving themselves all day. One of them, Jens, was already on his third piss: he cut the motor, turned his back to me, and whistled as he let loose a stream into the glassy water.

"Thirsty?" Jens asked. He had the relaxed look of someone who has just taken a particularly satisfying piss. He rummaged through the side of the boat, amongst the gun cases, and offered me a bottle of soda.

"No thanks," I said. Liquid was the last thing I wanted to put into my body. I scanned the sides of the boat for a place where I could hang off the side—the back of the boat, near the motor, looked the most promising—and squat awkwardly over the Arctic Ocean. Just in case it came down to that.

The closest most people get to thinking about Greenland, aside from documentaries about polar bears and ominous news reports of global warming, is on transatlantic flights, where a sleepy glance at the seatback flight map reveals the little white plane passing beneath Greenland's southern tip. In the groggy struggle to find the least uncomfortable sleeping position, between the jostle to the right against the arm rest and the toss to the left against the oversized stranger, some people probably have a fleeting Greenland-related thought: *That looks big. I wonder if people live there?*

Yes. People live there. Fifty-five thousand of them, to be exact. The size of a small city, except they're scattered across a frozen wasteland three times the size of Texas. Picture the whole of the East Coast as harsh, ice-covered rocky terrain— with 15,000 people in Georgia, several thousand each in towns flung to the far reaches of Miami, Charlotte, and Washington DC, and 1,000 in the lone northern outpost of Boston— and you'll get a rough idea of Greenland's "urban density." There are no roads between cities (and certainly not between the dozens of small hunting and fishing communities), few places have airstrips, and the piercingly cold winters solidify the surrounding seas, making them impassable by ship six months out of the year. All this makes Greenland's Inuit inhabitants—the people formerly known as Eskimos—some of the most isolated on the planet.

Something has always enthralled me about the Arctic. As a child, I used to spend hours staring at an illustrated book about icebergs, and as an adult, hours gazing at the black-and-white photographs of Polar explorers, the hardened lines on their grizzled faces conveying more than their trip reports ever could. Whatever strange force lured them to the northern latitudes—and it was strange, because no one in his right mind would be drawn, almost compulsively, to a land of frostbite, freezing cold, and almost certain misery—also exerted a powerful pull on me. There is something very bewitching about the Arctic.

I had just one problem: money. Greenland is expensive. Not just London expensive or New York expensive, it's Tokyo-times-two, your-slice-of-pizza-costs-twenty-bucks expensive. Why? Because if you live in Greenland you might as well be living on the International Space Station. Everything needs to be flown or sailed in. Few things can grow, let alone live, in such bitter conditions.

It took me six months to save for the plane ticket, supplementing my daily income as a science writer by working nights at a cheap dive bar, serving beer and refilling complimentary pretzel bowls for meager tips. When things at the bar became unbearable I would imagine Greenland. *This one is for the midnight sun*, I'd think, as I cleaned warm vomit off the floor or scrubbed a shit-spattered toilet.

I finally earned enough money to buy my ticket to Ilulissat, on Greenland's west coast, home to the most spectacular icebergs outside of Antarctica. With 5,000 people, Ilulissat is Greenland's third-largest town and even has some tourist amenities. I logged onto Couchsurfing.com, a website that connects locals and travelers, and contacted the only woman registered within hundreds of miles. She invited me to join her on a hunting trip with her boyfriend.

Hunting what? I wrote back, but didn't receive a reply.

I read that in the summer, Greenlanders hunted musk ox, reindeer, and seal. Then, a month before my arrival, the woman wrote that a work trip was taking her elsewhere in Greenland for the summer: the hunting trip was off.

Now I was more curious than ever. Was hunting still a major source of food? Did everyone, even people with day jobs, go hunting? And which animal was everyone after?

I barraged the handful of Ilulissat tour agencies with emails and phone calls, asking if they could help me arrange a hunting trip. Most wrote back that they'd be happy to arrange midnight iceberg cruises, helicopter trips to the icecap and dog sledding tours. But hunting? "Well, most people hunt," one wrote, "but we can't help you."

If having to pee was a color-coded alert system, then I had just hit Code Orange and was steadily working up to Code Red. It wasn't quite an emergency, but if I were on a cross-country road trip, I'd be keeping my eyes peeled for the next rest stop.

How long had we been out for? The constant daylight—the sun does not set in the summer—had robbed me of the intuitive sense of time I now realized I'd taken for granted at lower latitudes. Here there was no feeling that "it was getting late" or "the day was ticking away"; it was as if time had been liberated from the confines of the sun.

I checked the clock: we'd been out for nearly four hours and still had not spotted a single seal.

But there were other things to hold my attention: the sun felt impossibly large and near, as if it had decided to violate Earth's restraining order and come creepily close. The entire half-dome of the sky was lightly brushed with thin, wispy clouds, which provided the background to the most unusual sight of all: a massive rainbow ring that formed a magnificent halo around the sun. At first I'd been overcome with the same awe that accompanies the sight of a rainbow, but as the halo continued to swell—as if to commandeer the entire sky—my awe settled into a kind of constant feeling of wonder and elation.

Adding to the surreal effect, the glassy water reflected the entire sky, and towards the horizon everything faded into soft blues that gently blurred the boundary between above and below. The only hint of a border was offered by what appeared to be small ice cubes, demarcating the horizon. But as we neared, they morphed into colossal ice mountains the size of city blocks. The whole landscape had a mystical quality, as if we were floating through a painting of the heavens.

The silence was total. Stark. No animals, no people, no ambient noise, not even wind to rustle my eardrum or to whip up waves to lap at the boat. A plastic wrapper crinkled loudly as one of the men retrieved a chocolate chip cookie. Jens stood at the back, boots squeaking against the boat's floor as he scouted the waters for signs of life.

I'd met Jens by chance several days earlier, after I'd sought refuge from a torrential rainstorm inside the cozy restaurant at Hotel Icefjord. It was a slow afternoon. I chatted with the waitress, Ivalo, about how Greenland, which has long been a territory of Denmark, has never quite come close to its ruling country's education level and economic status, despite the Danes' many efforts (some woefully misguided) and financial injections. The waitress had been born in Greenland—she had the classic dark Inuit features and Asiatic eyes—but her mother had moved to Denmark to provide her with a better education. Like many young Danes, she was working in Greenland over the summer.

At some point I mentioned my cancelled hunting trip. Ivalo told me that it was seal that most people hunted during the summer, at least in Ilulissat. In fact, she'd recently been out hunting with the chef, the same man who had just brought out my lunch of musk ox burger.

"I think he might be going out again on Saturday," she said.

"Do you think I could join?"

She disappeared into the kitchen and emerged moments later with a phone number scrawled on a piece of paper. "Meet him at noon on Saturday on the harbor."

At the harbor I had difficulty recognizing Jens: he had traded his white chef's apron and poofy hat for blue overalls and a sweatshirt. He was probably in his mid-twenties, with shaggy black hair that spiked out as if surrounded by static electricity, and had slightly upturned lips that gave him a permanent smile. Jens introduced me to the others: a Dane, also named Jens, and another Inuit, his "very good friend" Ule, whose ski jacket, sunglasses, and knit cap made it look as though he was ready to hit the slopes.

We slowly wound our way out of the harbor—passing small boats, commercial fishing trawlers, and an occasional stray iceberg—and once outside we picked up speed, whipping around icebergs like it was a high-speed video game. This felt like the motorcycle version of the guided iceberg tour that I'd taken last week.

Jens didn't slow as we approached an area of densely packed smaller ice floes, scattered like puzzle pieces across the water's surface. He deftly maneuvered around most of them, but sometimes we'd hit the Greenland version of black ice—a refrigerator-sized berg floating invisibly beneath the surface—and it would scrape against the bottom with a kind of ominous grinding noise.

I tried conversing with the Dane but over the roaring motor and wind we had to shout, so all I could gather was that he was living in Ilulissat and working "with electric," which I assumed meant that he was an electrician. Eventually we settled into our own worlds, the Dane stroking his hunting rifle and occasionally aiming it out at nothing in particular, and Jens and Ule at the back, effortlessly standing tall, as if they were casually waiting in line for a coffee.

After some time Jens cut the motor. We drifted quietly, eight eyes darting across the water and icebergs in a furtive search—though for what, I wasn't exactly sure. I'd seen seals at zoos, and I'd come across a dead one in Iceland, the fat thing sprawled on the beach like an oversized football. Would the seals be sunbathing on ice floes or would they be frolicking in the water? Would they come close or would we have to sneak up stealthily from behind?

The day continued in much the same way—motoring to a new spot, drifting, searching, giving up, moving on—and my eyes quickly fatigued from straining at the same empty expanse of water. The initial thrill had faded. Now, even the Dane looked bored; he was no longer caressing his rifle.

Suddenly Ule pointed ahead: two black whales breached off in the distance, one after the other. "Minke whales," said Jens excitedly, as we changed course and raced towards them.

Surely they weren't thinking of hunting whales with those rifles?

"Where there's whale, there are seals," Jens yelled over the engine.

A few moments later: "Get down!"

I lowered my head. *Pop! pop!*

But either I was too slow in "getting down" or my sprawling ponytail of dreadlocks had gotten in the way (my hairstyle occupies so much airspace that I've earned the moniker "Sideshow Bob"), because Jens told me that I'd prevented Ule from taking a shot. So we switched places: I moved to sit on a blue fuel jug near the back, and Ule took my place at the bow, next to the Dane. They were on high alert—guns positioned against their shoulders, fingers on the trigger—and scanned the sea in all directions.

"Seals come up for water every five minutes," Jens explained. "Sometimes more, sometimes less."

Minutes passed. Then, in the distance, something broke the water's flat, glassy surface. At the first *pop!* I dive-bombed the floor like it was a war zone.

"Don't need to go that far," Jens laughed.

The next time I saw the seal's head: it looked almost like a duck, bobbing in the water about eighty feet away. It bobbed up once (*pop-pop-pop!*) twice (*pop-pop!*), three times (*pop! pop! pop!*), and it was gone.

I didn't see how it was possible to shoot such a small, quick-moving target from such a great distance. Even if they succeeded, wouldn't the seal sink?

"Sometimes," said Jens.

Round Four: the seal didn't pop up at all. Three minutes passed. Nothing. Five minutes, and we expanded our search radius, scouring the very distant waters for any sign of movement. Eight minutes and it seemed hopeless. Ten, still nothing. Fifteen. Twenty. The Dane traded his gun for a cigarette. Jens and Ule resorted to binoculars. Perhaps the seal held its breath for an extraordinarily long time. Or more likely, we hadn't seen it surface.

But the patch of water that we'd just stumbled upon seemed to be fertile seal territory, and we chased a few—or maybe the same ones—in a similar fashion. I learned to recognize the difference between a distant bird (a black blob that stays on the surface of the water) and a distant seal (a black blob that pokes its head out of the water a few times and disappears). Jens, on the other hand, could discern the seal's age and body type just by briefly glimpsing its head: "Baby one," he would say, or: "small but fat."

Seal hunting is a controversial topic that has received plenty of media attention, largely due to gory photographs of seals being clubbed to death, eagerly disseminated by organizations like PETA (People for the Ethical Treatment of Animals). Although seals don't inspire the same heartwarming *oohs* and *ahhs* as dolphins, they're not too far off: seals, especially the furry white pups, are cute. The anti-seal hunting campaign got a huge boost in the late 1970s when actress Brigitte

Bardot was photographed lying on some ice and cuddling with a baby harp seal. In one image, she is playfully—almost flirtatiously—caressing the area near its cheek.

In 2009, a parade of celebrities and wannabe celebrities— Pamela Anderson, Kelly Osbourne, Perez Hilton, and a slew of reality television stars—adopted it as the latest Hollywood cause du jour. In a sleek marketing campaign, they wore hipster "Save the Seal" t-shirts (in the case of Pamela Anderson, that's all she wore) that featured line drawings of innocent, helpless-looking seals. Bardot was back, blogging about the "sinister slaughter" on the PETA website. She wrote that "the gruesome bloodshed has only one purpose: to fuel the fur trade!" and vowed to boycott Canadian maple syrup until the government agreed to ban seal hunting "forever."

Aside from Bardot, who appears to be plainly misinformed, it's unclear if the celebrities have read up on the facts. If they had, they might have learned that up until recently, the Inuit relied on seals for heat and light (blubber was used for lamp oil), clothing and upholstery (seal skin), utensils (seal bone), jewelry and religious objects (seal teeth and claws), and food, both for themselves and their sled dogs. In older times, Inuit men would set out in a *qajaq*, a long, slender wooden boat covered with seal skins and designed to move quickly in the water. The men would harpoon the seals, and the women, who often followed in a wider boat called an *umiaq*, would load up the day's catches.

In modern-day Ilulissat I saw a strange mix of old and new: some people have desk jobs but go seal hunting after work or on the weekends, using outboard motor fishing boats and rifles instead of *qajaks* and harpoons. One woman I met— who nearly hyperventilated when she learned I was from New York, because it is the site of her favorite television show, *Sex and the City*—seemed just as excited about her recent seal hunting trip as she was about the green designer handbag she had just purchased in Copenhagen. And although there are two large supermarkets and several clothing stores, people still eat seal and many still use the skin for coats, gloves and furniture.

When Jens finally shot and hit the first seal, things moved fast.

Jens dropped his gun. Ule gunned the motor and we lurched forward. Jens retrieved a wooden pole with a hook at one end and leaned over the side. He kept his gaze on the water but guided Ule with his fingers, like a baseball catcher calling pitches. Just before we collided head-on with the seal—its black body floating in billowing pools of blood, its skin shiny in the glint of the sun—the boat veered sharply to the right and Jens deftly hooked the seal.

The whole thing, from shot to hook, lasted no more than several seconds. Like a well-choreographed dance, it was an impressive display of movement synchrony, clearly a result of many hours, days, and probably years of hunting together.

Together, Ule and Jens reached down and grabbed the seal by its hind flippers and with considerable exertion, hauled it out of the water. They slung it over the side of the boat like a piece of wet laundry, so that its bulbous head dangled over the water and the hind flippers rested inside the boat. A steady trickle of blood drained from its head to the sea.

"Ringed seal," Jens proclaimed.

I couldn't stop gaping at this creature, splayed out beside me at the back of the boat: its glassy eyes, its surprisingly long whiskers that skimmed the water's edge, and its stubby fins, with five finger-like segments, each containing an elegantly curved black claw that reminded me of a well-manicured fingernail. I touched its fur, which was dark gray with black spots—the spots are the "rings" that give it its name—and it felt like a soft, wet carpet. As we moved forward, I was mesmerized by the way the wake battered the seal's lifeless head, slapping it back and forth against the boat's hull.

Back on the hunt. The adrenaline subsided and I remembered how badly I had to pee. I crossed my legs and rocked back and forth. I focused all of my physical and mental energy on not pissing my pants. It became a song in my head: *I have to pee, I have to pee. Oh God, I have to pee.*

Jens must have noticed my discomfort. "You have to pee?"

"Yes."

"We'll find you some ice," he said.

Ice?

I thought of a conversation I'd had earlier that week, with a young Hungarian who'd been teaching English in a nearby fishing village. "The iceberg is finely balanced," he said. "One touch, one tip"—and here he stabbed the air with his forefinger like he was pushing a piece of a Jenga puzzle—"and the whole thing comes crashing down."

Yes. Icebergs were meant to be looked at. Not stood on. On the official iceberg tour, the guide had explained that huge chunks of ice often broke off the icebergs—a phenomenon known as calving—and caused waves large enough to topple a boat. For that reason we'd kept our distance from the bergs. Today I'd heard the thunderous sound of calving at least a dozen times (it echoed through the bay) and had witnessed a truck-sized chunk of ice crumble like fine powder and crash into the sea. Even land was not completely safe. A sign on the shore near Ilulissat read: EXTREME DANGER! *Do not walk on the beach. Death or serious injury might occur. Risk of sudden tsunami waves, caused by calving icebergs.*

I tried to imagine the logistics of my imminent iceberg piss, which quickly turned into me picturing the logistics of dying a very awkward death. It was like a *Choose Your Own Adventure* book, with divergent paths all leading to the same unpleasant ending. I tortured myself like this for some time. In the end I gave up, the way one does on those treacherous mountain bus rides in South America where a peek out the window reveals a straight drop over an impossibly steep cliff gorge. At some point you need to ask yourself: Are you going to get off the bus? If not, then accept your fate. If it's your time, it's your time. Anyway, it wouldn't be such a bad way to go, on an iceberg.

Is there anything more beautiful than icebergs? While mountains may have particularly sharp peaks or ridgelines scoured with hints of the past, a mountain's peak never crests like a wave, and a wave, though elegant and graceful, can never display the wrinkles and creases imprinted by years of geology. Not so with icebergs. Each berg is a structural marvel, abstract art on a colossal scale, a wholly unpredictable mixture of edges, fine lines, of stalactites and stalagmites, of Arabic archways and New York City high-rises, of domes, of lattices, of hills, of overhangs and undercuts, of caves and cavities, pillars and pyramids, of improbable balancing acts, of ridges and topographic lines, of peaks and dunes. Icebergs inspire a childlike sense of wonder; drifting through an iceberg-littered sea is like wandering through the most spectacular natural sculpture park on earth.

The icebergs are Ilulissat's claim to fame. The town sits near the edge of the Sermeq Kujalleq glacier, a slow-moving river of ice that runs from Greenland's interior ice cap out to the Arctic Ocean, depositing gargantuan icebergs in the bay surrounding Ilulissat. Sermeq Kujalleq is the largest glacier outside of Antarctica and the fastest glacier in the world. According to the Ilulissat Icefjord website, the glacier produces 46 cubic kilometers of ice each year, which if melted, would be equal to the USA's entire annual water consumption. The largest icebergs calved by the glacier are 1.5 cubic kilometers—equivalent to thirty football fields covered by a layer of ice as high as Mount Everest. After being calved, the icebergs journey south, often reaching latitudes on par with that of New York before they melt. The infamous iceberg that struck the Titanic is thought by most scientists to have originated in Greenland.

Ilulissat is the heart of Greenland's fledgling tourist industry, and it attracts a grab-bag mix of foreigners: elderly Danes who come on weeklong package tours, kayakers who come on organized trips, the ubiquitous German tour group, young Danes like Ivalo who come for seasonal work in the tourist industry, and other Danes who come for the same reasons mainland Americans move to Alaska—in search of solitude on an isolated frontier. My favorite foreigners, the middle-aged men who had served in the Canadian equivalent of the Navy SEALs, were living in Ilulissat and providing search and rescue services to an offshore oil rig. (Greenland has almost zero natural resources; finding oil would be like striking gold.)

One of the guys, Mike, seemed to have an endless inventory of stories about plane crashes, rescue dives, and helicopter missions. Before the hunting trip I had asked him what happens if you fall in the Arctic Ocean.

"You die."

"So why doesn't anyone wear life jackets?"

He explained that in the Arctic, both here and in Canada, the Inuit fishing communities accept that a few people will die each year. Wearing flotation devices would not only be unwieldy, but in many cases—such as those where the fishermen sail solo—they would "increase the time it takes you to die." The life jacket would keep you conscious for a bit longer, so that you could contemplate your fate as you slowly succumbed to hypothermia.

There were certainly no life jackets or flotation devices on this boat. As we headed towards "ice," I leaned over and dipped my fingers in the ocean, testing the temperature of my bath water. It was cool, but not as cold as say, dipping your hand in an ice bucket.

I spotted ice floes the size of surfboards: perhaps this was the ice Jens had been referring to? Maybe they would extend a piece of rope and I would surf-pee a floe. Even if I did fall in, they could haul me out pretty quickly: Jens was pretty handy with that wooden hook.

I must have been staring, because Ule pointed to a floe and shook his head, as if to say: *Don't worry. That's not your bathroom.* He put on his jacket, which I now noticed was emblazoned with the words "Qajak Ilulissat." He told me, in broken English, that there has been a recent movement to revive the *qajak*: mostly for sport, but also for reasons of national pride and cultural preservation. He was a member of the Ilulissat team and his girlfriend was Greenland's female *qajak* champion.

Suddenly he stood up and pointed: a seal. This one came unusually close and surfaced for an unusually long period of time, like it had a death wish. He exchanged some words with Jens, who turned to me. "We get this one, O.K.?" Jens said. "One seal for my family, one for his."

What could I say? Each seal could feed their families for at least several days. "Sure. But afterwards: bathroom, please!"

That seal turned out to be a difficult target, as we were now in a more crowded iceberg area and it kept slipping behind the bergs. It was like playing a grown-up version of hide-and-seek, with rifles and seals and icebergs. I trained my eyes desperately on the water, trying to spot the seal—anything to speed this up.

Finally, Ule shot the seal and we sped over. But by the time we arrived the seal had sunk below the reach of the hook. Jens tried to point out the sinking body. "See it? See it?" he kept asking, but all I could see was blood swirling into the blackish depths.

Back on track: to the bathroom. Eventually we approached an unusual iceberg: a flat island with multiple mounds of dirty snow that reminded me of New York City streets in January. This was the ugly duckling of icebergs. Ule cut the engine, and as we drifted towards it, I realized that this was my bathroom.

Maybe it wouldn't be so bad after all. The edge of the berg jutted out over the boat, forming a natural pier, and Jens hopped from boat to berg with ease. He extended a hand towards me, but I didn't need it: the ice provided such a perfect step that I, too, stepped off with ease.

On the berg the snow crunched beneath my sneakers. It was odd how normal this felt: the snow was like regular packed snow and the iceberg felt completely stable, as though we had disembarked on any old island. Hurriedly—both out of fear of this thing turning over, and because I didn't want to deprive them of more seals—I squatted, and let loose one of the longest streams of piss of my life. As my bladder emptied, the fear and apprehension of the previous hours were replaced with a kind of wild elation: I had just made the coolest pit stop ever.

Post iceberg-piss, the seal bonanza continued. My seal-spotting skills improved. When the others scanned the waters in front of the boat, I'd scan the back. "There!" I'd say, pointing at a bobbing head that they would have missed. They shot a third and fourth seal, but by the time we arrived they'd sunk. They hauled the fifth seal onto the boat. It was still alive. Jens held the wooden pole high over his head with two hands, paused, and then delivered a powerful blow that caused blood to spurt straight from its head.

Once we had those two seals the pressure was off. Jens and Ule spoke more freely, chatting in Greenlandic, a guttural language of "k" and "g" sounds. Jens even let me try his rifle. It was heavier than I expected, and I found it impossible to keep it steady on the undulating boat. Eventually I managed to hold a seal's head in the viewfinder—for a split second—and pressed the trigger. I imagine I didn't come close: Jens politely requested his rifle back.

They shot but failed to hook the seventh seal. We chased the eighth—injured, but not dead—endlessly through a jigsaw patch of small ice floes. Part of the seal hunting strategy, they explained, was to tire out the seal through continuous shooting and chasing. After an hour-long pursuit we finally approached the seal, which was floundering in the water several feet from the boat. Jens grabbed the rifle, aimed it point blank at the seal's head, and let loose one final *pop!* that spattered everything on the boat—even my camera lens—with seal blood. The final count? Eight killed, three hooked.

It was after midnight when we headed back, and the sun had sunk close to the horizon, assuming the position it would stay in through the morning. Summer nights in northern Greenland are an extended sunset, brilliant hues and streaks suspended in the sky for hours on end. But all I could think about was the cold. I stuck my fingers in my armpits. I wiggled my toes, then rubbed them through my sneakers, but nothing I did warmed them.

"Are you freezing?" Jens asked, in what I took to be the Greenlandic version of "are you cold?" He looked like he was out for a brisk evening stroll: no coat, no gloves, no hat, just a sweatshirt over his overalls. I took his suggestion to crouch on the boat's floor, which provided a (slight) respite from the bitter wind.

As the colorful houses of Ilulissat came into view, Jens turned to me: "We're going to cut the seal. Want to join?"

Even though I was freezing, starving, and pretty sure that I was losing a digit or two to frostbite, I couldn't say no. We dropped off the Dane at the harbor and headed back out to sea, where Jens waved and shouted something to a man standing on the iceberg. He waved back to Jens—with a machete.

The berg was flat, low in the water, and mostly submerged, the underwater ice a fluorescent blue beneath the water's surface. The man, a friend of theirs, stood in a puddle of blood at the center, and near his feet lay a dead seal. A single slit from head to flipper exposed its pinkish-red innards: fat, muscle, ribs, liver, and intestines. As we climbed onto the berg it felt like we were stepping onto an inflatable pool toy—it shifted noticeably with each footstep. Jens and Ule dragged the seals off the boat and anchored it to the most solid thing they could find: me.

Jens and Ule each got to work cutting the seals. After a few minutes, Jens placed a dark red organ off to one side: the liver. This, I had heard, was a delicacy here. "For good luck," he said, as he handed me a bite-sized piece. "It will make you a better hunter next time."

Even though I hate all kinds of liver—fried, grilled, chopped, or as pate—I accepted it. I braced myself to smile politely no matter how disgusting it would be. I took a bite, and my teeth sunk through the soft raw meat like it was a piece of sushi. Wait: it actually *did* taste like sushi.

"Wow," I said, surprised. "It's actually pretty good."

"Want more?"

"No thanks," I said. It was liver, after all.

Then, emboldened by the day's events, or maybe it was the rush of eating seal, or maybe I was delusional from the cold, I carefully walked a few paces to the edge of what remained of this very shaky iceberg, pulled down my pants, squatted, and took one last piss: a future hunter marking her territory.

❧ ❧ ❧

Anna Wexler is a writer, documentary filmmaker, and adventure traveler whose trip ideas are a continual source of concern for her friends and family. She has yet to top her solo bicycle ride across Mexico, but volcano boarding in Nicaragua, motorcycling northern Vietnam, and trekking the Himalayas all came pretty close. When Wexler isn't on the road, she writes about science and travel from her sea view desk in Tel Aviv. Read more about her work at www.annawexler.com.

TOM MILLER

~~ ~~ ~~

Precious Metal:
Me and My Nobel

The author takes his rightful
place among the immortals.

Every year the Swedish Academy awards the Nobel
Prize in Literature. The prize has been handed out
annually, with the exception of the World War II years, since
1901. Winners have included George Bernard Shaw, Pablo
Neruda, and Toni Morrison. It may surprise you, then, to
know that I myself received a Nobel Prize in Literature. No
one was more startled than me.

A good while back an online travel/adventure magazine
called Mungo Park sent me to Cuba to prepare a series of
reports under the general heading "Hemingway in Havana."
Now defunct, Mungo Park—named for a Scottish explorer
from two centuries ago—was owned by Microsoft and oper-
ated from the corporate campus in Redmond, Washington.
The series of dispatches I was to post daily would conclude
with reports from Mariel Hemingway, the actress who was
born some twenty weeks after her grandfather's death. She
was flown in for the occasion along with her husband, Stephen

Crisman, who was shooting footage of her for a documentary film.

I had considerable experience on the island, and made the best preparations I could, given Cuba's perennial suspicion of foreign electronic media. The country was just then emerging from its "special period in a time of peace," a euphemism for the economic free fall following the Soviet Union's implosion. Microsoft's reputation helped enormously as I arranged logistics along Cuba's informally dubbed "Hemingway Trail."

"Will Bill Gates be coming?" officials in the tourism and communications fields asked. "You never know," I replied with a wink.

My most daunting task was to convince Cuba's Catholic Church to take Ernest Hemingway's 1954 Nobel Medallion out of hiding so Mariel could see it. When Ernest won the 23-karat gold medal, he wanted to give it to the people of Cuba, off whose north coast his novel *The Old Man and the Sea* is set. Rather than turn the medallion over to the Batista government, he placed it in the custody of the Catholic Church for display at the sanctuary at El Cobre, a small town outside Santiago de Cuba on the island's southeast coast.

The sanctuary has been called the Cuban Lourdes, and remains a repository for mementos and prayers from the hopeful and hopeless. The medallion remained there until the mid-1980s when thieves broke into the glass display case and stole it. Police recovered the medal within days, but the Catholic Church decided to keep it under wraps rather than chance another theft. It was with singular pleasure, then, that I held a private meeting with Padre Jorge Palma of the Diocese of Santiago de Cuba to persuade the church to bring the medallion out of hiding for the first time since the theft.

When it came time for our series to begin, Mungo Park flew in a producer to oversee the project and handle the technical details, and a photographer whose digital work was to be posted alongside my articles. The day we were to go online the tourism minder assigned to us had unfortunate news: We had not yet received official clearance to begin transmission back to Redmond. State Security—which we later learned had a hotel room on the floor below ours—tried to sabotage us.

Producer Christian Kallen took a deep breath and went to work. Instead of using our hotel's monitored phone line to the States, he routed a line from his laptop to a Microsoft terminal in Canada, from which the stories and photos were dutifully forwarded to Microsoft's campus for worldwide posting the next morning. Every day the tourism fellow forlornly told us we had not yet received clearance to transmit, and we'd nod our sad acquiescence. And every night we'd mojo the package to Canada.

Finally, Mariel arrived with her husband and two facto-tums who seemed to have no function other than to regale each other with tales of how to extract cash from errant ATMs. I was only too pleased to guide Hemingway and her entourage around Havana and introduce her to people and places of note, especially locations associated with her father's father. Each time we came to such a site, I would recount the conventional wisdom about it, then explain that the popular story was at odds with the historical record.

A sign at a famous restaurant, for instance, had supposedly been autographed by Ernest Hemingway, but this was a complete invention, fabricated by tourism officials after his death. He was said to have written *For Whom the Bell Tolls* at one hotel, when in fact he wrote most of the book at another hotel where he maintained a room to escape his growing popularity. When Hemingway's old sea captain, then 100 years old at the time of our visit, was trotted out as the model for *The Old Man and the Sea*, I noted that, as a letter from Hemingway to his editor Maxwell Perkins reveals, the real fisherman was someone else who had died early on, leaving the way open for this new public face. Mariel's husband grew increasingly annoyed as I punctured holes in the grand myth he had come to film. At one point, he leaned over from the back seat of our rented SUV. "Miller," he said with irritation, "shut up."

We chartered a plane to fly to Santiago de Cuba, and when we arrived at the sanctuary at nearby El Cobre, Padre Jorge came to the chapel to greet us. I'd like to say he slowly opened a creaking mahogany box and carefully unwrapped a fringed silk tallit to produce the medallion. But no, Hemingway's celebrated Nobel Prize, which weighed almost half a pound, was stored in a large manila envelope.

Mariel knelt briefly and crossed herself, then received the medallion as the rest of the party watched from a distance. As interpreter, I discreetly stood a few feet back and to her side. Mariel held the precious medal, absorbing its essence. Then, as if a quarterback unexpectedly handing off to her halfback, she turned to her left and placed her grandfather's medallion in my hands.

After many books, through decades of writing, I had received the most hallowed honor in my profession, the Nobel Prize.

I do not know what followed. It seemed as if a ray of light had come through stained glass and struck me dumb. There was something heavy in my hands that reflected the sun, I know, but I'm not sure if I held it for five seconds or five minutes. I recall sweating profusely and wearing a goofy grin. Mariel's voice brought me out of the fog: "O.K., Tom, that's enough." I handed the 1954 Nobel Prize in Literature back to her.

On our last day in Cuba, the tourism flack, utterly clueless about the previous week's daily postings, excitedly told us we would be allowed to transmit to Redmond that evening. To make him happy, we reprogrammed the laptop and did it his way.

❧ ❧ ❧

Tom Miller's many books include Trading With the Enemy, The Panama Hat Trail, Jack Ruby's Kitchen Sink, *and* Revenge of the Saguaro. *His prizes include two Solas Awards and a Lowell Thomas Award for Best Travel Book of 2000. He was editor of* Travelers' Tales Cuba, *and wrote the introduction for* The Best Travel Writing 2005. *Miller is a member of the Thornton Wilder Society and the Cervantes Society of America, and lives in Tucson, where he serves as Adjunct Research Associate at the University of Arizona's Center for Latin American Studies.*

❧ ❧ ❧

The Babushkas of Chernobyl

"As long as the sun shines, one
does not ask for the moon."
—Russian proverb

Outside Hanna Zavorotnya's cottage in Chernobyl's dead zone, the hulking, severed sow's head bleeds into the snow, its gargantuan snout pointing to the sky in strange defeat. The frigid December air tingles with excitement as Hanna, seventy-seven, zips between the outlying sheds wielding the seven-inch silver blade used to bring the pig to its end. "Today I command the parade," she says, grinning as she hands a vat of steaming entrails to her sister-in-law at the smokehouse, then moves off again. In one hand she holds a fresh, fist-size hunk of raw pig fat—there is no greater delicacy in Ukraine—and she pauses now and then to dole out thin slices to her neighbors. "I fly like a falcon!" says Hanna, shuttling at high speed back towards the carcass. Indeed, falcons, as well as wolves, wild boar, moose and lynx, all species not seen in these environs for decades, have returned to the forests around Chernobyl. One particular falcon, however, has not fared so well. A large gray and white

specimen, it is strung up, dead, chest puffed and wings out-
spread against the slate sky, above Hanna's chicken coop as
a warning to its brethren. "He came and ate my chicken so
I beat him with a stick," she says. But if this falcon has not
survived, Hanna has—against all odds and any reasonable
medical prediction.

Twenty-five years ago, on April 26, 1986, Chernobyl
Nuclear Power Plant's Reactor Number 4 blew up after a
botched test, and the ensuing fire lasted for ten days, spewing 400 times more radiation than the bomb dropped on
Hiroshima. The government (then Soviet) declared that the
surrounding thirty square kilometers were uninhabitable,
and immediately resettled 116,000 residents with a pension,
an apartment, some pots and pans and sketchy information
about the health risks that lay ahead. In the months and years
that followed, these first resettlers were followed by a few
hundred thousand more, all displaced from the land where
they'd grown up. But Hanna, who'd been forced out in the
first group, did not accept that fate. Three months after being
relocated, she returned to her ancestral home with her husband, her mother-in-law and a handful of other members of
their collective farm, the main building of which now lies like
a carcass, silent and overgrown, its sunken roof collapsing, a
half-mile down the road from Hanna's house. When government officials objected, she responded, "Shoot us and dig the
grave; otherwise we're staying."

In the years following the accident, Hanna was among
1,200 returnees, called self-settlers, most over the age of forty-
eight, who made their way back in defiance of the authorities' legitimate concerns. For despite the self-settlers' deep
love of their ancestral homes, it's a fact that the soil, air, and
water here in what is now called the Exclusion Zone, or Zone
of Alienation, are among the most heavily contaminated on
Earth. Today, about 200 or so self-settlers remain, scattered

about in eerily silent villages that are ghostly but also strangely charming.

About 80 percent of the surviving resettlers are women in their seventies and eighties, creating a unique world of *babushkas*, a Russian word that means "*grandmother*" but also refers to "old country women." Why women? Radiation may know no gender preference, but alcohol and cigarettes do. The average life span of the Ukranian man is fifty-nine, and dropping. The consequences of vice—perhaps worsened by immune-damaging radiation—have contributed to creating this unlikely world of women.

Why, I wondered, would the babushkas choose to live on this deadly land? Are they unaware of the risks, or crazy enough to ignore them, or both? (These are reasonable questions from a Westerner who struggles in the aisles of a grocery-store over whether paying the extra $3 for organic almond butter is "worth it.") But babushkas see their lives, and the risks they run, decidedly differently.

When Reactor Number 4 blew up, roughly 30 percent of the initial fallout hit Ukraine and parts of Western Russia and 70 percent landed downwind in Belarus. The gamma radiation was death-dealing: some forty first responders were incapacitated immediately and died within weeks. But the explosion's long-term effect on the surrounding area was harder to quantify. Unlike the fallout from a nuclear bomb, which can be measured out circularly, and somewhat predictably, the radiation from Chernobyl's nuclear fire laid waste in a spotty, inconsistent manner. And that inconsistency was exploited by petty local officials. Which villages got doused? Which did not? Dosimeter readings (which indicate accumulated radiation exposure) varied wildly and sometimes the authorities accepted bribes to alter them. Confusion, bravery and corruption marked the post-explosion weeks and months, and hardly anyone on the ground fully understood the dangers they were facing. A nuclear fire of this sort was unprecedented and a secretive Soviet bureaucracy added to the cloud of misinformation.

Chernobyl ushered in a new chapter on the toxic vagaries of radiation. What is clear about the effects of nuclear contaminants (cesium, strontium and plutonium, and others) is that they enter the food chain through the soil, they spread via wind and fire, and their effects are cumulative and linked to, among other things, increases in fetal mortality and cancer. In some cases the contaminants stick around for thousands of years. Immediately after the accident, cows ingested grass contaminated with the short-lived isotope radioiodine 131 (contaminated milk largely accounts for today's sky-high thyroid cancer rates in the area). At the time of the accident, the babushkas may or may not have noticed that the birds fell silent and the honey bees ceased flying as the "invisible enemy" enveloped the spring countryside, but they were definitely alarmed when emergency workers made them dump out their cows' milk.

Maria Urupa was thinking about her cow when the soldiers arrived to evacuate her village of Paryshev on May 3, 1986. "I planned to take my cow and hide in the basement," she says. Instead, she and her neighbors were relocated to a hurriedly constructed housing project about two hours' drive away. Their new homes were outside Kiev (changed to Kyiv in 1991 after Ukraine became independent), on land where many people had died in the 1930s during the Holdomor (literally "death by hunger"), the massive genocide-by-famine that Soviet leader Josef Stalin instigated in order to subjugate Ukraine and move peasant farmers onto state farming collectives or into factories. Conservative estimates say between 3.5 million and 5 million Ukrainians died during this period, and many of the babushkas lost their fathers. Some almost died themselves, since during the Holmodor, starving villagers sometimes resorted to cannibalism, slaughtering one child to save the rest. Half a century later, the site where Maria and her family were relocated still held grim reminders of the Holodmor. "People's legs were sticking out of the ground, and that's where they built the village," she remembers. Three months after moving there, Maria and her family returned to their home in the Exclusion Zone.

When I meet the seventy-seven-year-old on a still December afternoon she's standing on her porch in twenty-eight degree weather, wearing only a cotton print housedress and a sweater so threadbare that a few of the buttons have been replaced by safety pins. With a small sled in tow, she's on her way to gather wood for her cook stove. "Would you like some soup with mushrooms?" she asks, diligently hospitable. I demure, knowing mushrooms, a regional favorite second only to pig fat, are infamous absorbers of radiation. She doesn't mind stopping to talk. She looks healthy and stout, if a bit stern due to the upside-down smile lines that crease her cheeks. Straining to be heard over the gobbles of a hefty reddish-brown turkey whose ruckus is meant to keep her chickens safe from the abundant wild animals, Maria tells me about the day Soviet troops under orders from Stalin marched onto the Urupa family farm. "They took away two bulls, two pigs and all the potatoes," Maria says. "They did it because my father was working for the church and that was not allowed then." When her father asked if he could keep a few potatoes, the soldiers threatened to kill him if he tried, saying, "Your soul will fly away and we'll wrap your guts around the telephone wire."

Indeed, for many of the women, Chernobyl was only the last in an unholy trifecta of hardship. After the famine came the Nazis, who, when the babushkas were teenagers, slashed their way across the Ukraine in the 1940s, raping women and killing another 2.7 million people, including virtually the entire Jewish population. Having survived all of that, the babushkas were not inclined to cut and run after the Chernobyl explosion created invisible threats in the air, soil and water. Hanna, who nearly became one of the infants eaten by their families during Holodomor, puts it succinctly: "Starvation is what scares me. Not radiation."

Most of the babushkas share the belief that "if you leave, you die." They would rather risk exposure to radiation than the soul-crushing prospect of being separated from their homes. "You can't take me from my mother; you can't take me from my motherland. Motherland is Motherland," says Hanna. Aphorisms slip matter-of-factly from the lips of the babushkas. "Replant an old tree and it will die," says one woman. "A pigeon flies close to his nest. I would never leave my home." One refrain I heard often was, "Those who left are worse off now. They are all dying of sadness."

What sounds like faith may actually be fact. According to United Nations reports, those who were relocated after the accident now suffer from anxiety, depression, and disrupted social networks—the traumas of displaced people everywhere. And these conditions seem to have health effects as real as those caused by radiation. "Paradoxically, the women who returned to their ancestral homes in the Zone outlive those who left by a decade," says Alexander Anisimov, a journalist I met who's spent his career studying the self-settler community. No health studies have been done, but anecdotal evidence suggests that most of these women die of strokes rather than any obvious radiation-related illnesses. Toxic levels of strontium and cesium in the soil are real, but so are the tug of the ancestral home and the health benefits of determining one's own destiny. And East or West, pig fat or organic almond butter, few would deny that being happy helps you live longer.

A lone fisherman hunches over a hole in the vast forbidden Pripyat River; abandoned gray metal ships on their sides and half sunk, languish in the landscape behind. For these women, environmental contamination is not the worst form of devastation, I think, as I stand near the river on an empty road snapping a photo of one of the massive storks' nests of sticks, hay and feathers that is perched atop telephone poles around Chernobyl. And that holds true for Chernobyl's wildlife, too. Storks may have dropped dead from the skies over Sweden days after the accident, but twenty-five years later they are ubiquitous in the Exclusion Zone. Their return illustrates the controversy among scientists and laypeople about exactly how living creatures cope with radiation. Do they adapt (as some scientists—and babushkas—claim people do)? Is survival of the genetically fittest at work? It's likely to be decades before we know. Scientists have discovered DNA mutations in the animals who have returned, but few visible physiological anomalies (one example: the local moose are having one calf, not two). Clearly, the mass exodus of human beings has been a boon to some animal species. In the Zone of Alienation, and in designated nearby areas, it is officially forbidden to hunt or eat wild animals, which can be highly contaminated. But that is the sort of edict people tend to shrug off in a country experiencing acute economic crisis and corruption, where there is a deep connection to the soil and, especially in the rural areas, a live-off-the-land culture.

"I often collect berries and mushrooms to eat," says one babushka. "It's forbidden, but I go anyway. When I see the police I hide in the bushes," she adds. Hunters also sneak into the Zone, and the contaminated meat from animals they poach ends up in the restaurants of Kyiv. Police charged with enforcing the rules in Chernobyl are rumored to shoot wild horses and other game from helicopters. And contaminated meat isn't the only dangerous item to slip out of the Zone. Pilfered irradiated metal from machines and vehicles used during the clean-up makes its way to China. "Hot" toilet seats, illegally looted from the evacuated ghost town of Pripyat, three kilometers from the reactor (where background radiation levels are a whopping 100; my visit there was brief) are now scattered throughout Eastern Europe. Twenty-five years after the accident, Chernobyl's legacy lives on.

At first, of course, the main victims were those who were initially exposed to extreme doses of radiation. After the first responders were felled, the Soviets deployed robots to put out the fire, but radiation levels were so high the machines went berserk. The government then sent in a phalanx of human beings, dubbed liquidators, the translation of a Russian word that can also mean "cleaner." Thousands of young soldiers were strong-armed into volunteering by being presented with the following choice: Spend two years on the bloody Afghanistan front or *two minutes* shoveling radioactive matter off the reactor complex. Most of them took a shot of vodka and the latter. Most of them are now dead, dying or disabled. (Call them what you will—heroes, pawns, soldiers who did their duty—the truth is they stopped a fire that, had it spread, could have caused the other reactors to explode, leaving much of Europe uninhabitable.) But these soldiers weren't the only liquidators that beautiful, tragic spring. The term also refers to the hundreds of thousands of women and men throughout the region who took part in the clean-up and support effort.

Galina Konyushonok, now seventy-one, was called to duty as a liquidator almost immediately. She worked in a nearby bread factory at the time of the accident and was charged with driving to the town of Chernobyl every day to pick up wheat so the government could feed the people working the disaster. Of course, the wheat itself was highly contaminated. Sitting today with three babushka neighbors in a kitchen bright with the reflection of the snow outside, Galina, who has thyroid cancer, looks strong and healthy; she's talkative and her thick eyebrows dance with almost every word. Her

friend Nadezhda Tislenko, seventy-one, has been bent over at
a right angle by osteoporosis, yet she is outstandingly gracious.

"Please, please have some cake," she offers.

"No *spasiba*," I say, deploying my standard response so as
to avoid potentially contaminated food. No local food, along
with "don't breathe deeply" were just a few of the warnings
on a release I had to sign at the Zone's police checkpoint. It's
hard to refuse food from any grandmother but here, where
traditions run deep and visitors are few, it feels extra rude.
On the windowsill, a white tin can labeled "Food Relief: in
the name of Christ" holds a well-tended houseplant. Galina's
house is located in the town of Zirka, a few hundred yards
outside the Exclusion Zone, a boundary demarcated by a
chain link and barbed wire fence. Her little village "used to
have seventy-six cows but now only has two," she says. The
arbitrary process by which Zirka came to be considered a
"normal" village despite high contamination levels is a common tale of misguided bureaucracy.

"All the villages around us were evacuated when the reactor blew. But a special strain of potato had just been planted in
the fields [of Zirka's collective farm], so they said our village
shouldn't be evacuated," recalls Galina, adjusting her purple
headscarf around her ruddy face. "They haven't checked for
radiation here in fifteen years," she adds.

Although it would be a stretch to call the babushkas a sis-
terhood, a deep camaraderie connects these women who have
spent their entire lives in the area. They help each other at
slaughtering time. They visit one another's homes (on foot;
they do not have cars) to play cards, and gamble. "But not
for money," Galina specifies. "I keep telling them, the more
you play the more your brain works," she says, laughing. The
women joke about moving in together if heating gas prices
get too high (they are on fixed, modest government pensions),
but emotional attachment to their homes runs too deep for

that; home is the entire cosmos of the rural babushka. The babushkas have electricity but most villages in the Zone have a single phone; nobody has running water. Those with a TV might sit down with handwork to watch a soap opera after the chickens are fed and the wood chopped. When I asked about the dearth of men, Galina responds: "The men died and the women stayed. I wish I had a husband to quarrel with!" The old ladies crack up when Galina tells a gallows-humor joke about a woman being gang-raped by Nazis. The babushkas are unfazed by how I squirm at the joke; they also ignore the *click click click* of my dosimeter, which is measuring ever-fluctuating background radiation levels.

In a corner of Galina's house, beneath a bright window, stands the bed where her husband died seventeen years ago after making her promise never to leave their home. Galina's exquisite needlework and embroidery, stacked in neat piles and framed on the walls, gives warmth and color to the three-room cottage where she's lived for fifty-two years and raised four children who visit her often—a pleasure denied her neighbors inside the Exclusion Zone. There, adult family members may visit after jumping through several administrative hoops, but children under eighteen are allowed in only once a year to see their babushkas and visit the graves of their ancestors, on a spring holiday called Remembrance Day.

On a small table in the same room, a dozen or so medicines, an identification card and a blood pressure machine tell a more somber story. An ID reading "Disabled, First Group," indicates her liquidator status and her thyroid cancer diagnosis. She waves away the table of meds, as if to shoo off its significance, and crosses the room to show me a piece of fabric embroidered with the message, "Bring happiness and health to my motherland."

"I'm not afraid of anything anymore. It's difficult to be old, but I still want to live," she says, folding up the embroidery.

"A gift," she says then walks into the other room to find a bag. I look out the window at her five-foot tall pile of chopped wood that rests in the snow next to a shed. Inside, the warm pungent air that is endemic to the cottages of Chernobyl wafts comfort—and fear. Burning Chernobyl wood releases radiation. It is illegal to burn wood from this region. When I put the dosimeter into the ashes of Galina's firebox it goes nuts; radiation levels shoot from fifteen to seventy-three in a matter of seconds.

Galina gives me a tour of her cellar, where the dim light of a single bulb reveals the antler racks of five roe deer. "My son shot them for me," she says. Local intelligence claims deer are the most contaminated species in the region, but Galina eats the meat from this land, as all babushkas do. The cellar is also heaped with brown eggs, beetroot, jars full of pickled foods, and of course, potatoes: the year-round, hardscrabble labor of the babushkas represented in a single room where Galina is laying in supplies for the harsh winter. "They used to not take potatoes from me, but now they do," she says of her son's family, whose vigilance about not eating contaminated food has apparently waned. Thinking of her son, perhaps, Galina looks upward, and with a mischievous, proud smile says: "In the attic I have forty liters of moonshine that I made. When I die my family will drink it! They won't have to buy any." We climb up to the attic so I can see the stash. A shaft of afternoon light blazes through the attic window, refracting through a dozen hefty glass jugs of hooch; stars of light bounce off the blades of old-school brown leather ice skates, circa 1940, hanging over a rafter.

There is a breed of heroic resilience, of plain-spoken pragmatism, specific to those who rise at 5 A.M. and work, with few modern conveniences, until midnight in subzero weather; to those who bury their two-year-old next to their own parents, as Hanna did; to those who've earned the hard way the right to joke about Nazi atrocities. It's not as if they wouldn't *want* things to be easier. Some acknowledge the radiation and its impact on their health. But as one eighty-two-year-old put it, with a patina of typical, simple defiance: "They said our legs would hurt. And they do. So what?"

Findings about the long-term health effects of Chernobyl are controversial and contradictory. The World Health Organization predicts 4,000 deaths will eventually be linked to Chernobyl, and reports that thyroid cancer rates have shot up in Ukraine, Belarus and Russia, largely among those contaminated in the weeks immediately following the accident. However, the WHO now considers the psychological impact to be just as or more detrimental than the physical. Being depressed and unmotivated, pursuing an unhealthy lifestyle and clinging to a victim mind-set, they say, has proved to be the worst fallout for the "Chernobylites" twenty-five years after the accident. Other organizations, such as Greenpeace, contend that Chernobyl is responsible for tens of thousands of illnesses and deaths even though these cannot yet be scientifically linked to the accident. All agree it will be generations before the full consequences of Chernobyl can be fully understood.

Meanwhile, life goes on. Until it doesn't.

Five babushkas bob in single file along a snow-swept, single-lane road, a squat platoon of hunched women swaddled in dark clothing and headscarves, marching home from the funeral. The second one that week. Their figures are all that moves in the frigid, bleak landscape. Lyubov Koval, 84, the mother of the deceased, describes her fifty-five-year-old son's final days. "He screamed, and screamed," she says, her narrowed blue eyes indulging pain for only the tiniest moment. "There was some problem with his kidneys," she reveals, regarding cause of death. "They won't say it was the radiation," adds his sister Olga Kudla. Six gravediggers sit at a long wooden table, eating wild goat liver, blintzes and dumplings and drinking. "He was a liquidator in the zone," one of them says. "They wouldn't give him the medicine he needed. He wouldn't have died if they had." The babushkas keep bringing piles of steaming food, brown bread and sweet homemade wine—pushing, pushing, pushing food as if it is love and life itself. Refusing is death. A full shot glass of moonshine sits in the middle of the table for the deceased.

The shelter covering Reactor Number 4, which so many lives were sacrificed to construct, sits cracked and rusty in winter's 3:30 P.M. dusk. I think about the lake of nuclear lava—20 to 30 tons according to experts on site—simmering below, then walk a few hundred yards onto a bridge and look down to see giant catfish, some more than ten feet long, trolling the waters of the now defunct reactor's cooling pond. After the explosion in 1986, the shelter was built to cover the reactor and prevent leakage of radioactive materials. The shelter was intended to last fifteen years, not twenty-five, but a mire of bureaucratic shenanigans, politics and economic woes have added up to little action in the construction of a new one. Part of the problem is that the shelter is leaking so much radiation that nobody wants to work near it. Collective fingers are crossed that the aging sarcophagus does not collapse and explode, the consequences of which could dwarf those of 1986.

While it has been possible since 1999 for visitors to pass the heavily guarded police checkpoints and enter the Zone with an escort, the Ukrainian government recently announced an idea, not yet executed, to open the Exclusion Zone for the first time to conventional tourism. For those who want to experience the Zone first hand, these babushkas could become a stop on an ethnographic tour. (Perhaps babushka moonshine will become the latest artisanal trend.)

For now, their spirit shines amid the bleak, silent dead Zone. A fearless babushka stands watch over a garden at night, poised to bang a gas bottle with a metal bar to ward off attacks from wild boar. Galina recently harvested twenty big bags of potatoes. "All clean. No worms this year!" she says gratefully. Flashing a glint of gold from her lone tooth, Hanna reveals that she has saved a pig to slaughter for Remembrance Day. "I only think of the good things in life," she says, rolling onto the balls of her feet. "Come back tomorrow," she tells me, holding up a chunk of thick, white pig fat. "We are going to party."

☙ ☙ ☙

Holly Morris is the creator/director of the PBS travel series "Adventure Divas," and author of Adventure Divas: Searching the World for a New Kind of Heroine, *which was named a* New York Times *"Editor's Choice." A former* National Geographic Adventure *columnist, she is a regular contributor to* The New York Times Book Review *and other publications, and her work is widely anthologized. She hosts the television series* Globe Trekker, Treks in a Wild World, *and* Outdoor Investigations, *and is at work on a documentary about the babushkas of Chernobyl. Visit her at www.thebabushkasofchernobyl.com.*

～*～ ～*～ ～*～

How I Got My Oh-La-La

You don't have to be born French.

By most accounts, I look O.K. My style, such as it is, mainly impresses the world with a mild, *she's nice*. Yet I had been in Paris mere weeks when Madame de Glasse, the French neighbor with whom I am friendly, announced some startling news. As we chatted in the launderette we both use on the rue de Passy, Madame eyed a washer's soggy wad of pajamas, long johns, turtlenecks and sweats I had plopped into a rolling basket. Then she said with some alarm, "Mademoiselle," she said. "Like many Americans, you are a prude, *non*?"

Moi? I stared at her, shocked.

True, Madame's wash was a jambalaya of plunging necklines, peek-a-boo intimates and colors the heart-racing hues of passion. There were lace bits and sheer slips and things that looked short and clingy. But who would have thought that what passes for hot where I come from—a whole sack of comfy stuff snapped up for a song at an outlet—would be seen by Madame de Glasse (if not all of France) as symptomatic of a horrible American malady: dowdiness. And I had it!

Was my frumpiness so far gone that nothing could be done? I squeaked. Suddenly, I was insecure in my one-size-hides-all hoodie. Madame swept a sorrowful look over the laundry I loaded into the dryer—a hefty cotton jogbra and the shame of some unraveling granny panties stood out—and rendered her opinion. I held my breath.

"It is grave, very grave," said Madame de Glasse, gravely.

I had no idea. Yet my wardrobe of saggy-ass sweats and what's-become-of-me tops certainly contrasted with the out-fits fresh from the dryer that Madame de Glasse was folding. Among them: a tiny lime-green thong, a demi-brassiere of transparent lace, and a sweet, sexy skirt no bigger than a wisp. Was it true I had no clue? That the art of feminine fabulous-ness French women take for granted had shut me out? There I was, roving around Paris in my take on cute—relaxed-fit jeans and U.S. Army t-shirt, while other women, *frump-free* women, were gracing sidewalk cafés in revealing décolleté, clicking down streets in chic kitten heels, or flaunting their flirty fig-ures in tight-fitting everything. Meanwhile, whatever wom-anly allure I might possess, Madame de Glasse pointed out, was obscured by my prude-wear. My vavavoom was repressed by my unisex dress; my pizzazz, she said, was hidden far, far beneath the sorry fact I did not, it seems, act French.

"What makes French girls as serenely self-satisfied as purr-ing cats . . . and catnip to the men who admire them?" asked Debra Ollivier, author of *Entre Nous—A Woman's Guide to Finding Her Inner French Girl*. I wondered! "The stereotypical French girl," she said, "is often insolently thin, casually chic, and fashionable despite a simple wardrobe. With or without makeup she is always put together and utterly self-confident, imbued with natural elegance and an elusive distance that is particularly, maddeningly French." I guessed such a woman would not be caught in a jogbra. *Especially* dead.

"*Chérie? Chérie?*" It was Madame de Glasse, interrupting my reverie in a chirpy tone altogether more cheerful than that she used over my giant, white panties. "To change the subject," she said, "have you been to that new gym at Beaubourg?" She meant Espace Vit'Halles at the Pompidou Center. "It is *trés flash*," she said. "Make a visit and tell me of your adventure."

"Yes, yes, I will; *au revoir* Madame de Glasse." I scuttled my uptight self out of the launderette as fast as my heavy duffle of now shameful frump's clothes allowed. *The French girl understands that sexy is a state of mind*, maintained Ollivier. Sexy is a state of mind . . . sexy is a state of mind. . . . Back at my apartment, I pondered this pearl and dressed for bed in the t-shirt, tights and full-body nightie the frigid night demanded. Surely Madame de Glasse, in my place, would not don her tiny lime-green thong and a babydoll peignoir! Then again, maybe she would. After all, such a get-up would guarantee she'd have a Frenchman keeping her far warmer than floor-length flannel ever could. If this wasn't reason enough to find my inner French girl, I didn't know what was.

"One is not born a woman," said author/philosopher Simone de Beauvoir; "rather, one becomes a woman." Now, there's a girl who sounds in touch with hers. Simone had a leg up, of course: she was, already, French. But still: her words gave me hope. If I were not born a woman who is catnip, perhaps I could become a sort of cat's meow—a woman so Frenchly serene and purring with self-approval that my laundry would tell of a total transformation. Hide my thighs? Disguise my derriere? Tent my tummy? Ha! No longer. My new dare-to-bare wardrobe of trim, tiny things would be as peek-a-boo as what have you. They would declare to Madame de Glasse, for one, that American shame has no place in my life now that my inner French girl is driving. No doubt she'll be dressed in something more form-fitting and flirty than my usual at-home outfit: the frump-o-wonderful caftan that Madame de Glasse surely would find more "burka" than "babe."

Then again, what would it take to achieve such body confidence? Such feminine self-acceptance? If only I could feel, as the French say, "*bien dans sa peau*"—good in one's skin. When American novelist Edith Wharton traveled to France in 1919, she observed that the French were "puzzled by our queer fear of our own bodies." So, I reasoned, my queer fear might be the cultural baggage of generations. But really, in these enlightened days? It was silly. Time to let it go. In the meantime, might as well try the new gym.

Day 1. The instant I entered Espace Vit'Halles, a friendly *monsieur* at the front desk bid me a big, grinning welcome. Yoga, dance aerobics, weights—I was encouraged to profit from them all. "The ladies' changing room is on the second floor, Madame," he said, and shooed me in the approximate direction. I found the door, clearly marked "Femmes," and entered a sanctuary of sensual splendor. Lovely lavender décor; chaise longues lined up for lounging; flowers blooming on the mirrored vanities: the room was a swoon of comfort and beauty. Showcased under spotlights, a hot tub as vast and artfully conceived as ancient Roman baths bid welcome. Such luxury. Such pampering! The gym-women who showered or soaked or otherwise performed their *toilettes* in various stages of undress flaunted their inner French girls exactly as Ollivier claimed. Women sinewy and women plump, women with goddesses' bodies and women with pocks and spots and skin that looked anything but good to be in: All got in and out of underwear that wasn't underwear at all, but rather, lingerie. There it all was, France's finest: lacy, racy and for sure, sensational. These confections, no doubt expensive, were also, let's face it: frightening. How would I ever undress in the presence of women so adept in the provocative art of underwear? Some of the self-satisfied purring cats of the changing room paraded . . . no, *swaggered* around naked. And down to their brazenly exposed French toes they seemed shame-free. Were I to strip to my big dowdy whities before their eyes, what

then? *So queer!* I feared they'd exclaim. *An American prude.*
Doesn't like to be nude.

I was in luck. There was a toilet stall that could serve as
a personal changing *cabine*. My strictly utilitarian bra sans
lace, plunge, pads, push-up, or the least suggestion of seduc-
tion could be kept secret. I scuttled in, did my business and
emerged dressed in workout-wear. Ta dum! Embarrassment
deflected. I headed for the exit and dance aerobic class, but
stopped dead when I heard a bit of catnip call.

"Oh, Madame! Madame!" I turned to see a raven-haired,
hipless thing holding aloft my favorite faded cut-offs—the
shorts that for a good thirty years now, I have found charming on me. "You dropped your . . . your. . . ." She did not have
words for what they were. But her sweet, sad smile and pity-
ing tone told me all that Inès de la Fressange already had:

"No *Parisienne* would dress mutton as lamb."

The ex-runway model and French fashion guru put this
rule in her *Parisian Chic: A Style Guide* to let me know *in
advance* of coming to France that shorts, like miniskirts, have
no business on any woman older than . . . young.

"*Merci beaucoup*, Madame," I said, sheepish. I waited until
she pranced off, pert ponytail swinging, and tossed my past
into the trash. *Mutton?!*

Day 2. "*Bonjour*, Madame," said the grinning *monsieur* when
I returned to try the gym's yoga. "The ladies' changing room
is on the first floor. Enjoy your class." *That's odd*, I thought.
Wasn't the ladies' changing room just yesterday on Floor
2? Yet on the first floor, as promised, there it was, the door
marked "Femmes." I entered and saw at once all *was* odd.
Where was the lavender? Where was the lovely? Loaded with
lockers, lacking a hot tub, the room was dim, dank, functional.
Testosterone chose the décor so sweat stains didn't show,
and from the télé turned to sports to the vanities equipped

with manly-looking man-things used by grooming men, this changing room clearly was meant for well, men.

And yet, there they were: Women. The *Parsiennes* flaunted their inner French girls like they had the day before; they paraded around queer-fear-free in brassieres like pasties and thongs if not sheer then small. Awfully.

"*Entrez*, Madame," said one, as I lingered at the door. The French girl had just contorted herself into a contraption of an electric-blue bustier, a towel on her head. "*Oui, oui*, Madame, come in. You've found the right place." I wasn't so sure. No toilet stall announced itself after my first look around, so I would have to strip and change into yoga clothes in full view of a man-cave full of catnip. My priggish panties! My not-hot bra! Never mind. This wasn't anything some serious French lingerie acquisition couldn't fix. Plus, it was no lace off *their* merry widows if, in front of the Frenchwomen, I got naked like the place had caught fire and I had better move fast or die. Which is how I did. But in the process? It was astonishing. There I was, whipping off my clothes and slipping into Spandex, and nary a glance went to my uncomely undies. I was a blur, sure. But snug in their absolute disinterest, smug in their elusive distance, the Frenchwomen paid my flash of breast and briefly bared behind no mind. Whatsoever. *Wow, self-satisfaction must be catching*. In the presence of such total nonchalance, I felt for one wild, nude moment . . . well, nude! It was awesome. I wanted more of it.

Day 3. I arrived at Espace Vit'Halles, today to try the weight room. "*Bonjour,*" bid the big-grinned *monsieur*, as expected. He then directed me to the ladies' changing room . . . on the second floor. The second floor? Seriously? Yes. The door marked "Femmes" had moved from the man-cave back upstairs; it opened again on the lovely lavender space filled with Frenchwomen changing.

Encouraged by my undressing success of the previous day, I was shy but excited to unveil my treasures. I had gone shopping. At the lingerie shop on boulevard Haussmann, I could find nothing frumpy whatsoever in a French granny panty; neither was there a single serviceable bra that would just do the job—as if such things in Paris existed. So standing before the display of wares both naughty and nice, a woman I didn't know spoke up.

"I'll take the panties in slinky pink with their matching bra of ruffles and bows—yes, those," she told the shop's assistant. I was stunned to discover it was I, myself, not just speaking but also pointing to items so cute that even Mademoiselle had to approve—endowed as she was with come-hither hips and considerable cleavage. This choice was so surprising that it meant only thing. There *was* a French girl in me—in me!— and she had been roused by ruffles. Here now, at the gym, I beheld this bold foreigner with cool suspicion and moved to the farthest corner of the changing room. There, I could undress apart from the purring cats and expose my newly-purchased pizzazz in relative privacy. I claimed a locker and settled-in on a bench. My queer American fears still lingered, but my new French bra of unabashed vavavoom? It almost busted out of my blouse to shout *Here I am*! And how my slinky pink French panties were pleased to sashay free of my jeans with a little wiggle of joy. Just then, the door. A man announced himself.

"*Bonjour, Mesdames*," he announced. "*Pardonnez-moi*." He begged everyone's pardon for the disturbance, but he was the plumber, he said, come to the ladies' changing room to solve the problem of the leaky sink. Beside him laden with tools and balancing a ladder stood his apprentice son; he looked about twenty-one. The changing ladies in the buff, or in some version thereof . . . well, did they shriek or run or faint or cover-up? No. "*Bonjour Messieurs*," they said, entirely nonchalant. The plumber and his son then passed through the friendly throng, clattering wrenches and whatnot. As they passed they muttered their manners, *pardon, Madame . . . pardon, Madame, pardon.* And the Frenchwomen stepped out of panties and shucked brassieres; they shimmied into shape-wear and stripped out of slips. *Plumbers?* Any one of them might have said. *So?*

Clad only in my new slinky pinks, I heard a *"Pardon, Madame"* so close it had to be directed to me. I froze.

Moi? I turned to stare at the hovering plumber, in shock.

Yes, he meant me. I was blocking the way to the sink which, he indicated with his whatnot, stood directly ahead in my corner. Leaking. The plumber's son scooched by with his ladder and tipped his hat, *"Bonjour,* Madame." Then the two, clattering, set-up shop on the bench closest to mine. The most miserable of moments arrived. I wondered: Did Edith Wharton ever have a queer fear of *her* naked self? If so, what protocol did she suggest for the presence of French plumbers when one has stripped down to intimates—silk bits that are the next thing to go?

"First of all," she once said, "the Frenchwoman is, in nearly all respects, as different as possible from the average American woman . . . The Frenchwoman is *grown-up.* Compared with the women of France, the American woman is still in the kindergarten."

What Wharton would say: *Oh grow-up.* If I didn't remove my slinky pink things without an ounce of shame, I would never make it to first grade. Really, what were the plumber and his son to me, except perhaps plumbers? In that flash of nudity between underwear off and workout-wear on, what harm could they cause in the midst of the changing room's entire *colony* of nonchalant nudes? On the count of . . . three: There I went. I squeezed my eyes closed and off with the ruffles, out of all bows. But I didn't even have to peek to know. My raw glory garnered less interest than a drip. The men, both bent over the sink and fiddling with a wrench, looked up at me and back at the leak like, *her? Her who?*

"There is in France a kind of collective, cultural shrug about nakedness," Ollivier said. Edith Wharton agreed: "The French," she said, "are accustomed to relating openly and unapologetically the anecdotes that Anglo-Saxons snicker over privately and with apologies."

I'm sorry, but the plumbers' total lack of interest in my body bare left me giggly with a secret, newfound freedom. Just think! Frump or no, I could flaunt my feminine fixtures and ask for nothing in the way of drama. Then, the plumber's son looked up, caught my eye, and winked.

Oh.

Day 4. When I arrived to attend class in Pilates, the ever friendly *monsieur* said the usual *Bonjour*, Madame and directed me to the ladies' changing room—on the first floor.

"But *Monsieur*!" I cried, by now perturbed. "Why does the ladies' changing room keep changing?" Second floor, first floor; first floor, second. "I don't get it."

"It's the hot tub, Madame. The men's changing room does not have one, so it's only *juste* that the men are given the opportunity to use the ladies' tub from the time to time, *non*?

It made perfect sense.

"Merci, *Monsieur*," I said. Today the ladies would change in the man-cave, so I found the first-floor door marked "Femmes" and entered. Empty. No purring cat so far had arrived. I claimed a sweet spot on the most spacious bench, flipped open a locker and proceeded to undress. Proud, yes *proud* I was to strip to my second shopping score—a brand-new sheer-lace brassiere and panties frilled in fancy fringe. Both were so pretty they should have been strolling the Champs Élysées. *Too bad no one's around to appreciate them.* Nevertheless, off they went so I could shimmy into the tight body stocking I wore for Pilates.

Just then, the door.

Too late to run, too late to hide; I thought for sure I was about to die. In they came, like kids let out for recess—a rambunctious bunch of buddies with gym bags over their shoulders. I stood stark naked, front and center, as the men bounded in and saw me. How could they not? Tied to the stake of shame, I burned to a shade of true prude pink and felt my inner American frump demand a good explanation.

Didn't these men see the door marked "Femmes"?

Didn't Monsieur at the desk think to direct them?

The herd dispersed around me, the men claiming lockers and dropping their gym bags on benches.

"*Bonjour*, Madame." It was the one whose bag landed closest to mine, and whose hunky, handsome self took a seat not three feet distant.

"*Bonjour*, Madame." It was the next, who scooted past to stake his spot before the télé turned to a game of soccer.

"*Bonjour*, Madame."

"*Bonjour*, Madame."

"*Bonjour*, Madame."

Too nude to speak, I could only nod my *Bonjour Monsieurs* in reply. If only I had dabbed on a drop of Chanel No. 5! As the legendary Coco herself once said: "A woman who doesn't wear perfume has no future." Then again, it hardly mattered if I had been scented by irresistibility itself. To the stripping Frenchmen, who soon had the place bustling with their good-natured fun, I was simply the naked woman among them who didn't get the message.

"*Désolé,*" said the front desk *monsieur* later, begging my pardon for his oversight. The ladies' changing room today was on the *second* floor and he didn't think to switch the door-signs until after I had arrived. Meanwhile, in the midst of men as blasé as the plumbers about the exposure—indecent to me for too long—I felt a queer thing, not fear, come to life. Could it be? Ah, *oui*. My inner French girl.

My body as is, just is. The idea delighted me. Since not a soul in the City of Light judged it lacking, since the people of Paris paid it no mind, why did I try so hard to hide it? To deny it?

Bring on the satin contraptions, France. I'm coming out.

"*Pardon?* Madame?" The Frenchman sharing my bench brought my attention to the fancy-fringed panties that lay on the floor between us like an unspoken question. I had flung them into the locker but missed. Who would pick them up? *Oh my God!* I lunged and snapped and swooped them into my bag. I may have been wrong, but was that the smallest flicker of a wicked smile.

"*Très belle*," he said. I dared to believe he meant not the panties but me.

At the launderette on the rue de Passy, Madame de Glasse stood with me at the folding table and eyed my neat stacks of items surely even Chanel had in mind. "A girl should be two things," she said: "classy and fabulous." Then Madame said with some surprise, "*Mademoiselle*," she said, "like many Americans who come to Paris, you have gotten over your problem, *non?*"

Yes. Now I've got my oh-la-la. And, oh, how even the plumbers of Paris would be proud.

Oh-la-la is a hard thing to hold on to when not in France but instead in the Monterey Bay Area of California, where Colette O'Connor lives and works. She's holding on to hers by the sheerest satin thread as she completes her MFA in creative writing at San Jose State University and writes stories that have appeared in a number of Travelers' Tales anthologies, among them Travelers' Tales Paris, Sand in My Bra, Whose Panties Are These?, The Best Women's Travel Writing (2005 and 2010), *and* The Best Travel Writing (2010 and 2011).

LAVINIA SPALDING

~&~ ~&~ ~&~

The Ghosts of Alamos

She brought her own with her.

T he sun is relentless, stalking me along the narrow, cobbled lanes of Alamos, Mexico, as I return to my hotel. I
unlock the heavy double doors and walk into the lush, untamed
courtyard, where weather-pocked stone cherubs guard a center fountain and rocking chairs sit motionless beneath electric
ceiling fans. It's quiet inside. Quieter, in fact, than any hotel
I've ever patronized, because I'm the only guest.

Which is not to say that I'm alone.

According to locals, my hotel is haunted by the woman it
originally belonged to: Señorita Marcor, a beautiful spinster
piano teacher who traversed Alamos only by underground
tunnel because the streets back then weren't cobbled, and she
refused to muddy her boots and long skirts.

This doesn't alarm me. For one thing, I like the sound of
Señorita Marcor. For another, I'm traveling with my own
ghost.

"I want to disappear," I told my mother a few weeks ago,
giving her a research project. My father had just died so I
thought she could benefit from an assignment that would
keep her busy, give her a purpose. As for me, I was desperate
to escape San Francisco—the endless hustle, the cold summer

weather, the impassive faces, and worse, the sympathetic ones. I wanted to retreat with my memories of my father to a place where no one knew us.

"Maybe Mexico," I said. "Somewhere pretty but not touristy—a quiet village with a couple of small hotels and coffee shops. And bougainvillea. Lots of bougainvillea."

It took her two days to return a verdict: Alamos, a seventeenth-century colonial town in the foothills of the Sierra Madre. One of Mexico's oldest treasures and a national monument, it was a tourist destination in the winter but would be disgustingly hot and accordingly devoid of visitors in June. A tourist destination in the winter, it would be disgustingly hot and accordingly devoid of visitors in June. I could take a first-class, air-conditioned bus from Tucson—where she lived—leaving at 6:00 P.M. and arriving at 6:00 A.M., for $80 round-trip.

"Alamos," I said, rolling it on my tongue like a Mexican candy. "I've never heard of it. Sounds perfect."

When I step off the bus at 6:00 A.M., however, I'm less convinced. It's quiet here, all right. The sun is just beginning its rise, exposing thin, dusty streets surrounding the station. Lifeless and bleak, they don't promise much—no bougainvillea, no inviting B&Bs, and not a single coffee shop brightens the pale, nondescript rows of single-story dwellings. Of the few local characters lurking about, none speak English, and I'm struggling with Spanish. I have only a few key words in my arsenal, and I'm hoping that if I can put them in the right order, they'll lead me to caffeine.

"Restaurante?" I inquire of the driver. He's leaning against the bus, pinching a cigarette tightly between his thumb and forefinger. No, he assures me, shaking his head once, definitively. No restaurantes. All closed at this hour.

So I camp out at the station and wait for the town to open its doors to me, miserably watching the ticket agent sip coffee from a thermos. Wishing I knew enough Spanish to engineer a transaction that would result in my getting a cup. Wishing I had pesos to offer. Wishing I knew the whereabouts of my formerly travel-savvy, super bad-ass self.

Finally around 7:30, I decide to strike out, following twisty cobbled roads into the center of town. For some reason, the sidewalks in Alamos are elevated a good three feet from the ground, almost shoulder height for me. Unsure of what to make of this, I decide instead to walk in the road, which means that each time a little pickup blows through I'm forced to press against the wall of the sidewalk to make room for both of us.

Within minutes my enthusiasm returns as I find myself surrounded by bright white Spanish colonial architecture, completely intact, and endless rows of tall, arched portals. I'm relieved by the absence of fast-food restaurants and scant suggestions of Western influence. No one is hawking blankets or tacky mother-of-pearl jewelry, or sipping Starbucks lattes while barking into cell phones. I see only a handful of locals beating dust from rugs, opening windows, calmly sweeping sidewalks. They cast shy looks my way, and something about them restores my confidence.

Soon I find myself at Casa de los Tesoros, a sixteenth-century convent turned tourist hotel. I spend the morning there, drinking Nescafe and nibbling on thick Mexican pastries delivered by clean-shaven servers in suits and ties. The manicured courtyard has café tables with umbrellas, a gift shop, a swimming pool, and an Internet station set up beneath massive, ancient-looking paintings of monks and saints.

Within an hour I've committed the very act I swore I wouldn't—I've made a friend: Jean-Philippe, a Parisian toy designer who came here to purchase a million jumping beans to sell in the pages of French magazines. Alamos, he informs me, is the jumping-bean capital of the world.

"Only, for the first time since 1982," he says, his face darkening, "they aren't jumping. The rain came too early this year, ruining the chances for a crop."

But he's solved the problem, he announces, turning cheerful again as he reaches for one of my pastries. He's invented a cardboard chicken that lays real, edible square eggs. This is exactly the sort of bizarre conversation I usually relish when traveling, but today it feels misplaced. I'm not in Mexico to make friends or conversation or be served poolside by well-coifed waiters. I'm not here to have a good time. I'm here for one reason: to lean into grief till I fall over and have no choice but to pull myself back up again.

My immediate problem is solved when I meet Suzanne, the owner of Casa de los Tesoros. After a brief conversation in which I explain that I'm a writer in search of simpler, quieter lodging (no need to tell anyone about my father), I find myself being led to her other hotel down the road where, if I stay, I'll be the sole occupant.

From the outside, Hotel la Mansion appears stark and pedestrian, and I brace myself to meet the dumpy little sister of Casa de los Tesoros. But Suzanne casually unlocks the heavy double doors, and I step past her into a wild, tropical, secret garden-like courtyard. A central stone fountain bubbles, surrounded by palm and mango trees, white pillars and statues. Slanted beams of sunlight illuminate thick curls of pink bougainvillea hanging from white arches, and birds circle the tops of trees. Hummingbirds buzz, and pale yellow butterflies flutter, and it feels like the doors have been sealed for a century. Suzanne offers me my choice of ten rooms, and then she closes the gate behind her.

My father would have been thrilled that I've come to Mexico to mourn him; he loved Latin American and Spanish culture. He collected Day of the Dead statues, Tarahumara pottery, and Mexican postcards of 1930s film stars; he devoured everything he could find to read about Pre-Colombian history, the Mayans, the mummies of Guanajuato. But mostly he loved the music. A concert classical and flamenco guitarist, he studied in Mexico with Manuel Lopez Ramos and in Spain with Paco de Lucia, and he once performed at the palace of Alfonso the XIII for the Prince of Spain. And when he was diagnosed with terminal emphysema and advised that he could buy himself six more months by moving to a lower elevation, my father immediately chose Tucson—he wanted to go to the Mariachi Festival.

I spend my first Alamos afternoon in one of the old Mother Hubbard rocking chairs outside my room, reading and writing in my journal. Finally around dusk I venture out to find food. In the town square I buy a book called *See It and Say It in Spanish* from a woman named Marta at Terracotta Tiendas, a co-op in the plaza, and study it over a bowl of tortilla soup and a Corona at Las Palmeras, a quiet, low-key restaurant across from the plaza.

Directly across from me stands the centerpiece of town, a gloomy, shadowy church called Iglesia de Nuestra Señora de la Concepción or La Parroquia de la Purisima Concepción or El Templo Parroquial de la Immaculada Concepción, depending on whom you ask. And right in front of the church, as if to cheer it up, is the Plaza de las Armas, with a delicate open-sided gazebo surrounded by flowers, a smattering of gangly skyscraper palm trees, and a wrought iron and white picket fence.

Like its church, Alamos has multiple names: the City of Arches, the Flower of the North, the Pearl of the Mountains, the Garden of the Gods, the City of Silver, and the Soul of the Sierra Madre—but Francisco de Vasquez Coronado first named it Alamos (or Real de Los Frailes de Alamos) in 1540.

The northernmost of Mexican colonial cities, it became one of the wealthiest towns in the country after silver was discovered in the hills in 1683. By the late 1700s, the town had more than 30,000 residents, some of whom traveled north to found San Francisco and Los Angeles.

By 1790 Alamos was one of the world's biggest silver producers and by the mid-nineteenth century, the capital of Occidente. But with riches came trouble; for two centuries, the people of Alamos suffered floods, droughts, plagues, and famine along with political unrest and continual Apache, Yaqui, Mayo and Tarahumara uprisings. Colonists, Federalists, Liberals, and bandits overran the town at one time or another. In the 1860s, under Napoleon's reign, Emperor Maximilian's troops occupied Alamos and drove away all the silver barons. Mexican rebels took it back the following year, and the Revolution drove away most colonial landowners. By the early 1900s the mines were closed, along with the railroad and the mint. The money was gone, and only a few hundred people remained.

But it still held some magic, because the story goes that when Pancho Villa's troops arrived in Alamos in 1915, intending to pillage the town, he gave orders not to burn it, vowing to someday make it his home. Villa was killed shortly after, so he never returned. Instead, after World War II, Americans began immigrating and restoring the old adobe mansions. Now Alamos is a national monument, with 188 buildings on the national registry, and home to some 15,000 people, of whom about 400 are expats (Paul Newman, Carroll O'Connor, Rip Torn, Gene Autry, and Roy Rogers all lived here). Still, it doesn't feel like an expat town.

From the window of Las Palmeras, I watch people mill about the Plaza de las Armas, settling into benches around the church and gazebo. Two handsome old mustached men in matching cowboy hats lean cross-armed against the ornate white fence that frames the gazebo, and behind them, a teenage couple holds hands shyly in the shade of a jacaranda tree. A woman sets up a hamburguesa stand, and a man carries a guitar case across the plaza.

My father was teaching guitar right up until he died, still patiently explaining to his students how to do a tremolo or a rasgueado, jiggling their wrists to make them relax their hands, scolding them for hooking their thumbs over the necks of their guitars.

I studied seriously with him from when I was five until thirteen and again in my twenties and thirties, far less seriously. Now that he's gone—and with him the opportunity to study—I'm already lost in regret for a lifetime of taking him for granted. It's not a surprise. I knew I'd feel remorse; I just didn't anticipate being so mad at myself.

My father left his guitar to me, but since he died, I've only removed it from its case a handful of times. I've held it in my arms, rested my cheek against the cool wood, played a few notes, and put it back. But suddenly I find myself wishing I'd brought it to Mexico. Perhaps here, in the haven of my hotel, I could make it through an entire piece of music.

The day he told me he was dying, I laughed at him.

"Dad, you're not dying," I said.

"Yes, I am. I have emphysema."

"A doctor told you that?"

"No."

"Then how do you know?" I asked.

"I Googled it."

I told him he was silly, but Google was right. His health declined over the next two years; he coughed and wheezed constantly, eventually barely able to breathe. Finally he was put on an oxygen machine, which he dragged around the house with him. He quit smoking, reluctantly, after forty-five years.

The last time I talked to him, I was in a rush to get off the phone. I had fifteen spare minutes before I needed to leave for work, but trying to carry on a conversation with him had turned painful; he was too often incoherent and rambled on.

"I've got to go, Daddy," I said.

"Well," he answered lightly, "when you gotta go, you gotta go."

The words stay with me.

The Plaza de las Armas is quiet tonight, but not so on Sunday evenings, when the age-old ritual of paseo is still practiced, as it is in virtually every small town in Mexico: teenage boys and girls promenading, walking in circles around the gazebo in opposite directions, eyeing each other openly. It reminds me of high school weekends spent at the shopping mall, except the laps these teens make around each other are much shorter, and the prowling more overt.

But the true distinction is the parents, sitting on sideline benches taking in the entertainment of their daughters walking arm-in-arm with girlfriends, being ogled by pubescent boys. I think of what Suzanne said about my hotel's ghost, Señorita Marcor: that she had dozens of suitors but never married because her parents didn't approve of any of them.

Maybe little has changed since Señorita Marcor's day, and parents still preside over their children's love lives here. I consider the scene in front of me. It's fairly self-explanatory, but for one thing: I see no pairing off, no conversation or flirtation between the sexes. What comes next for these teens loosely upholding the culture's dating traditions? Will they date? Get married? And if their parents disapprove, will they run off and elope as my parents did?

My mother first met my father at her art school graduation party in Boston when she was twenty-three and he was seventeen.

"That's the cutest boy I've ever seen," she said to a friend when my father walked in with his guitar, crashing the party. "I'm going to marry him."

"I'd better introduce you then," the friend said, ushering her over to him.

"Wally, meet Dolly," the introduction went. "You're made for each other."

Six weeks later they stole my aunt's car and ran off together, making it all the way to California. When they finally ran out of money, they called my grandmother and told her they'd eloped (they hadn't, but pretending to be married meant they could cohabitate). The following June they drove a borrowed TR3 sports car from Boston to North Carolina, where it was legal to marry at the age of eighteen without parental consent. This time they actually did elope.

Before my father got sick, he was the star of the family, the vibrant, handsome, brilliant performer, and we orbited his life, for better or for worse, like the gazebo these kids circumnavigate in Plaza de las Armas.

If the gazebo weren't here, would they still walk the paseo every night? What do we do with the traditions and patterns when our center is suddenly gone?

During the day not a soul visits my hotel, and I sit and listen to mangos drop from trees. I drink coffee, write, read, study Spanish, and nap. Sometimes I cry. Time spreads, expands.

But for a few hours each evening Ruben, a worker from Casa de los Tesoros, comes by in case I need anything. Twenty-two and bored, Ruben likes to bring things to my door. First, chips and salsa. Next, bottled water. Finally, a mango from the tree outside my door. I'm determined to be alone, but he doesn't know that, and his earnestness makes it impossible to resent the interruptions. Gracias, I say, again and again. Gracias.

An elderly security guard also comes at night. He sits on a chair just inside the main door, though to protect me from what, I have no idea. I can only imagine it's the town ghosts, for I've come to learn that Señorita Marcos is not alone; legend has it Alamos is teeming with them. There's the gray-robed monk who guards the treasures in the seven secret underground tunnels leading to the church, the ghosts of the silver mine workers, the "headless Chinaman," the unfaithful bride, the violet perfume ghost.

I find being in a ghost town soothes me. There's something about the way the people of Alamos so effortlessly preserve their past and coexist with their ghosts. I start leaving my hotel more frequently during the day, retreating to my air-conditioned room only when I get overheated. I strike up conversations with locals if only to ask them about ghosts. Everyone has a story. In this town, ghosts aren't a concept one does or does not believe in; they simply exist, almost as lively a populace as the living.

Out wandering one day, I poke my head into Casa de Maria Felix, a hotel and museum. One of Alamos's claims to fame is that it's the birthplace of Maria Felix, an iconic film star sometimes referred to as the Mexican Marilyn Monroe. This is the property where she was born. It's run by an expat named Lynda, who tells me she was unaware, when she bought it in 1999, that the film star was born there.

She was not, however, oblivious to Maria Felix's existence. Coincidentally, she'd been collecting the Mexican film star's photographs for thirty years. The casa now overflows with artifacts excavated during the construction of the hotel, and a room dedicated to images of Maria Felix runs the gamut from famous original portraits to what resemble middle school art class sketches. Altogether, Lynda has about 400 images of her.

Lynda's ghost story is that she came upon the ruin one night while taking a walk, during her first visit to Alamos. The moon was shining through a window, and behind the wall she could see mesquites and palo verde trees. Intrigued, she wandered to the back of the property, and turning to look at the ruins in the moonlight, saw the spirits of a woman and child. She bought the property the next day.

Later in the afternoon, I take a private walking tour with a man named Trini, who goes by Candy Joe (local kids gave him the moniker, he tells me, because he always has candy for them). We visit the cemetery, a study in shades of white and sepia. Elaborately carved statues of praying angels and weeping cherubs share sky space with towering, austere crosses, while beautiful old headstones are stacked on the ground like dishes in a cupboard. On one end of the graveyard, a tall block of aboveground family crypts all bear holes the size of grapefruits, evidence of a time when looting was standard practice.

Candy Joe also takes me by a mansion where a woman named Beatrice, a silver baron's daughter, once lived. The house was a wedding gift from Beatrice's father, he says. On the day she married, her father had the streets of Alamos lined with silver bars for a few hours. Leaving the church after the ceremony, though, the groom's horse was spooked and reared up; the groom was thrown and his back broken, and several months later he died. Beatrice subsequently lost her mind, and for the next six months could be spotted in the cemetery late at night, digging up his grave with a shovel and pick. Because her father was the most important man in town, the cemetery caretaker left her alone. She died not long after and was buried beside her husband, but people continued to see her ghost, in front of his grave, praying.

I find that the stories all intersect, weaving around each other, cross-pollinating. Is it the virgin bride, the woman in white, or the unfaithful wife who haunts the beautiful mansion they call Las Delicias? Or are these spirits one and the same? The legends are fused, details blurred. They have been repeated so many times.

The night before I leave Alamos, I have dinner with Suzanne, Jean-Philippe, and a few other travelers. As we swap stories, I realize that for the first time, I'm not eyeing the door, waiting for a break in conversation so I can escape. I'm content in the company of others. I even talk about my father.

For a place I hadn't heard of a month ago, Alamos has given me precisely what I wanted—gentle quietude and privacy, solitude without isolation, uninterrupted time and space to heal, no one asking anything of me. A summer season so slow and lazy that even the jumping beans won't jump, so hot and muggy it holds little appeal for tourists.

It's also provided what I didn't want but somehow needed. When I walk through town now, I know people. Jose Luis, the bartender at Casa de los Tesoros, is teaching me to conjugate verbs, Lynda from Casa Maria Felix has given me a driving tour, Candy Joe hollers "Buenos dias!" from his little tourist office, and Marta from the co-op waves exuberantly whenever she sees me.

I came here to be alone in my grief, but it's the people of Alamos who have helped me move beyond it. Without even trying, they've taught me to remember the dead in a way that keeps them alive—by continuing to tell their stories.

❧ ❧ ❧

Lavinia Spalding is the author of With a Measure of Grace: the Story of Recipes of a Small Town Restaurant *and* Writing Away: A Creative Guide to Awakening the Journal-Writing Traveler, *and is the editor of* The Best Women's Travel Writing 2011 *and* The Best Women's Travel Writing Volume 8. *A regular contributor to* Yoga Journal, *her work has appeared in a wide variety of publications including* Sunset, World Hum, Galding, Post Road, *and* Inkwell.

❧ ❧ ❧

Engagement Ceremony

It's all relative—that is, becoming family
in the Ecuadorian Amazon.

My son Mike and my assigned husband Bolívar explained to me what will happen during the pactachina[1], the *Quichua* engagement ceremony. They even told me why we must display to the future bride's family both humility and wealth—a kind of reverse dowry of subservience and material goods given by the groom's family in exchange for the bride. But I am not prepared for how long I have to petition for her, kneeling on the hard cement floor, crawling from one set of grandparents, godparents, and uncle-aunt pairs to the next, along an endless receiving line. Why is it taking so long to move down the row, especially since the ceremony was supposed to have begun hours ago? My knees and back are killing me, but all of Jacqui's relatives to whom I must appeal are sitting comfortably in chairs.

I feel sorry not only for myself, but also for the musicians, a violinist and drummer, who must sing, Greek-chorus style, a monotonous litany of what is happening during this

---

[1] Words in Quichua are underlined; words in Spanish are italicized.

supplication process called the *pedida*: "Now Angel, the groom's godfather, is asking the bride's grandmother for her hand. Now the groom's father Bolívar is asking the godfather and godmother. Here comes the groom's mother asking the bride's uncle and aunt." That very morning Mike had to take the bus to their village and drag the musicians here himself. Without the <u>visaru</u> and the <u>tocadur</u> and only the *discomóvil* for music, the ceremony would not be a traditional <u>pactachina</u>. To prove himself worthy <u>masha</u> (son-in-law) who is integrated into the Quichua community in the Ecuadorian Amazon, and not just any Peace Corps Volunteer, Mike wants to do the right thing, exactly as his stand-in godfather and actual village sponsor Angel has taught him.

I look down the line at the countless relatives I have yet to ask for the hand of my future daughter-in-law Jacqui, a hand I am not even sure I want or know what to do with. At my side, my "spouse" Bolívar, dressed like Mike and Angel in the ceremonial white vest and straw hat, is on his knees murmuring a lengthy solo *discurso* in Quichua, a language I have studied but still can't get a handle on, especially this lowland dialect. I would later have the daunting task of giving a speech in Quichua to these 250 of Jacqui's closest relatives assembled here in the largest grass hut I had ever seen. I am dreading my *discurso*—more apologizing and promising, but also expressing gratitude for accepting Mike into their fold. I would be reading the speech from a script that native Quichua speakers and Mike have already checked to make sure it makes sense and that I don't make a fool of myself and embarrass the groom's group or <u>cari parti</u>.

I can clearly understand, not all the words, but the tone of Bolívar's appeals—an attitude of humility and obeisance. I know that as a woman I have to act even more abject, even though, like many North American women and of course men, I am not known for my subservience. But the Quichua, an indigenous group subjugated for hundreds of years by the Spanish, have been forced to develop abjectness into an art form. They have had to serve their *patrones*, who look as white and European as I, in humiliating ways, even carrying them on their backs the day's journey up thousands of meters from Amazonía to Quito in the Andes. "Turn-about is fair play," as my (real) husband always says. I will make a concerted effort to act humble. My world suddenly feels like that map of North and South America I first saw in the New World Resource Center in Chicago—with the compass reversed so that South was up, placing South America on top where the U.S. used to be and North America on the bottom.

To each pair of relatives, I apologize—first, for even having to apologize in Spanish because of my poor Quichua. Then I apologize for the absence of that real husband, a homebody who works at home in his shop, rarely leaving the house even for the hardware store, let alone for the Amazon. Next I apologize that because of his job my other son hasn't made it to Ecuador either—these absences of our Caucasian blood relatives necessitating all this indigenous subbing in the cari parti. Then I beg them for their permission for Jacqui to join my family and come to the U.S., promising to help my son feed, clothe, and pay for the education of this woman-child I barely know who has not yet finished the 10th grade. In keeping with the Quichua custom, I acknowledge their profound sadness in losing her to another family and country. But I can't help thinking to myself that since every Quichua family has about nine kids and those nine kids in turn have another nine kids, would Jacqui really be missed that much? I figure that faced with my generous offer, they would graciously respond, "You are surely welcome to take Jacqui to your land of opportunity. And we will have one less mouth to feed." Then I could beseech the next in line.

No such luck. They initiate difficult discussions with me about cultural differences. They demand further promises. They want to give me a hard time.

"We have heard that the divorce rate in the U.S. is extremely high. What will you do when Miguel and Jacqui disagree? Will you take sides and make it worse, or will you mediate and help solve the problem?" inquires an uncle. I admire his deep knowledge of psychology as I fumble for a reply.

"We have heard that it is brutally cold in your land," comments the next elder. "When Jacqui gets sick from the ice and snow, will you attend to her and give her the necessary *medicamentos?*"

Only when I assure them that I will care for Jacqui as her own mother does, that she is indeed that daughter I have never had, which I silently hope is true, and only when Bolivar has finished his latest *discurso* can I crawl down the line to the next pair of challengers. When the pain in my knees and back has grown so severe that I am about to give up and stand up, ruining both the ritual and the image of my false humility, one of the youths from Mike's village brings me a chair, for which I quietly thank him.

The pachtachina is the second phase of the three-part Quichua marriage ritual. I have missed the first part, the tapuna, which, of course, I must also apologize for. During the tapuna, representatives from the future bride's family or the warmi parti meet and negotiate with those of the future groom's family. But when I was scheduled to fly to Ecuador, a three-day blizzard—the very weather the compadre referred to—hit the Midwest and most flights were cancelled. Mike felt abandoned when I could not participate in negotiations that quickly evolved into the traditional *borrachera*—meaning "Big Drunk." But when Mike could not meet me at the airport, I felt abandoned too, especially at the creepy Quito bus station; I realized that the youth I thought was a bus company employee had "helped" me get my baggage through the turn style and onto the bus by relieving me of the CD player and all the CDs in my backpack. I spent the six-hour bus trip to Jacqui's city, the gateway to the jungle, thinking of my revenge when he found my CDs were all Classic Rock rather than Latin Pop.

I am actually secretly glad to have missed the tapuna because excessive drinking is hard to avoid with the Ecuadorian style of alcohol distribution. Each person takes turns "hosting"— pouring a cup of beer or wine which is then passed around to each person sitting in a circle—a kind of secular communion celebration. Those plastic cups come fast; you can't linger with a drink and slowly sip because the next person is waiting for it. You can, however, pretend to drink from the cup, a strategy I was trying to perfect.

After the *pedida* finally ended and we in the cari parti had the freedom to stand up, there was traditional Quichua line dancing by the members of the immediate engagement party. Somewhat unsure of their moves, Mike and Jacqui watched what Angel and his wife were doing. Jacqui, who according to tradition had to be hidden during the *pedida*, was now dancing opposite Mike in a long, red Chinese-style dress with a slit up the side, her long, straight black hair done up by a beauty salon. She was smiling radiantly at him—the first time I had seen her looking so happy during their year-long courtship. Mike gazed back at her with adoration. I took lots of pictures, as Mike had appointed me the official wedding photographer. "No one else has a camera here, Mom." I was pleased to comply with a task I could perform standing up.

After line dancing came dinner, a welcome event because my stomach was growling. The first course though was authentic jungle meat flown in from the Peruvian Amazon, as the Ecuadorian jungle had already been hunted out. As the groom's only real family member, I had paid real money— hundreds of dollars for dozens of pounds of tapir, armadillo, alligator, and bush pig. My son's substitute relatives had awakened early in the middle of the night to make the long trip here from their village of Campana Cocha with the huge pots for rice and vats for *chicha*, the fermented yuca beverage the Quichua drink. In their servile role as members of the <u>cari parti</u>, they had been dutifully cooking all day. They handed me styrofoam plates of this foreign mammal meat, the shells of the armadillo chunks menacingly protruding. I carried the plates to Jacqui's mom Berta who distributed them to the relatives in their order of importance before returning to the kitchen area for more plates. Then, the Campana Cochans and I served the less important relatives, and finally Mike's Peace Corps Volunteer friends sitting at a table in the back of the hut.

Then it was time for the second course—chicken, rice, and salad. Jacqui's dad Sergio, carrying around for display and consumption a large bottle of brandy Mike had bought for him as a ritual father-in-law present, had assured me that I had gotten a good deal because I only had to pay for half of the chickens. He paid for the other half even though Quichua custom specifies that the groom's family pays for all the food. We observed the same routine for serving the chicken course. Angel's wife, aptly named Piedad (Piety, Devotion), informed me to my dismay that we in the <u>cari parti</u> were not allowed to eat a bite of food until everyone in Jacqui's family was served both courses. I was starting to feel woozy from repeatedly walking back and forth to the kitchen area without anything in my stomach. The familiar chicken smelled enticing, but my head was pounding and I thought I might faint. I hadn't had anything to eat since a light early breakfast, thinking that the party would start at two and I would have a late lunch. I would later learn that the delay is intentional; it accommodates guests who arrive via unpredictable buses from villages deeper in the jungle, and most important, it teaches the groom's family a lesson in patience, discipline, and humility.

Finally it was the <u>cari parti's</u> turn to eat. Not a morsel of jungle meat was left, which was fine with me because I was scared to try it anyway, but I managed to scrounge up a chicken thigh and a mound of rice with the typical delicious relish of purple onions, tomatoes, and lime. I wolfed it down and instantly felt better.

Next came the speeches: an extra-long one by Sergio, a medium-length one by Mike, and mine—short, sweet, and hopefully comprehensible, followed by drinking and dancing for the youth, and adults, and candies and cookies for the kids. The soda and beer I had purchased were conspicuously displayed piled up in *jabas* or cases, along with the guests' presents of cooking pots and bedding, which Mike and Jacqui would never be able to cram in their suitcases and take back to the U.S. The *discomóvil* alternated between danceable tunes in Quichua and mainstream Ecuadorian pop. Men and boys from Jacqui's family asked me to dance, and after a Pilsner, the most popular beer in Ecuador, I was happy to oblige. One of Jacqui's cousins, already inebriated and incoherent, shouted over the pounding music questions about where I had come from. All my answers—the U.S., America, North America, Up North, Iowa, New York—didn't seem to register with him. My new relatives from Mike's village also wanted to dance with me. Maybe I was such a popular partner because I was an exotic curiosity—like someone from another planet.

I ate and drank with the Peace Corps Volunteers at their table in the back of the hut. Nobody from Jacqui's family had invited me to eat with them, and after having to serve them, I didn't even know if according to tradition, I deserved to. My principal relatives seemed to be the cooking and serving villagers from Campana Cocha, whom I didn't know that well either. My mock mate Bolívar was engaged in some heavy drinking with a group of men, and it didn't seem appropriate to join him. One advantage of sitting with the Volunteers was that I could nurse my own beer since they didn't subscribe to the Ecuadorian drinking method—we each had our own private beer bottle. We could also speak English, comparing notes on what we thought was going on at the party and speculating about whether the cross-cultural relationship celebrated here would last. Mike had clearly "gone native," they observed, but would he and Jacqui make it to the third stage of Quichua marriage, the actual wedding? "Clearly they love each other, but she seems so young, always pouting until Mike buys her what she wants."

Various older male relatives took turns coming to our table bearing those dreaded plastic cups, which they poured full of artificially flavored peach wine for us to drink from and pass around, but we politely declined. We chatted with them, trying to be friendly. They were slurring their speech—as if they had already consumed a box of it themselves. I took more pictures—this time of Jacqui's immediate family: Sergio still waving around his brandy, and Jacqui's brothers dressed in the traditional black and gold Iowa Hawkeye apparel I had bought them—a curious cultural combo. One of the Volunteers posed hugging the smaller Quichua kids she knew from working in their village.

My favorite picture, taken by Angel, is of me, a very dark, Indian-looking Bolivar, whom I was addressing jokingly as *"mi esposo falso"* (my fake husband—that is, without benefits), and Mike—our blondish, curly-haired, impossibly blue-eyed progeny—*nuestro hijo, ñuka churi*—our son.

With the help of another Pilsner, I began warming up and socializing. I spoke with one of Jacqui's uncles about the political and religious situation in the small evangelical community where she had grown up before her family moved to the city. I listened to the Volunteers' stories about their assigned communities—the failures and successes of their sanitation and agriculture projects, and about their struggles to learn not only Spanish, but Quichua, Tsáchila, or Shwar. The crowd seemed to be thinning out. Where was everyone going? I ventured out to find a bathroom.

I was unprepared for the chaos outside the soccer-field-sized party hut. I wove my way through groups of drunken young men shouting at, tussling with, and trying to punch each other. Others were retching and vomiting off to the side. After locating the least objectionable porta-potty, I looked for Mike whom I found trying to separate two of Jacqui's cousins going after one another other. When they staggered off, I asked Mike if he could walk me back to the bed and breakfast after I said my good-byes.

"I wish I could, Mom, but I have to take care of Jofre," he said, pointing to one of Jacqui's brothers lying in a ditch moaning. "He fell down drunk. He's depressed about his girlfriend who left him. You'll be all right. By the way, thanks for the speech. Everyone was impressed."

I was happy my speech had gone over well, but I felt abandoned again and scared to walk back myself. I guess I would have to get used to sharing Mike with hundreds more of his, or rather our, new relatives. I thought of the reverse map of the Americas again. "Turn-about is fair play."

I went back inside and found Jacqui's mom and dad, Angel, my other Campana Cochan relatives, and Bolívar. I thanked them for all their hard work and their acceptance of Mike into their family and community. Jacqui's brother Danilo called me auya, extended family of in-laws—a term of endearment—and made me address them as auya too. I realized I had earned the right to receive that label, and ironically, I felt proud of my humility. I understood how we had all just enacted the merging of two lovers, two families, two nations, and two cultures.

I had to walk in the dark, through more brawlers, the quarter mile on paved road back to the bed and breakfast. They turned out to be harmful to each other, but harmless to me. It was good finally to be alone in my room with a view of lush jungle growth—huge leaves as big as kites shining green in the moonlight. Drifting off to the sounds of the rushing river below, the faint beat of the *discomóvil* in the distance, I dreamt of chicken and rice with tomatoes, onion and lime, and my new 250 family members in a world turned upside down.

≈ ≈ ≈

Carol Severino directs the University of Iowa Writing Center and writes about her travel and language-learning experiences in Latin America and Europe. Her essays have recently appeared in VIA: Voices in Italian Americana, The Minnetonka Review, The Broome Review, Writing on the Edge, *and other venues.*

~ ~ ~

My Black Boots

In her closet hangs a tale of footwear
and funny business.

The sun was setting, although it was hard to tell given the neon excrescences sprouting in the foreground—pink winking ladies and glowing palm trees, a crime against nature in the city of sin. I'd been playing slots for hours. I'd lost eighteen dollars in nickels, and I was queasy with fatigue and shrimp cocktail. So this was Las Vegas. Yuck. Only one night, then I'd hit the road for the last chapter of my own, two-week personal cliché: a Cross-Country Drive West. Specifically, I had left Boston (parents, Puritans, too much damn brick) bound for San Francisco (performance art? nudity? mind-altering substances?). Never mind that I'd never visited the city, nor had I lined up an apartment or job. I was twenty-five, and I was ravenous for . . . *something*—transformation, adventure. Until now, I'd never traveled this far from home by myself.

Dizzy from the mechanized clangor of the slots, I wandered out along the neon-saturated main strip. Sandwiched between a pawn shop and a convenience store was a shoe store. And there they were in the center window: the boots. *My* boots—sleek, wicked, inky-black cowboy kickers overlaid with a viridescent sheen, and tapering to a needle-nose point at the toes. I was sure they'd be banned in Boston. Embossed on the sides, heroic western riders lassoed unseen buffaloes. I went into the store, heart jumping, and strode out, two inches taller, reshod and reborn. This was exactly how I wanted to sweep onto the stage of my new life. Don't mess with *me,* yo. I gave myself a sultry look in the pawnshop window.

But there was a catch. As I discovered as soon I arrived in San Francisco and set foot on the pavement, my smooth soles were no match for the city's hills. I became a fallen woman—under the tree, slipping on some leafy slime; on the side of the street, as my sole slid off the curb; in the middle of a sidewalk, racing to keep up with the realtor. I minced up hills, feet sideways, clinging crabwise to the steep incline; downhill was a frantic soft-shoe routine as I gathered speed, flailing and careering through the crowds. I admitted defeat at Cala Grocery, where I had bought a bag of glorious California citrus and stepped into the sun. My heel slipped on the plastic entrance mat, and as I sprawled in the doorway, watching my grapefruits roll like guillotined heads through the parking lot, I had to admit it: my brief tryst, my *affaire de footwear,* was finished.

But how to dispose of my boots? I settled on a classified ad: "Black/green Vegas cowboy boots, ladies' 10, gently worn." Of the several responses on my voicemail, Carl's interested my the most. I was surprised to hear from a man; where I came from, men didn't inquire about ladies' footwear. His voice was soft, almost deferential. He sounded older than I. He sounded . . . safe. I called back.

"Tuesday evening?" he asked. "Wonderful. Where?" And I did something I had never done before: I invited him over, sight unseen. I chalked it up to the intoxication of trying on my new life, the giddiness of landing in a foreign land. My defenses were down, my exuberance up, and I felt invulnerable.

At 6:30 that Tuesday, the buzzer rang. I opened the door and shook hands with Carl, a middle-aged man wearing suit and tie and holding a briefcase. He was shorter than I, although his chest had breadth and heft for someone so compact. His face was finely drawn—caramel skin, long-lashed eyes, and a gentle mouth, with a deep smile line on either side. We shook hands and he handed me a card listing him as a consultant. His eyes swept my apartment—the Lilliputian living room, containing both the closet and the dresser, and the bedroom, just big enough to squeeze through, single file, into the kitchen. I got the feeling he didn't miss much.

I'd left the boots in the front room with the heels touching, toes pointing out. My guest knelt to look at them.

"First position," he said, smiling up at me.

"Yes! How did you know?"

"Oh, I know about dance," he said vaguely. His fingers moved slowly and sensuously over the leather of the boots, tracing the outline of the cowboys. I felt a frisson; no one had ever run his hands over me like that.

He stood and gave me a beautiful smile. "They're gorgeous!" he said. "May I try them?"

"Oh, they're for you! Of course." I'd assumed he was shopping for a wife or girlfriend. "Have a seat." I waved him toward the living room and headed to the kitchen. "Would you like a drink?" I called. "I have water, juice—"

"Wine would be lovely," he called back. Wine? Was he crazy? I wasn't going to serve wine on a first date. Date? Was I crazy? This wasn't a date.

I returned from the kitchen holding two jelly-jars full of wine. Carl was sitting on the couch, the boots peeking out from under his pants. His posture was perfect.

"Are you selling anything else?" he asked.

"No, just the boots."

"Done! I love them." He eased out of the boots and waggled his toes, beaming. "They were made for me." I felt a rush

of gratitude at his appreciation. I settled into the chair next to
him, my knees not quite touching his. My coccyx was still sore
from my falls, and I sat carefully.

He surveyed me for a moment and took a sip of wine. "So
what were you doing in Vegas? And why are you getting rid
of such fabulous footwear?"

Without warning, tears pricked my eyes. No one in San
Francisco had asked me about myself, other than to inquire
about my references and my bank balance. Carl had such a
gentle manner. I wanted to tell the truth, to confess. I told him
about the grapefruits, and my Mr. Toad's Wild Ride up and
down the hills of San Francisco.

"I just feel kind of . . . *unsteady*," I finished, sniffling.

Carl nodded sympathetically. "Yes, this town can keep you
off-balance." He unbuttoned his jacket. "May I?" he asked
politely.

"Of course," I said, feeling a little off-balance. He shrugged
out of his coat and folded it carefully next to him on the sofa.
I could see his chest stretching the blue fabric of his oxford
shirt.

"I'm not too worried about slipping," he said. "I won't be
wearing the boots outside." He spoke softly, and I had to lean
in to hear him. "I'll use them more for my work." He saw me
eyeing his suit, and laughed. "Not my day job," he said. "My
other work. I'm an erotic dancer."

I coughed and spat up a dribble of wine. "Dancer?"

He reached over and patted the wine from my chin with
his napkin. "Whoops," he said solicitously. "More?" I nodded.
He refilled my glass and held it up to my lips, and, like a child
drinking milk from a grownup's cup, I took a sip.

"Yes, clubs here are good," he continued. "Audiences are
pretty receptive. You probably haven't had a chance to get
out yet." He refilled our glasses. "But never mind that. What
about you? What brought you here?" He asked as if he would

rather be nowhere else than right here, with me. I wanted to curl up and be held, like a pearl, in the palm of his hand.

So I talked. I talked about my parents back in Boston. I talked about their parents. I talked about the friends I had left behind. Carl listened. I told him I'd studied classical piano, and described how I'd become enamored of jazz after hearing a Coltrane recording in college.

"Oh," he sighed, "I love Coltrane. Do you have *Ballads*? No, don't get up." I was quite tipsy at this point, and relieved that he was taking charge. He moved to the stereo and plucked *Ballads* from the pile of cassettes.

"Lovely collection," he murmured. He caressed the case with the same attention and tenderness he had touched the boots. "Excellent taste, young lady." I beamed.

Saxophone wafted over us as Carl sat back down, a little closer to me.

"So which was the song that made you fall in love with jazz?" he asked. I fought the urge to clamber over the arm of the sofa into his lap. I confided that it was actually the dissolute guitar player at the local jazz club who had opened my ears and initiated me to the ways of the world. Coltrane was only part of the picture. Carl's face didn't change, but he leaned a bit closer.

"Really," he purred. "That's very interesting. Hold that thought. May I?" He gestured toward the bathroom.

While I waited, I took the opportunity to open the window. So hot in here! En route to the kitchen, I checked my reflection in my tiny bedroom mirror. I looked flushed and bright-eyed. Drunk. But beautiful, I thought.

Carl emerged. "I definitely want the boots," he called. "Did you say you had anything else to sell?"

I was puzzled. "You mean . . . mmm . . . housewares? Crockery?" I swept unsteadily back into the living room brandishing a bottle of wine and a white dinner-plate, one of my four. "Plate?" I asked, toppling into my chair.

He looked at me for a moment then laughed, and reached over and touched my cheek.

"No, sweetheart, thank you. No plates." I placed the plate on the table in case he changed his mind. He leaned over so that his knees touched mine lightly.

"So you haven't finished your story," he said. "About the guitar player." His attention was irresistible. I told him how my relationship with the guitar player had led to liaisons with his equally unsavory friend, and how I'd finally met a nice boy but had renounced him to come west. I made it sound like I was an old hand at love, when in reality, my previous commitments had ranged from three hours to three months. This latest boyfriend was young, I explained, and lovely but— well, maybe just a bit boring. He was unformed; I was look- ing for someone closer to my age—a little more worldly, I explained with a blowsy wink. Maybe a foreigner. Or perhaps a woman—I was quite intoxicated by this point—women didn't kiss women in Boston, as far as I knew, but I'd heard . . .

Carl laughed. "You're looking for adventure!" He put one hand on my arm, and gestured toward the world outside the window with the other. "You've come to the right place, sweetheart. This is a fabulous town for that kind of thing."

"Like what?" I asked.

"Oh, you know, really anything you can think of," he said. I didn't know, and couldn't think, and sat in silent agony that he would not elaborate.

He smiled. "I mean, any kind of . . . kink. Fetish. Orgies, S&M, sex parties. Things like that." He held my eyes. "What do you think? Does that sound . . . adventurous?"

I drained my glass. It was so very hot in here. I rolled up my sleeves, and Carl took my hand and ran his fingers up my forearm. I hoped he couldn't see my heart pulsing through my t-shirt.

"What beautiful hands," he murmured. He caressed my fingers. "Real pianist's fingers. Strong. I actually have a bit of a . . . thing for hands." He gave a playful nibble. Perspiring and over-stimulated, I began to expound. I explained about the importance of finger span, and how I used to only be able to play an octave but could now reach a ninth. I'd started in on the difference between pianos and harpsichords when he put his finger to my lips.

"Shh," he said tenderly. He lifted the wine bottle to my lips and waited while I took a draught. Then he stood and moved to the dresser. "May I?" he asked. I nodded mutely. He opened the middle drawer and surveyed the contents.

"Look at this finery! Darling, you must have *something* for me. Maybe this number?" He pulled out a lavender baby-doll T-shirt.

Ah! The clouds parted. Clothing! He was one of those men I'd read about in women's magazines—"I came home early and found my husband in bed with my camisole"—a cross-dresser! In my apartment! I stood and reeled to the dresser.

"Yes," I burped, hanging onto the furniture to keep the room from rotating. It was a tiny t-shirt that barely stretched over my ribcage, but I had held out hope and transported it from Boston. Carl took the shirt and retired to the bathroom. The universe did have a grand structure, I realized: I'd bought the t-shirt in high school, saved it all these years, and toted it all these miles because it was *meant for Carl*. I leaned on the dresser, stunned by the beauty and gravity of the world.

Carl emerged, the fabric stretched tight across his chest. His stomach was far more toned than mine. He ran his hands across his ribs.

"I love it. What about something for the rest of me?"

I reached into my drawer.

"Ta da! What about this?" I produced a tiny blue-and-white gingham skirt-shorts combination—a "skort," the saleswoman had told my, a pederast's dream. I'd had my doubts—I thought it made me look like Dorothy—but again, I understood that I had bought the outfit for Carl. Not to pass it on to him would defy the laws of gravity, physics, fate. Everything was falling into place.

I handed over the skort, and Carl disappeared back into the bathroom. When he emerged, clad in his tiny outfit, he looked like a muscular and slightly deranged member of my girls' school field hockey team. We moved on to other items: a yellow tank top, a striped sailor bateau-neck (*tres* Cannes, said Carl), a pink cardigan abloom with daisies. When we had exhausted the dresser drawer, Carl inquired about my closet. I stumbled over and threw open the door, ushering him in.

"What about this?" he asked, holding up a black velvet dress.

"Oh no, that's my favorite!"

He sighed and replaced the hanger.

"This?" (long purple dress, spaghetti straps, beaded bodice).

"Sure, try it." I was flattered at our similar tastes.

"What's this?" he asked at one point. He was standing close to, but not touching, a black velvet shawl fringed with intricate glass beading.

"Oh, that was my grandma's." I never wore it, but I loved knowing it was in my closet—a memento to the imperious and generous family matriarch, long since gone. Carl and I stood together for a moment in respectful silence.

I'm not sure who suggested the underwear drawer. Coltrane was on his nth round, and I on mine, as I rummaged through my lingerie, Carl standing respectfully to the side. My clock showed midnight. The night outside was dark, but inside my overheated apartment, lights blazed and clothing lay flung over sofa and chairs like a church sale. My anxiety

rose. Would my undergarments pass the test? I hesitated, ago-
nizing, and finally settled on a peach camisole, a pair of lacy
panties, and a satin atrocity, a crimson teddy sticky with black
faux-fur trim that I'd bought on impulse one Christmas.

I took a breath and presented the items.

"Well?"

Carl caressed the teddy. "I must," he said simply, disentan-
gling the straps from my fingers. "May I?" He emerged from
the bathroom a few minutes later, resplendent and volup-
tuous, the satin straining over his chest—a Folies Bergeres
dancer gone bad, all sinewy arms and barrel chest. His mus-
cled legs protruded from beneath the furry trim.

"Well?" he asked, with the flirtatious satisfaction of one
who already knows the answer. He executed a pirouette. "I'd
love to do my nails to match. Do you have any polish?"

I tottered to the bathroom cabinet and selected a coral pink,
"Prude," and bore it out to Carl. "Voila!"

He took my hand and led me to the bedroom. We knelt by
my bed, and Carl painted his nails, then mine, with the same
sensuous, unhurried care that seemed to mark all his interac-
tions with the world. I envied his approach.

"Beautiful," he murmured, holding my hands like precious
artifacts. He blew gently on my nails, then, holding my hands
carefully so he wouldn't smudge the color, pulled me closer
and looked directly at me.

"We don't have to sleep together," he said kindly. I stared
at him, mouth open.

"Sleep. Together," he enunciated a little louder. "I'm not
against it in principle; I like men, and I like women, and you
have the sexiest hands I've ever seen. But it really doesn't
have to be about sex. I really—well, what I really like is to be
watched. You know?" I didn't, but I wasn't about to let on.

"Wisdom is knowing what you don't know," I intoned,
deeply drunk, and shook his hand.

On some level, I did understand. The feeling all night had been one of curiosity and sensuality, not animal attraction. Nonetheless, even at this stage in the game, I thought it honorable of him to make his intentions clear. What a gentleman, in his red teddy.

"Fabulous!" he exclaimed, and stood up. "I thought you'd understand. So you wouldn't mind . . . watching?" He surveyed my bedroom. "I feel so comfortable with you, I'd love to dance for you. May I?"

I nodded, stepped back, and tripped onto my bed. I had a feeling he didn't mean a court gavotte. "Carl," I said too loudly, "I would be delighted—no, honored—if you danced for me."

He smiled his beautiful, untroubled smile and clapped his hands. "Wonderful! I think you'll enjoy it. Let me go put on some music." He dimmed the overhead light and moved to the living room in a rustle of red satin, and I heard the music change from Coltrane to Marvin Gaye. I sat on my bed and thought longingly about my friends in Boston, wondering how I was ever fully going to convey the mise-en-scene.

"Sexual Healing" was wafting from the other room as Carl emerged wearing the boots. Just the boots. I squinted. Was it possible I didn't *see* his clothes? No, Carl was definitely nude, as naked as the day his pan-sexual, exhibitionist Creator made him. I sat on the bed and watched as he glided to the tiny corridor in my bedroom and began to undulate. His hands moved over himself as he swayed, his back arching and bending like a reed in a tide. In the dim light, the muscles in his legs stood out like the grooves in a tree trunk. He was a sensual and evocative dancer, throwing sinuous shadows on the walls, dancing as if lost in a trance. It excited me to think I was watching someone who no longer knew I was there.

At some point, he began to jump. His dancing grew more frenzied, and the boots made a loud *smack!* each time they hit the floor. I could see sweat beading on his temples. The boots banged out a rhythm, faster, as his hands carved the air. He spun and gyrated, and for one tense moment I thought he might erupt into a squatting Russian kick-dance. I thought anxiously about my downstairs neighbor. It would be a shame if he called the police before we'd even met. Finally, at fever pitch, Carl stopped—arms outstretched, head thrown back, full priapic splendor on display to his stunned audience. He stood, chest heaving, and we stared at each other. I pondered the etiquette. What now? Did I stuff dollar bills into his boots? At a loss, I fell back on my years of good upbringing and started to clap.

"Thank you," he said with mock solemnity, bowing.

"Bravo," I croaked. "Bravo."

Carl took my hands. "Thank you," he said gently, and gave me a kiss on the forehead. "That was fabulous. Thank you. And now, if you'll excuse me . . ." He disappeared into the bathroom, leaving me limp on the bed. When he came out a few minutes later, he was wearing his pants and shirt, and holding out the boots.

"Do you have a bag for these lovelies?" he asked anxiously. "I don't want to get them dirty." How much dirtier could they get, really, but I kept my mouth shut and went to the kitchen for a plastic bag.

"I, er, got a little excited in the bathroom," he called. "I just couldn't help it. I cleaned up, of course. I used the small towel, not the bath one. I hope that's all right?"

"Of course," I replied expansively.

Carl retrieved his jacket and briefcase from the living room. "You've been wonderful," he called. "You know," he added, "I'd love to dress you up and take you out sometime. You could put me on a leash. I know some places we could go." I thought for a moment. It was the logical next step, wasn't it.

"We'll talk," I said confidently. The wine was wearing off and my coccyx was throbbing. I got more bags from the kitchen, and together we piled in the rest of his loot: dresses, t-shirts, panties, camisoles, the teddy. I wedged in the dinner plate when he wasn't looking.

He reached for his wallet. "So what do you think?" he asked. "How much?" For a moment, I was confused. Wasn't I supposed to be paying him?

"Seventy-five? A hundred?" He peeled the bills from a wad in his pocket and pressed them into my palm. "What a wonderful evening," he sighed. "Thank you." He kissed my hand, and playfully nibbled my fingers. "Gorgeous," he said. "I'll call you. We'll go out." He touched my cheek. "Don't worry, I'll let myself out." I didn't argue. And with a rustle of plastic bags and a last lick of my fingers, he was gone.

After the door shut, I turned and surveyed my apartment. The living room blazed with a startled, caught-in-the-act air—lights burning, music playing, but no one there. Empty wine bottles stood on the coffee table, and a few dresses lay on the sofa, the rejects. Panties, camisoles, and bras hung from the dresser drawers, festooning the knobs like the silken fall-out from some sartorial apocalypse. The floor of the front room was littered with more clothes—dresses, skirts, even, inexplicably, my winter coat. I was sorry I'd relinquished my smart brown velvet blazer.

I turned off the stereo, and let the silence ring in my ears. The clock showed three a.m., and the front window glowed a deep, impenetrable black. Black, like my boots. I sighed, and wandered into the kitchen. All that wine had left me light-headed and ravenous, but the fridge yielded only apples, scallions, and a bag of potatoes. I thought about calling my best friend back east, but she'd still be in bed. I could regale my co-workers in a few hours, but as most of them didn't yet know my name, it seemed a bit forward. I'd briefly met the young mother down the hall, but it seemed unwise to wake her up and introduce myself.

I leaned against the fridge, overwhelmed by a need for normalcy. I stared at the potatoes. Bland, wholesome, soothingly starchy; they'd do. I heated a pot of water and examined my Prude-pink nails while I waited for the water to boil. I had a new appreciation for my hands after this evening. When the potatoes were soft, I transferred them to a bowl, took out a fork, and set about mashing them with fervor. I was ferocious, purposeful, as graceful in my dance of the potato as Carl had been in his. When I finished, I ate a few spoonfuls, shoveled the remainder into a plastic takeout container, and stuck a post-it to the lid: "We met downstairs the other day. Enjoy the spuds. #5." I opened the door, tiptoed down the dark hall, and left the whole mess at the door of #6. Then I tiptoed back, maneuvered through the piles of clothes on the floor, and fell into bed fully dressed. Potato caked my lips and my teeth were sticky with wine, but it didn't matter. My universe had expanded, gloriously. A pair of boots was a small price to pay.

≫ ≫ ≫

After stints in San Francisco and New York, Juliet Eastland has landed right back where she started: Boston, Massachusetts, where she lives with her husband and children. Her work appears in anthologies, magazines, newspapers, and on the web. Since this trip, she has crisscrossed the country several times.

❧ ❧ ❧

Zombies on Kilimanjaro

A father and son walk above the
clouds and discuss many things.

We had wound our way slowly down a steep slope to the bottom of a valley when we heard a sound like rolling thunder. A cloud of dust appeared far above us on the slope of the volcano.

"Rockslide," said Fred, our Tanzanian guide, shielding his eyes with both hands to look up.

Fred had copper skin, a pencil thin mustache and an easy-going manner. Nothing seemed to upset him much; he applied the Swahili catch phrase, *hakuna matata*, "no problem!" to almost every situation. Even now, he seemed weirdly relaxed.

Not me. I could see what looked like small pebbles bouncing down the side of the volcano, careening like billiard balls into the top of the valley through which we were climbing. These tiny pebbles were a few kilometers away. Were they going to roll all the way down to where we stood? I looked around. Giant boulders littered the valley floor, some big as cars, some big as houses. Do we run? Do we hide? I watched, transfixed. I had to keep thinking of them as pebbles to keep myself from panicking. So this was why the Tanzanian government had closed the Western Breach trail to Kilimanjaro's summit.

These frequent slides, I later learned, were the result of a "freeze-thaw" process. Subzero nights and hot days make the top centimeters of the rock face contract and expand, creating tiny fissures. It's the same process that creates potholes on city streets. Water gets into the cracks. It freezes then thaws, again and again, forming wedges of ice that widen the cracks with each cycle. Like a slow-motion jackhammer the process fragments the outer shell of the volcano, eventually popping loose giant boulders just like the ones rolling our way now. It's a fascinating geological phenomenon to observe, though at the time I was more interested in whether or not we were going to be crushed to death. I watched Fred closely for some clue to our danger. He seemed in no apparent rush to escape to higher ground. I couldn't tell if this meant we were safe, or if we were in danger, but could not escape no matter how fast we ran, so *hakuna matata*.

The dust and the rocks eventually settled in place well above us. The thunder halted. Fred picked up his pack again and led us forward without a word.

We climbed up the far side of the valley, hand over hand up a steep slope. Fred put Josh in the middle between us. Josh was my son, age twenty. This was the trip of a lifetime, climbing Kilimanjaro, a cool father-son bonding adventure. But he had been whacked with altitude sickness, and was suffering. On this our third day on the mountain we had climbed to just over 4,000 meters above sea level. The ascent had given Josh a massive migraine. It was painful just to watch him shuffle along with slow deliberate steps. I could see how each jarring slip on the trail sent needles of pain through his skull. He didn't want to talk, didn't want to stop. He kept going, his face pinched, mouth tight. Fred assured us relief would come as we got to lower elevations. Our camp for the evening would take us down 500 meters, and give us more time to acclimatize before our push to the summit.

Kilimanjaro is the highest point in Africa and at 5,850 meters (19,341 feet) above sea level it's the world's tallest free-standing mountain. While there are higher peaks in the Andes, Rockies and Himalayas, they are all part of mountain ranges. What makes Kilimanjaro so amazing is that it is a solitary, staggering mass of rock that rises straight up from the Serengeti plains where elephants and lions roam. It starts at near sea level, and soars to a glacier-fringed cone. The trek to the top is like walking from the equator to the North Pole in a week.

The other thing that distinguishes Kilimanjaro from the rest of the Seven Summits (the highest peak on each continent) is that one does not need ropes or mountaineering skills to climb it. Kilimanjaro is just a long, exhausting, but technically simple trek, and for this it has gained a reputation as "Everyman's Everest." Each year, as many as 40,000 trekkers attempt to make it to the volcano's rim. Fewer than half succeed, however, mostly due to altitude sickness. Almost everyone suffers mild symptoms such as exhaustion, nausea, headaches and coughing. But in the worst cases, high altitude can kill you, fast. Fluids leak into your brain and can put you in a coma, or into your lungs and you can drown in your own juices; on average, altitude sickness kills about ten climbers a year on Kilimanjaro—many more than die in rockslides.

Over the crest, the trail dropped steeply, making the descent slow and tortuous. We passed a strapping young Danish man and his Tanzanian guide, taking a rest. The guide was carrying the young man's pack (emblazoned with the red flag and white cross of Denmark). The Dane, seated on a rock, held his head in his hands.

"How's it going?" said Josh.

"Bad," the Dane groaned. "You?"

"Terrible. But we are all on our way down now. It's sure to get better."

The Dane smiled feebly. Josh turned to go. He hesitated, turned back, and gave the guy a big hug.

"Good luck!" said Josh.

"I feel like part of a club now," Josh told me. "Brotherhood of the Splitting Headaches."

The joke was a good sign. Another few hundred meters down, he was moving quicker, his head up.

"Dad, I've got a question," he said, his voice suddenly upbeat. "Mythologies are memeplexes, too, right? Like the ancient Greeks?"

"Of course," I said. I could hardly believe he was bringing the conversation back to memes.

For a good part of our hike I had been discussing with Josh this new theory of ideas that had captured my imagination. We had talked about how memes—ideas that replicate—can build up into whole systems of thought—religions, philosophies, political systems. That Josh was bringing the topic back to what I wanted to talk about seemed a real sign that he was feeling better. Or else he was succumbing to delirium.

"What we call 'mythology' is really just the religion of other people," I continued. "We commonly use 'myth' to mean 'something other people believe that we know is not true,' like urban legends. In fact, the real characteristic of a mythology is that it explains the world in a coherent narrative. A mythology tells stories about how the world came to be the way it is, and why we are the way we are. In this sense, every religious system is a mythology."

Josh described in detail a mythology-based video game he enjoyed playing, *God of War*, in which the player takes on the identity of a man bent on avenging himself against the Greek Gods. He kills them off, one by one.

"So it's the thrill of being a mortal man," I said, "and killing the immortals?"

"And he's also having this fling with Aphrodite at the same time. He kills a God, then goes and screws the Goddess."

"Well, I guess the makers of the game know how to hook their target audience," I said grimly.

"No kidding," laughed Josh. "My point was, you were saying how religious belief systems were memeplexes. Wouldn't each video game be a memeplex, too?"

"I guess so," I said slowly. "The idea never occurred to me."

"Sure, each game creates its own world, defined by hundreds of memes. The player has to figure out for himself the rules of the game. He has to learn the strategies and skills to guide him along the way."

"Ah, I see," I said. "A game's internal coherent reality is its mythology, just like any religion."

We had to break off talking for a few minutes where the path dropped so vertically it felt as if we were scrambling down a dry waterfall. One or two quick steps could put you out of control and into a tumble. It put strain on a completely different set of leg muscles. My knees ached. Fred positioned himself at key spots and held our hands as we clambered down. I needed his support. I'm fifty years old, I thought, but I feel like a ninety-year-old trying to negotiate my way down a fire escape.

The valley into which we descended had a silver stream running down the center of it, bringing back plant life that we had not seen all day on our long walk through Moonland. For the first time we encountered a weird, new kind of tree, the giant groundsel. Fred said it was called the "Kilimanjaro Tree" because it only grew here and on a few other mountains in East Africa. These trees were shaped rather like giant cactuses, growing up to about fifteen feet tall, with huge branches that curved upwards from a single trunk at odd angles. The trunk and branches were covered with a thick mat of dead leaves. It looked almost like they were wearing puffy fur coats.

Green, living leaves sprouted from the tops of the branches in big, fan-like, circular tufts. Some of these tufts had a straggly, flower-covered spike sticking up from the center towards the sky like peculiar, whimsical antennae.

"They look too wacky to be real," I said to Josh.

"Like something out of Dr. Seuss," he replied.

The small plain at the bottom of the distant valley was studded with hundreds of these crazy Kilimanjaro trees, but also speckled with dots of bright blue, orange, green, and yellow fabric. Some seventy tents were already pitched for the night. Fred explained that at this valley the Lemosho route to the summit merged with the Umbwe route. The trekkers from both trails converged here for the night, making a tent town, rather than a village. Seeing our destination gave Josh and me a final boost of energy. As the path eased off into a level walk, we picked up our pace.

As we walked I pondered these unknown and complex virtual worlds my son so effortlessly inhabited. As a teen, he had wanted to share his favorite video games with me. He would sit at my side in front of the computer and coach me through various levels. My hand-keyboard coordination was painfully slow, nowhere near fast enough for many of the tasks that came as second nature to Josh. Sometimes he would step in when I was failing and getting frustrated, and complete the task for me. I appreciated him for wanting to share what he loved. But I had not really appreciated until this moment that these imaginary worlds he navigated with such ease were meme systems potentially as complex as any mythological epic. I could see now that these role-play video games were very much like visual novels in which the protagonist could move about freely, discovering and exploring the landscape and characters within. How dull it must seem to gamers that a written tale has only one single pathway from beginning to end. I realized that for Josh the experience of coaching his struggling, ill-coordinated father at the keyboard must have been something akin to trying to teach an illiterate man how to read.

We strolled into the valley, flat as a dry riverbed. The weird loopy-branched trees and the angular, bright-colored tents created a perceptual clash, as if Pablo Picasso and Salvador Dali had painted the scene together on a single canvas.

Our little bowls of warm water were waiting for us beside our tent, as they were every day at the end of the trail. We splashed the dust and sweat from our faces, then went straight to dinner.

"Welcome macaroni and tuna!"

Our waiter, Sully, beckoned us to another surreal Kilimanjaro meal. I had thought perhaps this dish would mimic that old camping staple I had eaten round so many campfires in Canada: a box of Kraft noodles, a packet of cheddar cheese powder, a tin of tuna, and voila! Not so on Kilimanjaro. The noodles were served plain, like spaghetti. Onto it Sully ladled chunked tuna in an orange sauce that looked like cheese sauce but was in fact vegetable soup. The mixture looked remarkably like a bowl of vomit. But it tasted amazing: soupy and fishy and chewy with a hint of tomato and little bubbles of fat. Josh started slurping it down like a dog at his dinner bowl, the first real meal he had eaten since altitude-sickness hit him the previous day.

"Sully, this is the most delicious, fabulous meal I have ever had in my life!" he said.

Sully beamed with pleasure as we helped ourselves to seconds.

After eating, we sipped our tea by the light of the mushroom-tin candelabra and talked about the day. Fred entered the tent. He held in his hand an orange prescription bottle filled with little white pills.

"Diamox?" I asked.

Fred nodded. This was the only medication that alleviated the symptoms of altitude sickness. It could only be taken below 4,000 meters though, so Josh was not able to take it earlier in the day.

"Josh, how is your head?" he asked.

"Oh, I still have a headache. But compared to what I felt like at lunch, I feel like now I'm dancing in a field of buttercups."

"You should take pills," Fred said.

"Can I read the label for side effects?" I asked.

Fred handed the bottle to me.

"'May cause drowsiness. Don't operate heavy machinery.' Hmm . . . Josh, you think you can operate your walking poles?"

"*Hakuna matata*," said Josh.

He mimed going spastic with invisible walking poles, stabbing and smashing into everything in the tent. Definitely, he was feeling better.

Fred turned to me. "So, give him half a pill after dinner, another half in the morning. Make sure he takes it with lots of water."

I nodded to Fred. I had my hand on the top to pop open the bottle and break a pill in two. Wait a minute, I checked myself. One of the reasons I had wanted to take the trip with Josh was to bond in a new way with him, man to man. But here I was, compulsively slipping into daddy-mode. I looked across the table at Josh. Our eyes met. I handed the bottle across the table to him. Yeah, he's old enough to take his own medicine.

Day 4: No doubt about it, I stank. Bacteria do not thrive at high altitudes. Theoretically, one can go a long time this high without a bath. But waking up the fourth day on Kilimanjaro with all the odors of the mountain zip-locked inside my sleeping bag with me, I knew it was time to take action. When

Josh went out to visit the potty-tent, I rummaged through my duffle bag and found the special item I had been saving for just this moment. While shopping for trip supplies a month earlier, I had been thrilled to find a camping accessory that was new to me: man-sized wet wipes. Wet wipes are a parent's best friend. These little moist tissues with a slight antiseptic sting make changing diapers easy and sanitary, and can also clean a dirty face or sticky hands. But these beauties I found at REI were made for head-to-toe adult body rubdowns. Each napkin unfolded to the dimensions of a laptop keyboard. Using both sides, I found I could wash about one quarter of my carcass before the wipe turned gray and grimy. Four wipes and ten minutes later I felt clean and fresh as the proverbial daisy.

Josh, while appreciating my change of skin color, declined to use them on himself, no matter how enthusiastically I promoted the daisy-fresh feeling. Though he did not smell as bad as I did, he looked frightful. His hair seemed to be made of solid clumps that stuck up from his scalp at odd angles like palm fronds, like some Claymation-cartoon version of himself. And he was covered with feathers. His down sleeping bag was leaking. Since he was sleeping in his fleece jacket and long johns, white tufts of down had gotten stuck in the fibers.

The walk today would be a short one, Fred explained after breakfast, just five kilometers. But there would be a lot of steep climbing up and down at high altitude, so we would go slowly, covering about a kilometer each hour. To start, we would scale the cliff on the far side of the valley, known as the Barranco Wall, a climb of 200 meters (600 feet), straight up.

A little glacial stream flowed alongside the base of the cliff. The morning sun glistened off a thin layer of ice that covered the stream's banks. Mist rose from the ice like a translucent veil in front of the wall. As we drew near we saw that the ice had given the stepping stones in the stream a glossy sheen, making it difficult to cross without slipping and plunging ankle deep in the frigid water—not a great way to start a day's trek. Fred hopped nimbly across and then steadied each of us so that we only splashed our waterproof boots without soaking them.

Where the wall begins, the trail turns into a steep switchback etched upon the rock face. We picked our way slowly over jagged chunks of lava. In some places the footpath disappeared and we had to climb straight up, one careful handhold at time. Our conversation dropped to nothing as we struggled to keep our breath and focus on each grip. After hauling ourselves up a particularly challenging stretch, we rested on a broad ledge. We gulped water, gulped air. I was sweating profusely. Looking straight down, we saw the icy stream, just a thin, white line at the base of the wall far below us. Across the valley we watched the last of the tents coming down, the patches of colors folding up and disappearing amidst the trunks of the crazy, tufted Kilimanjaro trees. Our porters started coming up behind us, precariously balancing their heavy loads on their heads while they used both hands to pull themselves up. It was insane to watch this take place without the use of a single climbing rope. Josh and I could barely manage to haul our own asses up the cliff, let alone loaded down with groceries and gear bags. Fred bent over and grabbed each of our porter's loads and hauled them onto the ledge as one by one they joined us for a brief rest.

As we reached the top of Barranco Wall, Kilimanjaro's southern glacier slammed us in the face. The sun glinted from the brilliant mass, a hard white light that hurt the eyes. The mountain filled the sky, too big, too close to comprehend. I felt disoriented, as if hit with a weird kind of vertigo. Not dizziness from looking down, but from looking straight up at that wall of glaring ice. Standing on the mountain's neck, I knew with my rational mind that the glacier was still at least two kilometers away, more than a mile. But it seemed poised just above our heads, so close I felt I could reach out and touch one of its long white toes.

I recalled reading that the first mountaineers on Kilimanjaro were turned back by massive ice sheets so thick they covered Kibo's cone down to 4,000 meters, which was about our present elevation. The men who first summited, Hans Meyers and Ludwig Purtswcheller, spent days cutting ice steps in a 100-foot ice wall of that blocked the way to the top. Though these glaciers still looked crushingly majestic, I realized I was in the last generation that would ever see them.

The previous night I had pulled out the papers that Mike had given me. He was a geography teacher we met our first day on the mountain. He had passed on to me an article on the most recent research of Kilimanjaro's glaciers, published in the science journal *Nature* in September 2009. It was written by a team of scientists from the University of Ohio and University of Massachusetts who have spent more than a decade on Kilimanjaro measuring the exact dimensions of the ice fields.

They had discovered that the rate of shrinkage of Kilimanjaro's glaciers more than doubled in the past half century: from one percent per year between 1912 and 1953 to 2.5 percent per year between 1989 and2007. The researchers also learned something new from drilling core samples all the way to the bottom of the ice. These cores, some of them 50 meters long, revealed huge amounts of information about the climate of East Africa. Like the tree rings on a giant Redwood, one could count the layers of ice laid down year after year, like pages of an 11,700-year-long calendar. This was the history of the continent frozen in ice. For example, a 300-year-long drought was marked by a 30 cm layer of dust in the cores. Tiny air bubbles trapped at various depths in the ice could be analyzed to reveal the levels of carbon dioxide in the atmosphere at specific moments in time. Given how little data there was about Africa's climate in ancient times, the cores from Kilimanjaro's glaciers were something akin to unearthing the climatological Dead Sea Scrolls. But this unique record is being rapidly destroyed as the glaciers shrink, literally erasing 11,700 years of information. In just a few decades, this record will be gone. Because of this threat, the scientists decided to drill and remove additional ice cores to be stored in freezers for future generations of researchers to analyze with more sophisticated methods.

The most alarming thing that they discovered was that the top sixty years of ice is missing from the record. In the past few decades, instead of adding new layers, the surface of the glaciers has started to melt from the top down. At high altitudes such as Kilimanjaro's summit, the temperature stays below freezing, so glaciers typically don't melt to water. Instead, the intense rays of the sun turn surface ice directly into vapor. The ice gradually evaporates in a process called sublimation. But these most recent cores showed that the top 65 centimeters of the glaciers had turned to water and then refrozen. Elongated bubbles and tiny channels in the ice provided certain evidence of melting in modern times—a phenomenon not found anywhere else in the glaciers' 11,700-year history.

Furtwängler Glacier, on the plateau inside the cone of Kibo, was actually discovered to be waterlogged and shrinking at a rate of five percent a year. The scientists measured its decrease at fifty percent over the past decade alone. It recently split in half, increasing the area exposed to the sun and further hastening its inevitable demise over the next several years.

"Hence, the climatological conditions currently driving the loss of Kilimanjaro's ice fields are clearly unique within an 11,700-year perspective," the researchers concluded in the *Nature* article.

I explained to Josh what I had read about the glaciers in the article.

"You are looking at an endangered species," I said.

He looked up silently, taking in my somber words.

"It's sad," he said.

"How do you and I even begin to absorb what this means, Josh?" I said. "I think of the thousands of people who walk up to these glaciers as we are doing, they take a picture, a snapshot. This single moment, it's enough to capture the grandeur. But we don't see the time lapse photography, how over decades the glaciers are disintegrating. If we had the perspective of a glacier, perhaps we would see the climate changing at a pace the planet has never experienced before. This is definitely something we humans cannot afford to respond to with *hakuna matata*."

We both looked up at the glaciers in silence.

"I am looking forward to the snowball fights, though," Josh said.

≈ ≈ ≈

Tim Ward is the author of six books, including Zombies on Kilimanjaro: A Father/Son Journey above the Clouds, *from which this excerpt has been adapted. Disclaimer: please note that there are no actual zombies on Kilimanjaro. It just looks that way when you see hundreds of exhausted, brain-dead trekkers on the crater rim at dawn. Zombies also serve as a metaphor for the book's main theme of how we can become enslaved by the stories we tell ourselves. Tim has also written about Thailand* (What the Buddha Never Taught), *India* (Arousing the Goddess), *Greece* (Savage Breast), *and is the author of a collection of stories about Asia* (The Great Dragon's Fleas). *He lives in Maryland with his wife, Teresa. You can visit his websites, timwardbooks.com and zombiesonkilimanjaro.com.*

✧ ✧ ✧

Traveling to Mary

Wandering through London, a young scholar finds
inspiration for life and love in warrior women of the past.

At the foot of Westminster Bridge in London rides a
bronze woman bent on war. Drawn in a chariot
behind two rearing horses, she sweeps her arms vengefully
high, clutching a spear and beckoning some Fury from the air.
She is Boudicca, Celtic warrior queen. In 60 AD, after Roman
soldiers flogged her, then raped her two preteen daughters in
front of her eyes, she did her damndest to kill them all. "Let
us, therefore, go against them trusting boldly to good fortune," she shouted to her troops. "Let us show them that they
are hares and foxes trying to rule over dogs and wolves." Boudicca nearly beat the Romans, but when her defeat became
inevitable, she poisoned herself rather than accept it. Now she
guards the entrance to a bridge, a place of crossing, of something new on the other side. In this city, pressed by a dying
first love and the soft clamor of ancestral voices at my back,
any bridge might be the bridge I'm looking for.

When I stare up at Boudicca, I'm a twenty-six-year-old
graduate student in nineteenth-century British literature on
my first trip to England, alone. It's a landscape I'm already
primed to read: a native of rural Alabama, I breathe the

charged air of the not-quite-dead past as naturally as oxygen. At age seventeen, Dicey Langston—my great-great-great-great grandmother—swam across the frozen Tiger River near Travelers Rest, South Carolina to warn local rebels, including her brother, that a local band of British loyalists called the "Bloody Scouts" were about to attack their little settlement. She saved them all. When the same "Scouts" came to harass her father about his son's whereabouts, she sprang—Pocahontas-like—in front of him and dared them to shoot. Later, she married Thomas Springfield, the leader of her brother's rebel group, and had twenty-two children before her death at age seventy-one in 1837.

Dicey is, of course, short for Laodicea, the name of a Christian community cited in Revelations, chapter three, as being "lukewarm," destined to "spue" out of an angel's mouth. Yet a teenage girl who could ford a frozen river to warn a whole settlement of disaster, flirt with the rebel leader (and marry him), and save her father is far from lukewarm—she's a role model. As a child I never waded into a creek on our family's farm without thinking of her; bookish and late-blooming, I loved the thought of her blood bracing up my own. As I got older, I feared lukewarmness more than anything. I smoked and drank and told riotous stories in bars. I wrote all night and went to rock shows and seized any chance for what I thought was love. I held on too tight to the first boy who said he loved me, because I feared there might never be another one. I looked so bold, so strong. Inside, I was so afraid.

Now, at twenty-six, I'm walking alone in one of the oldest cities of the Western world. It's the year 2000, the millennium celebrated by the brand-new London Eye revolving just beyond Boudicca's outstretched hand. This is a city built on the sites of women's battles. Ravens stride the Tower yard where I gaze on the execution block that cradled Anne Boleyn's neck. From a Thames-chugging tourist boat I study the dank stone of Traitors Gate, where young then-princess Elizabeth I craned up at the dripping archway as she passed underneath. In Westminster Abbey I shuffle in a line toward her marble deathbed effigy, its sharp profile softened like a cow-licked salt block by all those centuries of touch. I study the surprisingly small and ordinary Coronation Throne with its three hundred years of carved graffiti, a script date marked by some then-tourist: 1763. They filed past then just as I do now: *even a cat can look at a king*.

Having just read the work of the great English feminist Mary Wollstonecraft for the first time, I'm also looking for traces of her London—dark and rickety, racked by gin and crime and the decades-long clash with upstart colonists and French regicides one slim Channel's-breadth away. Wollstonecraft was born in 1759, the same year as Dicey Langston. She approved of both these revolutions against what her future son-in-law Percy Shelley would call "an old, mad, blind, despised, and dying king." But in 1795, age thirty-six, weeping after a rakish American speculator named Gilbert Imlay deserted her, she was walking up and down on Putney Bridge to let the rain soak her skirts before she flung herself into the Thames. Dicey swam a swollen river to save lives; Wollstonecraft jumped in to kill herself. Peering down into the suck and gurgle of the brown water, I wonder: was this where they fished her out, or here?

In 1795, Dicey Langston, also age thirty-six, was happy at home in South Carolina with her own rakish American, nursing the fifth of her soon-to-be twenty-two children. But Mary Wollstonecraft would bear only two children, both girls. The first, Fanny Imlay, committed suicide at an inn in Wales, her body buried anonymously by the parish. The second, Mary Godwin, ran away to the continent with a sexy married nobleman named Percy Shelley, grieved the deaths of three of her four children, and began, in the summer of 1816, a novel called

Frankenstein. Mary's birth caused an infection that killed Wollstonecraft at age thirty-eight, when Mary was ten days old. For her whole life, the younger Mary yearned toward the memory of her famous mother, tracing the invisible maps of grief: a creature bumbling and stumbling, looking for love, looking for a parent, blind to the rules and laws everyone else seems to know by instinct. This is non-lukewarm life: you always seem to want too much or try too hard or reach too high. You're always crossing some line everyone else seems to see, always getting it wrong. Especially in love—which seems to me, as I study the lives of women, so frighteningly deterٰminative for something so chancey. Wollstonecraft—like her daughters—would never be lukewarm.

Technically, I'm in love on that first trip to England, in a long-distance relationship with a sweet boy, Allan, from Mississippi. He is the first man to whom I ever said *I love you,* and the first one to say it to me. But three years after our first dizzying summer together, we're carrying on lives a thousand miles apart, and without admitting it, we're losing the will to stitch them together. I look back toward Allan in my mind as I walk in London, but I can't imagine him closer anymore. That effort used to feel like love. Now it just makes me sad.

More real than Allan in my mind are the people who have walked here before me, especially the dead. A scholarly-historical tourist walks through a double world, half-known and half-imagined, maps of what used to be or might have been laid over the clattering, honking reality of the present. She sees the place as palimpsest, imagining the traces of other footsteps, other words, only half scraped away beneath the inscriptions of the present. All these ghosts are in such vigorous coexistence. But this cloud of stories, imaginings, and dreams is clarified by fact: a woman traveler's body is vulnerable as a man's is not. Yet my body, I tell myself, is an exception. Roman historian Cassius Dio described Boudicca as "very tall, in appearance most terrifying, in the glance of her eye most fierce" with "a great mass of the tawniest hair" that "fell to her hips." I'm Boudicca-sized: six feet tall, with a similar mass of curly hair, with wide shoulders and long arms and legs. Like Mary Wollstonecraft, I pride myself on my physical strength: "In the name of truth and common sense," she wrote irritably, "why should not one woman acknowledge that she can take more exercise than another? or, in other words, that she has a sound constitution; and why, to damp innocent vivacity, is she darkly to be told that men will draw conclusions which she little thinks of?"

Yet I'm confused, then, at twenty-six, about the gap between my physical health and an emotional self-sufficiency I can't quite reach: I can't seem to get strong in both ways at once. Years later, after I've become a college professor and avid cyclist, a different boyfriend will listen to me plan a study-abroad tour of Shelley-and-Keats-related sites in London, Switzerland, and Rome. "You're as big as most men," he remarks. "Bigger than most people, in fact. I don't imagine you'd be afraid *anywhere*. That *anyone* would want to bother you." That man will leave me abruptly on a cold November night, breaking my heart as no man ever had. At that time I'll be thirty-six years old, Wollstonecraft's age on the night when despite her books and intellectual achievements she decided to die from disappointed love, from depression that knew no outlet, from the yearnings and urgings of the sensual body she believed no man would ever want to touch, again. I've tried so many times to fashion my strong, unruly frame into something more delicate. I've tried to anticipate a man's desires and call them forth out of him, before he even knew them himself. I've kept doing everything Mary Wollstonecraft did to try to keep Gilbert Imlay in love with her, and more. And like her, I've failed. Boudicca fought to keep her country, not a man.

Was her battle more important? Then, I would have said I
wasn't sure.

On my own in London, I walk, I wander, I look. And I let
my mind wander too, to women, and the bridges they threw
themselves from. Warriors, and who they stride into battle
against, and why. Their struggles to harmonize the urges and
sensings of the body and the mind. The men they settle into
contented lives with, or not. The swollen rivers they cross in
the dead of night, the warnings they shout. When they stand
and fight, and when they walk away.

Mary Wollstonecraft was a warrior from birth, and never let
up. *A good hater*, her husband, William Godwin, described
her. She grew up witness to what she would describe as the
"tyranny" of a bad marriage: her abusive father farmed half-
heartedly, gambled, and drank. Young Mary Wollstonecraft
slept on the landing outside her mother's bedroom to protect
her from him, and once her mother died, she lit out to cobble
together an independent existence. "It is a happy thing to be
a mere blank," she wrote, "and to be able to pursue one's own
whims, where they lead, without having a husband and half
a hundred children to teaze and controul a poor woman who
wishes to be free." The patriarchy of society, she saw early on,
was just the patriarchy of the family writ large—one big bad
marriage in which everyone was trapped.

London, of course, was her destination: the eighteenth-
century version of the "creative class" centered around her
publisher, Joseph Johnson, in St. Paul's Churchyard. She
plunged into a self-fashioned intellectual life, arguing with
men around dinner tables, including Godwin, who didn't like
her the first time they met. Eventually she wrote the pair of
political treatises that made her name, *Vindication of the Rights
of Man* (1790) and *Vindication of the Rights of Woman* (1792).
The latter, in particular, made her notorious, although its

central theme now seems too obvious to state: the mind is not gendered—or limited—by the gender of the body in which it resides, which is bound by a society organized from top to bottom to benefit men. Therefore, social and educational institutions must be reformed to let women live up to their full potential. "[T]he most perfect education, in my opinion," she wrote, "is such an exercise of the understanding as is best calculated to strengthen the body and form the heart. Or, in other words, to enable the individual to attain such habits of virtue as will render it independent. In fact, it is a farce to call any being virtuous whose virtues do not result from the exercise of its own reason."

Drawn by the bloody drama of the French Revolution—like any journalist drawn to Afghanistan today—Wollstonecraft went to Paris intending to write her own history of it. There she met Gilbert Imlay—a tall, charming venture capitalist and professional trader in sentiment, including Europeans' yearning for an unspoiled New World and Wollstonecraft's for a man who understood her. But his mode of love, unlike hers, was to enjoy himself and then move on. Wollstonecraft fell in love anyway, meeting him during the height of the Terror at the barricades of the city and conceiving her first child, Fanny. She dreamed of traveling back to America with him, of starting a new life on a farm in the former colonies—sturdy and self-sufficient as Dicey Langston. Yet the relationship foundered, then soured. But still, on his behalf, Wollstonecraft traveled.

Go to Scandinavia and find out what happened to my ship, Imlay asked. *I trust you.* The ship was full of silver to rescue him from debt, and it had disappeared. Perhaps they both knew this was his way of distracting her from what was coming, as some men do: pile on compliments and signs of trust to raise a woman's spirits before you let them drop. Because if you can't get away to see to your own ship, and you have access to a smart, tough, and tough-minded woman like Mary Wollstonecraft, wouldn't you take advantage of her?

Letters Written in Sweden, Norway, and Denmark—aka *Letters from Norway (1796)*, drawn from her actual letters to Imlay—shows Wollstonecraft in that strange sort of limbo travelers enter under a weight of emotion: called out of preexisting preoccupations by the new scenes and challenges, half-reminded, by the contrast, of what she's trying to forget. Her body is active, and her mind continually slips back to what is elsewhere: Imlay, and the relationship that may be already dead. Yet you can also see her fighting that other effect of travel: the dreamy instinct to let go of that tether connected at the other end to home, the need to let that lingering obsession or emotion go. Here, anyone in her shoes might wonder, does it matter anymore? Here, can't I just let it go? Because the world is bigger than what that side of your heart, tugged by that cord, connected to that man, would suggest. Is it disloyal to let yourself let go of your old self and travel toward a new one? To choose solitude over a man who can never really give you love?

"Talked to Allan on the phone last night," I wrote in my first day's journal of London. "Don't know why talking about this departure on the phone should feel so much like a departure in person." Only now, approaching the age Wollstonecraft was when she died, have I learned to let go of men rather than beg and plead and cling to them. Only now do I see how I held onto the tiny thread of something that was real and spun it so far out it became too thin to hold.

Like Wollstonecraft and Imlay at the barricades, Allan and I couldn't get enough of touching, talking, breathing the same air, that first summer we fell in love. We waded into a spring-fed waterhole, giggling. We lay in the grass as crickets and frogs tuned up and lightning bugs flashed in the trees, and his face over mine blotted out the moon. In his apartment, we'd prop ourselves up against the headboard of his old maple sleigh bed and smoke, dropping our ash into a tiny china dish set on his chest. When we moved the little dish and put out all the lights I'd kiss him there, again, right over his heart, with a fierce tenderness. This boy, this man, was the sweetest I had ever known.

Like Lot's wife, I will turn to a pillar of salt, weeping, if I look back at this too long. Anyone does, looking back at feelings you can't know then will change. But they do, as people do.

What happened to us? What happened?

We hung on by emails and phone calls and grueling drives between our separate states, where we trudged up our forking career paths. We both ate mindlessly and smoked a lot. Increasingly I felt too big around my boyfriend, too exuberant even in the toned-down version of myself I adopted to please him. I reached for him and he turned away. I picked him wild onion flowers—the bright stars in the grass I had always brought my mama, when I was a little girl—and he snorted, complained of their smell, tossed them in the trash. "Well," I said weakly, "I didn't know . . . I mean, I thought . . ." And I let it drop. *If a woman were to tell the truth about herself,* wrote the poet Muriel Rukeyser, *the world would split open.* If I told him I was angry and hurting—if I let that righteous strength roar out—the fragile bark of this relationship would split open and drop me into a cold bottomless sea: falling, falling, with nowhere to land.

Any relationship is work. Any marriage is work. And we do have to work, even to fight, for what we want. But we also have to choose when to stride, Boudicca-like, into battle, when to risk swimming that creek to warn the rebels, and when to walk away. Some love is sustainable; some has been prolonged beyond its natural life, out of fear. Some marriages are theoretical, the wouldn't-it-be-good-if, white-lace daydreams of good little Southern girls and boys. And some are built on real passion, sturdy enough to take honesty, anger, the occasional burst of outrage or pique or immaturity from one or both. A relationship should be able to withstand the human frailty of the humans it shelters. And if it can't, then both those humans are better off alone. I know that now.

This is what Wollstonecraft learned. And what she helped me see.

Shadowed by her dying love affair, *Letters from Norway* is Wollstonecraft's most wistful and haunting book, and the one that enraptured even previously unwilling readers: as Godwin later wrote, it was "calculated to make a man in love with its author." Mary presents herself as wandering the overlaid tracks of the present—the landscape in front of her—and the imagined and remembered past, where the lover who has sent her here is absent. She tracks back and forth from commentary on the customs and appearances of the people she meets and the landscape she's passing through to veiled, melancholic renderings of her own emotions (meant for Imlay, displayed to the public) and thoughts about the future of the soon-to-be-fatherless little girl traveling by her side. "I would then, with fond anxiety, lead you very early in life to form your grand principle of action, to save you from the vain regret of having, through irresolution, let the spring-tide of existence pass away, unimproved, unenjoyed," she addresses little Fanny directly. "Gain experience—ah! gain it—while experience is worth having, and acquire sufficient fortitude to pursue your own happiness; it includes your utility by a direct path. What is wisdom too often but the owl of the goddess, who sits moping in a desolated heart . . ." Back in London, discovering that Imlay had moved on to another woman, she rented a boat to row herself to Putney Bridge, where she walked up and down on the bridge for half an hour, letting the rain weight her clothes, and then jumped in. Yet she was rescued, and made the determination to live. When Imlay wrote her, claiming that "he knew not 'how to extricate' them from the 'wretchedness into which we have been plunged,'" she scornfully replied, "You are extricated long since." It is as the sadder-but-wiser independent woman, her beauty deepened by the "experience" she had half-sought, that Wollstonecraft re-encountered Godwin and began to see him regularly, leading to their marriage in the spring of 1798.

The path marked by low points, broken places, wide bends where it stalls out, is the easier one to set your own feet on, if you're looking for ancestresses to guide you. Boudicca is inspiring but the steep grade of her path—victory or death, by her own hand—can also seem intimidating. Wollstonecraft knew how the right models can enable the women who follow them: "In fact, if we revert to history," she wrote dryly, "we shall find that the women who have distinguished themselves have neither been the most beautiful nor the most gentle of their sex." Remember, she implies, only shallow men admire the merely pretty and sweet, the stereotypical sterling ideal. Similarly, pure achievement leads straight up, on a grade no one but that distant, now-dead figure can climb. When you're seeking the women who've gone before you, this is important.

The train carries me into Victoria Station through a suburban-industrial landscape of high-rise project housing, chain stores and parking lots, rows of brick Edwardian-era houses with tiny back gardens, graffiti slashed onto stone tunnel walls. Mary Wollstonecraft's grave seems like the appropriate destination for a pilgrimage. Her daughter and Percy Shelley thought so too: every biography says there's a strong possibility that they made love for the first time on that grave, within sight of the little stone church where Wollstonecraft and Godwin were married. *St. Pancras* is the only name I know, and there it is: an Underground stop on a map. I've never been on a subway before, but I navigate the Underground with no problem. Can this really be so easy?

Wollstonecraft never intended to get married. Nor did Godwin. For a while, even after she became pregnant, they kept their relationship, and then their marriage, a secret—sensing, correctly, that friends would tease them, since Godwin had written confidently of marriage as "the most odious of all monopolies" and she wasn't much more positive. But these two prickly, self-sufficient intellectuals had really fallen in love. "You do not know how honest I am," he wrote her. "I swear to you that I told you nothing but the strict & literal truth, when I described to you the manner in which you set my imagination on fire on Saturday. For six & thirty hours I could think of nothing else. I longed inexpressibly to have you in my arms." And she felt the same. "I have seldom seen so much live fire running about my features as this morning," she wrote in a morning-after note, "when recollections—very dear, called forth the blush of pleasure, as I adjusted my hair." So, on a late-March morning—with Wollstonecraft three months gone in pregnancy—she and Godwin went to their small neighborhood church and got married, with only one of Godwin's friends in attendance. His diary records only one laconic notation, amidst books read and friends visited: *Panc.*

Climbing up out of the Underground station into busy Euston Road, my eyes fall right on a tall marble building: St. Pancras Church. A dry-mouthed excitement takes hold of me as I hurry across the street and up the shallow steps into the church. On a weekday morning, the church is quiet, its vestibule low-ceilinged and cozy, smelling of wool coats and old carpeting. I step forward into the sanctuary and a black man in minister's garb comes down the aisle. "Can I help you?" he asks with a Jamaican lilt. When I explain I'm looking for Mary Wollstonecraft's grave site, at the church where she and

Godwin were married, he frowns, and then his face clears. "Oh," he says, "you want *Old* St. Pancras." Rummaging in the stack of brochures and devotional books on the side table, he draws out a small Xeroxed map and hands it to me. There it is, a small square far to the right of the page, at the end of a curving line: *Old St. Pancras.*

Down the street I walk, passing the great reddish-brown sprawl of the British Library and heading into a neighborhood of densely packed row houses, small grocery stores, more graffiti on underpass walls. A trio of Indian women in bright blue and pink saris passes me, walking in the other direction, and we smile at one another. This neighborhood still feels as it might have in Wollstonecraft's time, a scruffy, busy enclave of hardworking people, sun peeking into narrow streets through fitful clouds, trees in leaf in their sidewalk cages in front of dark brown brick buildings. Wollstonecraft and Godwin each kept their own apartments here, even after they were married, in the name of work and independence, sending food and notes and books up and down the street by messenger during the day and rejoining in one or the others' rooms at night. Somewhere in this neighborhood Mary Shelley also grew up, in the building where Godwin and his second wife and their menage of children kept a faltering bookshop after Wollstonecraft's death, but I don't have the presence of mind to remember or look for the addresses. I'm in a fog, a haze. I walk.

And suddenly, there's the little gray stone church, on a slight rise above the street, surrounded by big trees and a graveyard with stones tumbling left and right. It's not hard at all to imagine Godwin and Wollstonecraft in a little cluster of people at the church door, gathering their wits about them before going inside to get married at last. Nor is it hard to imagine Percy Shelley, tall and skinny and excitable, walking under these trees next to a slight girl with her father's serious, downward glance and her mother's light auburn hair.

It isn't hard, even though the whole site is surrounded by orange plastic construction fence and crisscrossed by growling, beeping machines. Old St. Pancras is under restoration. The door is barred, the whole site looks forbidding. But I slip through the barriers anyway and find the big, square monument quickly: Wollstonecraft's name and dates on one side, Godwin's on the other, and Godwin's second wife's on the side opposite: *Mary Wollstonecraft Godwin, Author of A Vindication of the Rights of Woman: Born 27 April, 1759: Died 10 September, 1797.* But the bodies aren't there. Wollstonecraft's granddaughter-in-law—Percy Florence Shelley's wife Jane, zealous to preserve her husband's family's literary legacy—had Wollstonecraft and Godwin dug up and reinterred in Bournemouth, near their daughter's grave, and this monument left here in apology. Still, past and present slide together and apart and back together here, like overlapping lenses in a viewing glass. The air under these big trees is dim and cool and welcoming. The stone church hunkers comfortably on its little hill. How old are these great trees? Maybe they were here at Wollstonecraft's wedding, even if they were just little saplings. Maybe Percy Shelley leaned against one. Maybe he looked at Mary as their flickering shade fell on her face, searching for some sign of her mother in her eyes.

"Excuse me." A construction worker in a yellow hat—her blond ponytail sliding over one shoulder—approaches me. "You can't walk about in here, you have to go." She points with Wollstonecraftian firmness at the barriers. The machinery is too loud for her to hear the explanation I try to give, so I smile and walk away. I found it, after all.

Wollstonecraft and Godwin both expected her second child to be a boy. As with Fanny, she wrote jokingly of the "little animal" poking and prodding her belly from inside, complained affectionately of its "liveliness." Yet when that baby was born on August 31, it was a girl—also named Mary. And complications immediately ensued: a retained placenta, leading to infection that grew worse. Wollstonecraft floated between consciousness and uncontrollable shivering, so strong that it shook her bed and the ceiling of the downstairs room. No one expected the new baby to survive. And soon, they knew her mother was dying. "Talk to her of Fanny & Mary," records Godwin's journal. Then, at twenty minutes to eight in the morning on Sunday, September 10, Mary Wollstonecraft died: Godwin recorded the time and scratched three solid lines underneath. A month after her death, he described his grief to a friend: "I partook of a happiness, so much the more exquisite, as I had a short time before had no conception of it, and scarcely admitted the possibility of it." The irony hurts: Dicey Langston, in a cabin on the American frontier, survived the birth of twenty-two children. Mary Wollstonecraft, in the major city of the then-known world, died with number two.

The baby Mary Wollstonecraft Godwin—later Mary Shelley—grew up in a household that would come to include the increasingly cold and taciturn Godwin; his second wife, Mary Jane Clairmont; and five children including herself, no two of whom had the same two parents: her older half-sister Fanny Imlay, Mary Jane's two children, Charles and Claire, and her half-brother, William Godwin Jr., born of Godwin's second marriage. By all accounts it was a chilly, bookish, and genteelly impoverished childhood, presided over by the invisible ghost of the dead Wollstonecraft, whose portrait hung over the fireplace in Godwin's study. In graduate school, ever since I had learned about Mary Shelley's life, my imagination had snagged on this detail. Over and over I pictured the slight girl with light auburn hair—trained from birth to the knowledge that she would uphold her mother's and father's intellectual legacies—slipping into her father's sanctum to gaze at this picture: her only connection, aside from books, to her mother, whose death she must have felt she had caused. Perhaps this is the birth of the braided strands of horror and yearning and guilt that surround sex and childbirth in *Frankenstein*; perhaps this is the source, a daughter's secret conviction of her own monstrosity. Perhaps Godwin punished her, in any minor transgression, by shutting her out of the study, not allowing her to gaze on her mother's face. Perhaps this was the way she punished herself.

That portrait of Mary Wollstonecraft still hangs in the National Portrait Gallery in London. It was painted by the Godwins' friend John Opie in 1797, when she was pregnant with Mary. A few years before, Opie had painted *Boadicea Haranguing the Britons,* in which a classically robed Boudicca, arm upraised, exhorts her male soldiers to go forth into battle. Her two daughters—as in the statue—huddle close by, sad and drooping. Boudicca's gaze is firm, her long hair is chestnut-red: comparing the two pictures, I wonder if Opie used Mary Wollstonecraft for his model of Boudicca, consciously or unconsciously. It makes sense.

I dawdled through the slowly ascending levels of the National Portrait Gallery, shy and intent. There was something loverlike in my approach to Wollstonecraft's image, because I longed for what it represented: an echo of a woman in that past in whom I could recognize myself, a shadow of a face that could look into mine, a smile that could surround and gather me, speak to me of its own experience and teach me how to meet it. I was naïve. But I wasn't wrong. We look in lovers—and in friends, and in mentors, and in mothers—for what they can make us into, how they can call us onward and upward out of ourselves, how they can make us into something more.

And suddenly, there she was. In the upper right corner of the main wall of Room 18 of the National Portrait

Gallery—surrounded by portraits of William Wordsworth in the center, Godwin in the upper left, Mary Shelley on the bottom left, and Percy Shelley on the lower right—hangs John Opie's famous portrait of Mary Wollstonecraft. She sits looking slightly down and to the left, with a small, preoccupied smile. Her auburn hair is gathered under a plain dark cap, her gaze soft. Her hands rest in her lap, one arm curved near her pregnant stomach, which just shows under her simple white gown. Mary Shelley must have stood looking up at this picture too, knowing she was the baby sheltered in her mother's arm. Standing in front of it, I smiled even as my eyes filled with tears, remembering Wollstonecraft's words in *Letters from Norway:* "It appears to me impossible that I shall cease to exist, or that this active, restless spirit, equally alive to joy and sorrow, should only be organized dust. Surely something resides in this heart that is not perishable—and life is more than a dream." Wollstonecraft's eyes seemed to shift and shine, the corners of her mouth to quirk deeper into a wry smile as she looked down me, another young female petitioner. *Well?*

Compared to her earlier portraits, this is a compassionate face. Mary Shelley's gazing is so understandable: I would stand and look at this portrait if Wollstonecraft were my mother, too. In a sense, she is, as Boudicca is, as Dicey is. Yet this search for our mothers is complicated. In his account of Boudicca's army's initial raids against the Romans, Cassius describes the Britons' treatment of aristocratic Roman captives: "They hung up naked the noblest and most distinguished women and then cut off their breasts and sewed them to their mouths, in order to make the victims appear to be eating them; afterwards they impaled the women on sharp skewers run lengthwise through the entire body. All this they did to the accompaniment of sacrifices, banquets, and wanton behavior, not only in all their other sacred places, but particularly in the grove of Andate. This was their name for Victory, and they regarded her with most exceptional reverence." Pro-Boudicca historians swallow

hard and speculate that maybe Boudicca herself was not present at these "banquets," that surely she never could have done
such things to fellow women. Yet this is disingenuous essen-
tialism: the idea that women are "naturally" more nurturing
and supportive of one another than men, that women are
"naturally" nonviolent, that women "naturally" express their
strength in non-physical, non-masculine ways—which can
lead right into a benignly bigoted ghetto, policed by women
themselves. Obviously I don't think skewering enemies is the
best sign of womanly strength. But as we search the past for
ancestresses who guide us to be the strongest women we can
be—physically and emotionally—we need to remember that
strength has a range, that violence is present even where we
don't want to see it, that difficulty and complexity and mistakes and historical contingencies are as much a part of our
foremothers' lives as they are of our own. Boudicca wanted
to drive the Romans away. She wanted to win. These were
the rituals her tribe had been performing against captives for
years. She likely saw no reason for things to change.

Obviously, in my dreamy search for my own ancestresses in
America and London—including Dicey Langston, Boudicca,
and Mary Wollstonecraft—I've been as guilty of idealism as anyone. All I can do is try to be guided by what I think I see in these
women at their best moments, and what enables me to keep
reaching for it myself: a self-reliant strength of body and mind,
tempered with a righteous appetite for justice and with mercy
to others and to our own erring, wandering selves. In the Meth-
odist South of my childhood, the Biblical image of "a virtuous
woman" held sway, yet it wasn't until I attended my first Jewish
wedding—with Allan—and heard this same scripture trans-
lated as "a woman of valor" that its meaning came truly clear.
"Virtue" is cloistered and mealy-mouthed compared to "valor,"
which suggests the same straightforward, temperate, and mer-
ciful courage of body and mind that Wollstonecraft advocated
in all her work. The woman of valor not only buys and sells

her own land and provides thriftily for her whole household, she is charitable and wise: "she stretcheth out her hand to the poor; yea, she reacheth forth her hands to the needy," reads the King James version of Proverbs, which both Wollstonecraft and Dicey Langston would have known. "Strength and honor are her clothing; and she shall rejoice in time to come." The way to not only survive but to be able to give to others is to become a woman of valor, not afraid to act—including, when necessary, in righteous anger—and to acknowledge complexity. It might not be legal or morally comfortable or right, but I know this about myself: hard as I strive for mercy and peace, I would, like Boudicca, do my best to kill men who raped any daughters of mine. And I would not be afraid.

Wollstonecraft's portrait still floats in my mind, right beside the gleam of sunlight off Boudicca's Thames-side statue. I still see Boudicca's daughters, too, huddled in her chariot behind the rearing horses, peering around her in a gesture both fearful and supportive. They are bound to her furious, loving onward course, bound to their mother's path as, in one way or another, daughters always are. In John Opie's painting of Boudicca, the daughters lean dispiritedly against her, hoping she can incite the men to take up their cause, knowing that as ever she will probably have to do it herself, but for them, she will. Yet his portrait of Wollstonecraft gives us still another image of a mother, pointing us along what seems like a good way for a woman to keep on traveling: go forward in mercy and wisdom, and a little bit of humor, looking both behind you and ahead, always remembering that a woman of valor is strong in more ways than perhaps even she will ever know.

❧ ❧ ❧

A native Alabamian, Amy Weldon is currently associate professor of English at Luther College in Decorah, Iowa. Her short fiction and essays have appeared in The Carolina Quarterly, Shenandoah, Story Quarterly, Southern Cultures, Fiction Southeast, *and others. She has recently completed a novel,* Eldorado, Iowa, *and her weekly meditations on sustainability, spirit, and self-respect can be found on her blog, cheapskateintellectual.wordpress.com.*

❦ ❦ ❦

Hiking in Grizzly Country—Or Not

The author wrestles with existential issues.

Is it possible to be scared out of your wits and profoundly grateful at the same time? Those competing emotions are racing through my brain, although at the moment "scared out of my wits" is out to a commanding lead.

It's nearly dawn, and in two hours I'm supposed to be hoisting my backpack onto my shoulders and setting off on a fourteen-mile hike to a backcountry lodge in the Canadian Rockies.

Alone.

Through country teeming with grizzly bears.

A guide was supposed to have accompanied me, but he canceled and no backup could be found.

"Ah, there's nothing to be a'scared of," said the lodge owner. "I've been around those bears my whole life. I've been this close to them"—he held his hands 3 feet apart—"and I've never had any trouble. None at all."

I couldn't help thinking that he sounded just like Timothy Treadwell, star of the documentary "Grizzly Man," right before he began his journey through the gastrointestinal system of a lip-smacking *ursus horribilis*.

It had been shaping up as a bad summer for grizzly encounters. At the moment, four teenagers from an Outward Bound course were recovering in an Alaska hospital after being attacked by a mama grizzly. A couple of weeks earlier, a man had been killed in Yellowstone National Park—to go along with the two killed just outside the park last year—and a few days after I got home from Canada a hiker was mauled in Glacier National Park.

Everyone I talked to in Jasper agreed that the trail I would be walking was one of the most reliable places around for coming face-to-face with a grizzly. Someone pointed me to a YouTube video, shot two weeks earlier, of an enormous mother and two cubs lumbering alongside the path.

My courage needed some serious bucking-up, so the night before the hike I went to a lecture on bear safety. The naturalist began with a scary story about a close call she'd once had with a grizzly—on the very same trail I'd be walking, naturally—and stressed that the safest thing hikers could do was travel in a group of four or more.

(Hiking alone, it occurred to me, deprived me even of solace in the old joke that ends, "I don't have to outrun the bear; I just have to outrun you.")

The naturalist didn't think much of my two main lines of defense: Some jingly bear bells designed to prevent surprise encounters—they're not even remotely loud enough to do any good, she said, but they make great souvenirs—and a canister of "bear spray," a weapons-grade version of the Mace women carry to fend off muggers. "Sometime it deters the bears," she said, "and sometimes it just makes them mad. And sometimes the wind blows it right back in your face while the bear is charging."

So I think I've got the "scared out of my wits" part of my dilemma covered pretty well. What about the "profoundly grateful" part? That's a little trickier, but hear me out.

Everyone has his own personal definition of wilderness, and this is mine: A place where humans are not at the top of the food chain. Or, to put a finer point on it: A place where there are creatures who can, and will, without even giving it a second thought, eat you.

I'm grateful such places exist, and I wish we had more of them. I've walked through grizzly country before, always in the company of other people, and it's a profoundly humbling and energizing experience. Instead of swaggering like the lord and master of your domain, you walk lightly and modestly: You're just one insignificant creature among many. You're part of nature—part of the food chain—not aloof and apart from it.

The potential danger, no matter how statistically slight (and it is slight), triggers a gusher in your adrenal glands that puts your senses on high alert. Your eyesight grows sharper, your hearing more acute. You feel an extra, nervous, spring in your step.

Normally we are so accustomed to being unchallenged as apex predators that we barely give it a thought. To see things from the other side, to become potential prey, however temporarily, forces us to rethink our place in the world. Which, I suppose, is one of the reasons we travel.

Now the sky outside is growing light and my alarm clock has just gone off—quite unnecessary, because I haven't closed my eyes all night. I've been too scared. I make a decision, or, rather, admit to a decision I now realize I made hours ago: I'm not going.

I vow to come back and do the hike another day, when I can line up some partners and won't have to run the grizzly gauntlet alone. But for now I'm grateful that the bears have a place that is theirs, not ours.

A truly wild place.

୬ଈ ୬ଈ ୬ଈ

John Flinn is the former travel editor of the San Francisco Chronicle.

❦ ❦ ❦

Escape

Is it really so bad today?

Not long ago a blogger friend posted, "As a business, travel writing is now in even worse shape than during the Great Depression." In their desperate need to hear themselves type, some bloggers write silly things and hope no one pays close attention. But as a guy who grew up hearing from my dad how I, a soft, spoiled, English-major dunderhead, would have starved to death during the Depression, my friend's assertion caught my eye. Was this just self-pitying hot air—a callous flip-off to our travel-writing predecessors who may have suffered hardships my glib blogger could not even imagine? If, on the other hand, what she said was demonstrably true, I would stick the evidence under my father's Depression-withered face, and finish him off with a resounding "Ha!"

I liked the prospect. Dad, having always been the cheapest human being on the face of the earth, has saved a few bucks for his old age, and as far as I know, murder by exclamation is not a prisonable offense. Times, indeed, are tough.

So I decided to get to the bottom of things.

Between 1929 and 1933, U.S. unemployment exploded from 2 million to 15 million—nearly a third of the country's labor force (today, nine percent unemployment is almost grounds for impeachment). In those five years, our national income dropped 50 percent—from $80 billion to $40 billion (these days, even a drop of a few percentage points for three consecutive months is considered a full-fledged recession). The sale of durable goods fell two-thirds, and foreign trade was off 65 percent. More than 6000 banks failed, wiping out life savings (today we're protected by FDIC). Three years after the 1929 crash, the combined income of (formerly) middle-class families had been cut in half, their income from investments reduced to zero. Two families out of five had multiple working-age members unemployed. Bank deposits were drained by 76 percent, and all assets were depleted by 78 percent. Fully half of all homeowners could no longer retain their homes (bought, unlike these days, with substantial down payments) and were forced to walk away with nothing. Unpaid doctor and dentist bills increased 150 percent. The average family income in this group dropped to $1600 per year, the equivalent of only $10,000 today. Former lawyers, bankers, and architects scrambled for the best street corners on which to sell apples.

And this was in relatively cozy middle-class America. Those in lower income groups (like my dad's) were in much worse shape. Nearly half of this work force was unemployed. Shack slums sprang up on the outskirts of every town. When they weren't standing in bread lines, men, women, and children were scouring big-city garbage dumps like vermin.

Even the wealthy couldn't hide. Utility magnate Samuel Insull, before 1929 the second richest man in the United States and a decade later on the lam for unpaid debts in the millions, died in a Paris subway in 1938 with 84 cents and an unpaid laundry ticket in his pocket.

No one—professionals, laborers, housewives, or their children—was immune. Everyone was scared, desperate, and suffering. This, the gravest economic times the United

States had ever known, had come without warning and without social safety nets (the federal government didn't create its
unemployment compensation program until halfway through
the Depression, and even then it was useless to those already
unemployed). Rich and poor alike were wiped out. There was
no place to go, no relative's, friend's, or softhearted employer's
doorbell to ring. Even churches closed by the hundreds. No
one was home.

Infrastructure collapsed. In cities, winters were perilous.
Electric power often failed for days and weeks at a time,
people freezing and groping in the dark, some families (like
Dad's) nearly starving. The countryside fared no better. The
cash income of all farmers had dropped from $11 billion in
1929 to $5 billion in 1932. That same year, wheat, cotton, and
beef saw their lowest world prices since the mid-seventeenth
century.

During the 1930s, the U.S. population growth fell to an all-
time low. People simply could not afford children. The Sears,
Roebuck catalog began listing contraceptive wares for the
first time. Children already here were (like my father) pulled
out of school to make a living as best they could. Elementary
schools in New York City, for instance, lost 150,000 pupils.
Boy and girl hoboes wandered the roads and rode the rails by
the tens of thousands.

Week after week, newspapers carried stories about people
who had lost hope and jumped to their deaths from rooftops
or spent their last nickel on razor blades to kill themselves.
Despair hung over the land.

Yet, with seeming paradox, Depression-era travel writing
flourished. In the maelstrom of economic collapse, escape provided a certain kind of economic, philosophic, and psychological analgesic for what ailed writers and their readers.

For readers, escape through travel literature assumed an
almost spiritual urgency: flight from the shattered American

dream. To read about unfettered excursions and intrepid adventures was to vicariously escape the despair of their Depression struggles. Tramp-steaming through the Panama Canal, freighter traveling to Europe, luxury lining to the Orient, sailing around the Caribbean, hiking through the Alps, busing across America, visiting Russia for firsthand accounts of "ideal" Soviet life, dodging headhunters in the equatorial Amazon (no, not the Internet one), spellbound and despair-bound Americans eagerly escaped to other places, if only aboard paper and ink.

To imagine a world where on ocean liners, "The blankets were soft, wooly white, bound with red satin and pleated into marvelous shapes," and where writers "stopped here and there, sometimes to watch indolent Mexicans dozing upon their doorsteps, and, when turning the knob of the radio, to listen to a Chopin polonaise," was to dreamily flee, for a little while at least, real-life hardships.

A different kind of escape was when readers sometimes discovered there were others even worse off than they: "Our bunks were so thick with bedbugs that if you shook out your mattress they would drop off in chunks. For the first time in my life I knew what it was to envy the lot of another man."

Indeed, for writers escape was not a luxury born of boredom, wanderlust, or avocation. It was, in fact, actually cheaper and more secure to live on the road than in the city. One recalls that "In my part of the country, the physical network collapsed. To leave the city was to survive." Another writes, "In New York not possibly did we seem to be able to afford to marry and live together. On the evening we decided to find an island, there must have been at least a million other young couples talking of precisely the same thing. We chose St. John because it was forgotten by everyone and therefore cheap." Still another: "Can you spare four dollars a day for a tour of the globe? It's as cheap to go traveling now as it is to stay at home." And: "Anyone could see from the patches on our tent and the model of our car, that the Depression had not gone very far around the corner from us."

It was true that—in the last half of the 1930s anyway—the government's Works Progress Administration (WPA) did support more than 6000 otherwise jobless men and women who had some claim to expertise in putting pen to paper. Unlike today's dilettante blogs and magazine freelance contributions, though, those were not ego-driven, hobbyish enterprises but matters of putting bread on table. What's more, whereas today's travel-book writers have a fighting chance to make a few bucks from royalties, back then Americans seldom bought books, but, rather, borrowed them from libraries (indeed, did so in astonishing numbers).

Not all travel writing took their readers to foreign shores. Car travel through the Old South offered an appealing kind of time-travel escape—to a simpler, kinder America that managed to find apparent pleasantness under every rock: "We sometimes found little picture-book jumbles of decayed wooden dwellings, their courtyards full of washtubs, carts, and pickaninnies, their piazzas loaded with flowers in tin cans and alive with the sounds and guffaws of merry Negro women." And, without the slightest hint of irony (take note, my egalitarian blogger friend): "I liked colored people, of almost every race. [Before the crash] I had had them for my servants in many countries."

America's rugged West, too, found an enthusiastic Depression-era readership. Tales of gunslingers, outlaws, and lawmen were common subjects, often as their writers were themselves hightailing to Mexico in order to outrun Prohibition (which my blogger pard should keep in mind the next time she's slurping a margarita at her keyboard). No GPS then, naturally. Writes one intrepid car-traveler: "We stuck the compass to the dashboard by its little suction cup and watched the small disk, floating in oil, turn and turn again, its spinning needle bearing absolutely no relationship to our direction."

Bus travel offered substantial savings over train fares and the cost of car ownership (the Depression had, by the mid-1930s, put the few national rental car companies out of business, and even the new concept of installment buying could not revive auto sales). The popular Gable-Colbert movie *It Happened One Night* (1934) romanticized overland bus journeying. The number of bus passengers rose threefold in the '30s, and those who could not themselves get away experienced vicarious escape in travel books that glamorized what one author called "luxury inland ocean liners": "My reasons for taking such a journey by motor bus," she wrote, "was to go Marco-Poloing . . . it was my spice of escape." Indeed, by 1931 cross-country motor coaching had evolved into a safe and comfortable way to see the country and write about it: "[My bus] contained sleeping accommodations for twenty-six people, with two dressing rooms and a kitchen and four levels of berths, a shelf in each room to hold toilet articles, reading lights, thermos bottles of cracked ice, even—final miracle—basins with hot and cold running water." But before my blogger bud waxes too nostalgic, that Depression-era writer also lists among her bus amenities "ashtrays for each and every berth."

With the perfection of the diesel engine and the introduction of other technological innovations, the 1930s also saw a leap in rail travel. In 1934 the Union Pacific pioneered a completely diesel-powered train constructed of duralumin, and its competitor, the Burlington, quickly followed with the first of its flashy stainless-steel Pioneer Zephyrs. Those Art Deco beauties, running at speeds up to 100 miles an hour, brought the East Coast and Rocky Mountains within overnight range of Chicago—whose World's Fair was the great escape destination of 1933-34. The benefits of these vintage bullet trains, though, was also their (sometimes tragic) downfall: rail curves had not yet been built to accommodate their kind of speed—with consequences, after a moment's reflection, you might have expected. What's more, the lightweight bodies of these dashers folded like tissue in even minor collisions with other trains and even with terminally stupid (not much has changed there) car and truck drivers. As profit sources, they weren't successful. Zephyrs were truncated trains with only one and a half coach cars each. To be profitable, their fares would have to have been prohibitive in any age, let alone during those hardscrabble times. So those rolling works of art, designed principally to reignite the public's interest in rail travel, worked much better on paper than in real life.

Ditto aviation. Yes, the late 1920s saw the invention of stressed-skinned aircraft construction and air-cooled engines that allowed for bigger and lighter planes, and improvements in aerodynamics were enhanced by the use of alloys like magnesium and aluminum. New high-octane fuels were developed, as was, in 1937, the pressurized cabin, allowing higher-altitude, more comfortable flights. Coast-to-coast travel in (relatively) large, 200-mile-per-hour planes with overnight sleepers and navigation by radio beacon (a recent innovation), serviced by a proliferation of airports and improved weather service, all helped to make aviation no longer just an amusing novelty. But air transportation was enjoyed only by a relatively few wealthy businessmen and politicians (First Lady Eleanor Roosevelt crisscrossed the country by air, checking out poverty). To suffering families like my dad's, whose own father had died penniless, hopeless, and miserable in 1936, reading about recreational sky travel wasn't so much vicarious escape as it was a cruel joke.

And the next time my blogger pal whines in print about getting "groped" by horny TSA agents and the cost of onboard

snacks, I hope she also notes that in 1936, with stops, the fastest planes took as long to fly from New York to Los Angeles
as it now takes to fly around the world, and with a lot more
bumps. The 1930s saw an aviation fatality rate of one person
per each *million* miles flown, as opposed to today's one in two
billion. (The '30s rate extrapolated would today mean 7,000
fatalities a year.) No surprise, then, that in those days a $5,000
insurance policy for a plane trip cost $2, compared to an insur-
ance premium of twenty-five cents for the same trip by train.
Also for good reason, the first airline stewardesses, introduced
in 1930, were required to be registered nurses.

Those Depression-age readers and writers who had a more
practical (and safety-minded) side to escape, vicarious and
literal, found refuge in freighter travel, a common topic of
Depression travel adventure. One writer notes, "Five years ago
only one or two freight-boat lines had anything even remotely
approaching a travel folder. But now [1937] Americans are
discovering freighter travel as offering something different
from cruise-liner journeying . . . Most of the newer ships are
diesel-motored, practically all of them burn oil instead of coal,
making them faster and more efficient." Here, then, was at
least a theoretically attainable means of escape for young men
and women—and had my dad not accepted the responsibility
of working to help his widowed mother, he might have run
away on one of these oil-burning clunkers to whatever exotic
life waited for him at distant ports, instead of merely turning
oily library book pages.

My blogger friend yaks ad nauseam about the shallow-
ness of American commercialism—the blight of suburban strip centers, Viagra ads, the constant "You'll like the
way you look . . . I guarantee it" reminders of our capitalist depravity—and, conversely, the superiority of slower, less
acquisitive lifestyles: Caribbean beachcombing, Left Bank
wine-sipping, Medieval-history- Rhine River barge-cruising.

There's a certain charming and harmless hypocrisy about her lecturing the rest of us about the evils of avarice, considering her growing list of sponsors (more power to her, I say). But during the Depression, ideological escape could be a perilous thing indeed, hardly victimless. Beleaguered Americans, sick of feeling useless, enthralled by stories about the glories of communism, queued up on the dream of Soviet utopianism. Said one travel writer: "Our world is a mess. The only thing to do is escape. Escape from a fake society, from the antics of the maggots on a decaying [capitalist] corpse." And many, to their later (and sometimes inescapable) sorrow, did just that. A disillusioned expat in Russia wrote: "The elevator operator was tired, unhappy, hopeless, dissatisfied, and hungry. He mentioned casually that he had been riding up and down in that airless contraption, going nowhere, for fourteen unbroken hours and had no idea when he would be relieved. But surely he must have been mistaken. For I had been told, and came to believe, that the seven-hour, or less, day is now universal in the Soviet Union."

My blogger friend means well. She just wants to be read, like the rest of us. Someday the best of our blogs will be rediscovered, as I rediscovered some brilliant, elegant, poignant Depression-era writing. Maybe hers will be among the archival travel-writing treasures of future scholars. Fifty, a hundred years from now, someone will know she existed. A future history student will write a term paper comparing and contrasting travel writing of the early-twenty-first century's economic downturn with that of the 1930s. And in one of those Great Depression travelogs the student might come across this observation: "In Heidelberg I registered my first presentiments that something was rotten in this picture of perfection. Behind the light and shadow I felt and shared a nameless disquiet." And, a little later, "I have never known a shipboard journey as melancholy as this. When I left England, we were still suffering a stink in our nostrils over refreshed attacks on the German Jews." And the student might scratch his head wondering what, exactly, about our times was in "worse shape."

So I have to go with Dad on this one. No "Ha!" in my immediate future. I'm not saying we baby boomers wouldn't have survived those terrible days, and I'm not saying our own mini-version hasn't taken its toll. We staycation; we walk away from our mortgages; we go bankrupt. We download at $3.99 instead of hardcopy $14.95; we rediscover libraries; we fly standby; we read blogs; we blog.

Dad doesn't read blogs. He doesn't even own a computer. My brother and I offered to buy him one and teach him how to use it. We thought it might take his mind off being alone. He's eighty-seven and refuses to live in assisted living. He can't see very well and is as deaf as a potato, but he still creaks around, accepts lifts to Walmart and PetSmart—although he hasn't had a pet in thirty years. He used to love the Fremont Township library, but his eyes have gotten too bad to read much. Although he lives in an adult community, it is not an old-people's home. Most of the residents are younger than Dad. They all live in maintenance-free, single-family ranch houses, small but adequate, with little front lawns, stubby, white fences, one-car garages, and inviting rear decks. Very American dream.

Dad doesn't want to be a burden on anyone, and that's his American dream, too. He's a child of the Depression. He doesn't want to be on the dole. He was on charity once, and he won't do it again, ever, financially or otherwise. "If you were poor once, you're always poor," he likes to say. He's been talking about his childhood more and more lately. So my brother and I thought introducing him to the Internet might be a good way to take his mind off whatever seems to be drawing him

backwards. But after pretending to think about our offer, Dad
politely declined. Instead, he goes to Walmart and PetSmart
and comes home to sit by himself and think.

When he was a young man, Dad wanted to be a writer,
but that never happened. He dropped out of school to work
and later went to war. After that he began a family, found
one sales job after another, and before he knew it, writing
was just a distant dream. We thought he would be amazed
and delighted with the world of the Internet. We thought
it would give him a new lease on life, make him feel young
again, that with a big screen, he'd be able to read well enough.
We thought he would want to visit the exciting worlds of
Facebook and Twitter and YouTube and the thousands of
interesting sites to which people surf to escape their otherwise humdrum lives. We thought he might like to see how
the modern world talks to one another. We thought he might
like to read some travel blogs.

But we were wrong.

What he mostly does is, he sits in his old Naugahyde chair
and thinks. He's so deaf now that ringing his doorbell does
no good, so my brother and I just walk in and usually find
him sitting, thinking. His Rolodex file has very few cards on it
anymore, his friends having mostly died. There isn't anyone to
call. So he sits and thinks. We know he's thinking about the old
days because he talks more and more about his boyhood during the Depression. But something has changed. Now when
he mentions those days, there's a hint of nostalgia in his voice.
This never happened before. Before, he was always bitter.

There are different kinds of travel, different ways to escape.
Going places is one, reading and writing about it another.
"Writing books is the only real immortality," said a (now forgotten) sage. Spending endless hours online, we forget dirty
dishes and snoring spouses and overdue bills. Blogging may
be the best some of us can do to escape oblivion. Wandering

Walmart and PetSmart, searching for something, you forgot what, may be running away, too—from what, though, might escape you.

Sitting alone in the dark, you might remember.

≈≈ ≈≈ ≈≈

Gary Buslik writes essays, short stories, and novels. He teaches literature, creative writing, and travel writing at the University of Illinois at Chicago. His work appears often in Travelers' Tales anthologies. He is the author of A Rotten Person Travels the Caribbean, *and* Akhmed and the Atomic Matzo Balls. *Visit him at www.garybuslik.com.*

MARDITH J. LOUISELL

꙳ ꙳ ꙳

Mahnmal

As a resident of many camps, I can say that Guzen was
the worst. This is not to say that the conditions at the
other camps were not dreadful. Compared to
Guzen, however, one might almost say
that those camps were paradises.

—Rabbi Rav Yechezkel Harfenes, *Slingshot of Hell*

I had never wanted to go to Austria because of its Holo-
caust history but when my partner had to go to Linz for
business, I went. If I had to go to Austria, maybe I could gain
a small understanding of how ethnic cleansings occur. When
I saw an audio tour of a concentration camp offered as part of
the Linz Arts Electronica Festival, I signed up.

When the bus arrived at the site of the Gusen concentration camp, instead of concrete walls and barbed wire, I saw a
yellow church steeple on a hill and beige houses with gerani-
ums in window boxes—this concentration camp was now a
middle-class housing development dotted with parks, newly
built houses, and remodeled camp buildings on roads like
Gartenstrasse where I would soon walk—as nondescript as
the small town in which I grew up.

Fifteen kilometers from Linz, the Gusen complex is the
only extermination camp of significant size not memorialized

as a site. Administratively the Gusen complex was catego-
rized as a satellite of Mauthausen, but the three Gusen camps
covered an area large enough to include four towns and in
1945 held 25,000 inmates, double the number of Mauthausen.

Audiowalk Gusen, The Invisible Camp, is an art project
by Christopher Mayer who grew up in St. Georgen an der
Gusen, which adjoined Gusen II; Mayer's grandfather had
joined the National Socialist Party and his parents still live in
St. Georgen. Mayer hadn't known about Gusen until he was
fourteen years old when a neighbor asked him if he knew
the town had been a labor extermination camp. In not knowing, Mayer wasn't unusual—Austrians didn't speak of Gusen
for decades. The interwoven voices on the audio belong to
Gusen camp survivors, past and current residents, former
air force soldiers, and SS camp guards, all of whom Mayer
interviewed.

Mayer sets me up with my iPod. Two blocks separate each
audiotourist so I walk alone. I press the iPod button and hear
a narrator provide directions.

*Walk in time to the footsteps on the tape. Turn left at the end of
the road. Keep walking.*

Beside a stone wall that lines the main business road of the
village, I see terrain that seems innocent, orderly, even boring,
but walking alone into a strange town with earphones, I can
be singled out, almost as though I were wearing one of the
ugly yellow stars of the Reich. How quickly I absorb what I
imagine is the prevailing norm. I feel I'm braving peer pressure—a nice person doesn't investigate the detritus of other
people's neighborhoods. I try not to make a wrong turn on the
spotless road, try not to annoy anyone.

Turn left here. Continue. . . . Stop, here at the iron gate.

Two surveillance cameras. NO TRESPASSING signs. A
clean gray garbage bin on wheels, except for color exactly like
one in San Francisco.

This was the gate to the camp. Prisoners were deposited and informed the only way out was through the chimney of the crematorium.

This was true. At first, the camp worked prisoners to death in stone quarries; later inmates excavated cliffs to build a factory to produce jet fighters. When inmates' bodies were spent, they were exterminated, usually within four months of arrival.

The iron gate rests between two stone columns, probably supports for the original camp gates. A two-story affluent house rises on a hill at the end of the long driveway.

Look up to the top. The basement of that stone house was the camp torture chamber.

Nothing suggests its past. Only now do I notice that the stonework seems slightly older in the lower left portion of the house. The current owner had wanted to tear down the basement, but his engineer said, "Use it. It's a good foundation." Is it now a breakfast nook? A family room? Who walks down those steps and watches television there, perhaps with a cup of good Austrian coffee? On the tape two men argue about whether the walls remember. One thinks the walls do, another thinks not—it's just a building.

Continue walking down the road to the right. Stop here. Number 14. This was the whorehouse.

I imagine Austrian guards walking into a small cubby-hole to have sex. With German prostitutes? Camp prisoners? Jews?

I was done with my shift, time for someone else's. I walked up the four steps to the brothel.

A small gray plaque neatly outlined in white, 14 UNTERE GARTENSTRASSE. One window of the barracks-style house ajar in the casual way of early fall. White petunias. On the front porch table, a green-and-white checked cloth. Two chairs—the owners' hope for a last meal outside before

winter. A man walks out the door and down the four steps.
Mayer hadn't told us what to do were we to meet residents.
I look at the man. He looks back. His face betrays nothing.
Keeping my face also expressionless, I avert my eyes as though
what I'm hearing has nothing to do with him, but it's his story
on the tape.

*After we moved in, we wanted a party room so we tore down
the walls because the rooms were so small. Getting a reasonably
priced house in Upper Austria was a lucky break. Now I would
never live anywhere else.*

Silence on the tape. I try to understand how landing an
experimentation camp whorehouse in Upper Austria was
such a good deal. Footsteps.

*I got my first job at the camp. Back then, everyone had been
poor. The working people, even factory workers, had so much
more with the Party. They could take their families for picnics on
boats down the Danube, something no one had even dreamed of
before.*

They could also take weekend trips to Munich, train trips
to Lake Garda and cruises to Madeira, all thanks to a Party
sponsored tourist agency that kept costs low.[1]

In this village where people flirted, gardened, and took
boat trips down the Danube, where everyone wanted to fit in,
inmates were gassed, beaten to death, bathed in cold show-
ers until they died, drowned, and killed with experimental
heart injections (420 Jewish children between the ages of four
and seven in February 1945). In the winter of 1944/45, more
inmates arrived than the work consumed so new prisoners
were left at the train station in locked railway cars. Left to
freeze, they died in days.

---

[1] *In Europe, Travels Through the Twentieth Century.* Geert Mak, Pantheon, 2007,
p. 248

Where could a villager intervene? Could one give food to prisoners? On the tape, an old man said that as a boy he tossed an apple core into the woods; when a male prisoner grabbed it, he was killed.

Walk down Gartenstrasse. To your right you see the cement walls of the quarry where prisoners dug stone for Munich and Linz buildings. Turn left and continue down the street.

My feet scurry to keep pace with the prodding of the tape's footsteps. I learn that locals remember dogs and SS on horses chasing men and children, forcing them to run from the camp to the work site.

Look at the house in front of you, Number 4.

In 1985, I was twelve, I learned to play the piano there, in the former SS-kitchen barrack.

I turn the corner. Suddenly I see three women chatting on the front sidewalk. They look up and stop talking. I have to decide whether to greet or ignore them. I paste a pleasant look on my face, implying that I don't judge. Embarrassed, I keep moving, head bowed, preserving some tacit agreement I hope I have with them, although I'm not sure what it is or that they feel the same. Most of them were children during the war. For what exactly would I judge them?

I would like to condemn the people who lived here in the 1940s, but I have to consider my own desire to fit in, the small events where I didn't speak up for fear of sticking out, the times I asked if it was really my responsibility to act. I wonder how I would have stacked up in St. Georgen in 1943. Because my mother is Jewish, I wouldn't have had the choice, but it's easy to say people should have objected and fought. It's less clear when I'm the one who must act. Lynchings were normal in the United States until the 1930s and people went along to the extent that they didn't stop them.

I feel uncomfortably vulnerable when the women look at me, but as a villager in the 1940s such vulnerability would have been not merely uncomfortable but terrifying. Some residents must have been horrified, but could they say so? To whom? By 1940, the Austrian handicapped had been gassed at Hartheim Castle just forty kilometers west of Gusen. The gassings, the camps, and the smells were already familiar as part of the daily lives of Austrians.

I took the tour hoping to gain insight about how this atrocity happened and the experience has thrown me deep into the mind of a run-of-the-mill Austrian in World War II. I can see how things creep forward, how you don't know when to say "Stop, enough!" and when you do, it's too late, you're in danger. German writer W. G. Sebald, trying to understand his countrymen's actions, wrote that under the apparently inexorable power of the Nazi regime, "a basic stance of opposition and a lively intelligence . . . could easily turn into more or less deliberate attempts to conform. . . ."[2]

Yet I also know Austria's history of anti-Semitism, that some Austrians might have been eager for a Reich that would eliminate Jews and that the economic well-being they so treasured came in part from looting the houses of Jews whom they knew would not return.

Look on the building on your right. In 1943 I went to get my teeth fixed. We used the camp dentist and when I walked by the front to get to the side entrance, I saw guards unload sacks from a truck and throw them against the wall. I heard screams. I found that guards were smashing Jewish children to kill them.

I look back at the three women. I'd like to stare, examine them, interview them about their moral compasses. Instead I look down.

---

[2] *On the Natural History of Destruction.* W.G. Sebald, Modern Library, 2004, p. ix.

Pink chalk on the cement—kids' hopscotch. Laughing ten-year-olds whiz by on bikes. It almost seems that Mayer has orchestrated the scene, the contrast between the kids on bikes and the fact that sixty-two years ago Jewish kids were being murdered. I remember the black-and-white remoteness of war photos. I realize that this war, which I had imagined in grainy shadows, didn't happen that way at all but in color—yellow water hoses, red petunias, pink chalk, gray garbage cans.

As I avoid the bikes and slow-moving BMWs, I wonder if the camps inform a residents' every thought. Or are the camps as remote as slavery is for some Americans? Do Austrians think, "It's true our ancestors killed but that was years ago. We live here now." Austrians I spoke with after the tour saw parallels in U. S. history. "Look at what you did with Native Americans," one said. "You finished them off."

Mayer clearly intended the piece to be a confrontation with the townspeople, and at first they refused permission for the tour. He could have sued to gain access to the public streets, thereby generating substantial unfavorable publicity for the town; instead he requested a discussion with the town council. There the residents made the size of the tour groups the issue. Mayer countered that individuals would walk alone, no more than eight in a two-hour period. The residents' real issue was their belief that this kind of remembrance shouldn't occur, but since no one could say that publicly, the tour was allowed.

Continue. This gray concrete to your right was the camp crematorium.

I was a young boy in St. Georgen and I lived half a mile from the camp. I remember being in the house when they fired up the ovens. My grandmother paced restlessly. "The smell," she said to my mother. "I can't stand the smell. Why do they have to burn them?" "But what can we do?" my mother answered her. "They

*can't work anymore, we can't keep them." "Oh," my grandmother
said, "I guess so. If they can't work, what can we do?"*

Walk on. Follow the curve in the road.

A railroad track: Trains deposited 10,000 prisoners daily
at the underground factories where they manufactured the
Messerschmitt Me262s, the first operational turbojet fighter.
Sputnik-generation American teenagers worshipped this jet,
it was "cool," way ahead of its time. However, this glorious
airplane was built in thirteen months in factories carved out of
stone by prisoners worked to death. *Vernichtung durch Arbeit*:
"Destruction through Work," used more during the Third
Reich than ever before in history. Already the Reich had
planned that slaves would produce 1,250 jets a month through
the year 1955. The raised rail bed, now a leg of the Danube's
cycling path, curves through the countryside of Upper Austria, green and fresh from the past week's rain. Sixty years
ago, the rain would have eased the stench of burned fat from
the ovens.

*I've lived here for sixty-five years. It's so peaceful here now, isn't
it? Quiet. Hard to believe, almost like the past is no longer true.*

In 1945, the Russians looted the Messerschmitt underground plant, then locals looted what was left, and in 1947
the Russians blew it up. In the 1950s, when the terrain was
privatized, Austrian authorities planned to raze the cremato-
ria too but French, Italian, and Belgian survivors purchased
the ovens and built a small memorial to those less fortunate.

Mahnmal is a word that means "memorial" and "warning"
simultaneously. It doesn't appear in a dictionary until after the
war. At the Mahnmal Memorial against War and Fascism in
Vienna, two white stone monoliths represent, on the one side,
Jewish victims of the Nazis, on the other, all victims of war
and fascism. The figures are generic and stand on a granite
pedestal cut from the Mauthausen quarry. The monoliths are

controversial—they don't mention perpetrators and imply that Austrians and Jews alike were victims.

Close to the base of the white stone monoliths, a miniscule black statue made of bronze and the size of a German shepherd shows a man flattened on the cobblestones and scrubbing the pavement with a brush. This man is neither large nor generic but obviously and stereotypically Jewish, downtrodden, bearded, as clear as a Kathe Kollwitz print. The statue memorializes an event that took place immediately after the Anschluss: Jews were forced to eat grass and remove anti-Nazi graffiti from the streets of Vienna with toothbrushes. Onlookers cheered. In fact, "couldn't get enough of it,"[3] The small statue of a Jewish man scrubbing is demeaning and controversial, because who would want to be debased, then have that debasement memorialized in a statue in which you look like a dog? But the sculptor got it right. In Austria, even in a memorial, the worst job, the worst caricature, goes to the Jew. When the statue first appeared, people sat on the man's back, so the statue is now covered with barbed wire.

The one-third of all registered Gusen II victims who were Jewish, including children, lived about half as long and were given the worst jobs—residents saw naked children emptying the latrines with buckets and standing in excrement up to their waists. People knew.

Yes, my parents' generation built memorials, Mayer told me, and Austria now takes some responsibility for these crimes: "Annexation" is no longer an accurate translation of *Anschluss*. "Joined," Mayer said, "not annexed. And Gusen, formerly a 'labor camp,' was recently declared an 'extermination camp.'" But, he went on, no one has done much research on perpetrators, and conflicts still smolder about post-war history and

---

[3] *In Europe*, p. 280

what to do with leftover camp buildings. Why, he asked, even now do so few people in Austria talk about Gusen?

Although Mauthausen is one of the forty-five concentration camp names chiseled in the base of Rachel Whiteread's mausoleum-like memorial in Vienna's Judenplatz, Gusen is not—it was only an auxiliary, although it killed at least 37,000 persons—one-third of all victims who died in the forty-nine concentration camps in Austria.

Yes, I was a guard. Hitler did a lot of good things. I don't feel so bad. You had to have been there. All in all we can say we fulfilled this difficult task of love for our people.

I stop, sit on a bench and look across the field, corn stalks turning beige in early autumn. Peaceful. I think about parallels in the United States, remember how during the Depression Americans benefited from FDR's policies. Some loved him like he was God, couldn't imagine not supporting him, no matter what. Would they have followed him had FDR gone the same direction as Hitler? Maybe not, but what would have been the difference?

Walk across the road to the end of the short road on your right.

Behind me the cornfield, in front the underground Messerschmidt factory hollowed out of sandstone cliffs to hide it from the Allied pilots. It's an abandoned air raid shelter now, a locked iron gate across the door.

On the iPod, a guard hesitatingly describes prisoners who pick up dead comrades, inmates left to die in the cold, torture. It's what I've been waiting for—an acknowledgement of the enormity of Gusen. He talks of guilt. I ask myself how he lives with this. The narrator wants to know as much as I do and presses him.

What else did you see?

But the guard won't be goaded.

You can't imagine. You had to have been there. I've taken you as far as I can.

The narrator and I crave absolution, for ourselves, for the guard, for humankind. Or maybe it's justice we want. A tilting of the scales a millimeter closer to balanced because the guard suffers. But the guard doesn't have these illusions.

There's nothing that can help me. It's as though I go through a door to an empty room where no one can join me. Then there's another door. That, too, I must go through by myself. And another. And another.

The narrator asks again.

What do you think about now?

You cannot know.

≈ ≈ ≈

Mardith Louisell's essays include "Toccata and Variations on Venice" in Italy, A Love Story, *"Shadows" in* Lady Jane's Miscellany, *and "Big Basin or Two Reasons for Couples Therapy" in* Minnesota Magazine. *Her fiction includes "Had They Learned about Jayne Mansfield" in* Solstice Literary Magazine. *She works in San Francisco in the child welfare field.*

ERIKA CONNOR

✢ ✢ ✢

Desert Convoy

Between past and present is the sheerest of veils.

The moon is a golden crescent above us. In Morocco's Anti-Atlas mountains a blowing smoke and the head-lights of the bus dust the edges of the banks and drop off into darkness, thousands of feet down into clefts and canyons, then long up into the walls above. The shadow hills among us are something living, brown-pelted, knit with bone and bristle and somehow the road climbs its way through them, slowly, slowly to the pass. No barriers, nothing to keep us from fall-ing. And then we descend. At each crest the driver releases the brakes and we are given to God and wind. No one can speak, listening to the wailing wandering song on the radio, the clap-ping hands and drums of the prayers.

At dawn a roadside café appears like a stage set in the night, a bright-lit room of tables, plastic chairs, painted tiles, posters and knick-knacks. The cook and a few young boys, a girl waitress, awaken, and the driver and passengers go in. I am not one of them, nor am I alone, standing in the doorway.

"Yalla!" someone calls. Come. They are holding up their glasses of mint tea, inviting me. The sea is here, somewhere close. Salt, stench of grilled fish, two dogs skulking on the periphery, a bone in the sand. One takes it in his mouth, then drops it again, afraid. They flinch at the least movement.

By morning light the cold mountains are only shadows behind us. We skim along in the heat of a flat gravel desert, riding through bleak towns partitioned off into grids of telephone lines and metal towers, cement buildings and houses, factories, desalination plants. Any gardens or colours are held back within walls. Chimneys smoke on the oceanfront, a silver pipeline snakes inland.

For long hours between these outposts is the other desert: soft golden expanse patterned with wind rings, smooth as warmed skin. The dunes are the outline and sensual surfaces of giant bodies submerged, sleeping. Blue dust weed is strewn with black plastic. Shale fragments are bleached and porous as bone, some are cairns laid in long lines and patterns. Who built these? And for what? Some are statues facing out to sea. The band of the sea is always on the right shoulder with the lines of chalk cliffs and canyons sun-spotted and speckled. Two old iron ships sag in the surf abandoned. Far away, blowing on the cliffs are tent cities of plastic and cardboard. Men sit on the side of the highway or go walking and disappear over the cliffs, or come from the desert on the other side, come out from nowhere.

The bus slows and comes to a stop in the dust.

"*Voilà, les marins*," the man beside me says as two men get on. Look, the seamen, the fishermen, their dark baked skin lined as the waves on the sea. Every year they come to live here on the desert coast, hauling in the fish from the wild sea.

Hour after hour, on the final stretch to Dakhla, southernmost town of Morocco, the highway runs dark and smooth and straight, bands of sky, sand, sea, perfectly planar, sun and light, rhythmic music moves us in and out of sleep and the desert is always there upon waking.

I have been here before.

Four years ago it was a bus ride with a dreaded television, some American Kung-Fu movie, and people pulled the curtains shut against the sun and I felt enshrined, caught forever in the modern invasive world. When the film ended the curtains were drawn open again and the Moroccan music began, and another film began for me. I saw camels spilling onto the horizon for the first time, blue plastic floating along the ochre earth, glittering glass and locusts.

Because I knew nothing then I was blessed. Don't we always in life try to go back to find those same moments? You never find the same place twice.

There were locusts, red-winged, metallic gleam, a shrill song, flying north in clouds, miles thick, hitting the glass panes. When we came to a stop I saw the bus, the shacks, the ground fluttering blood red, alive, and we crushed them underfoot. Later the swarms were gone. All along the way from Tarfaya into the old Spanish Sahara the bus stopped at the police checks, and each time a military man came on board and the driver and passengers turned to look at me. I was the only one who had to get off to show my passport. At the last check in Laâyoune, while I waited in the dust and all the passengers looked down at me through the bus windows, a new green Land Rover pulled in with two white surfboards strapped to the roof. A man came out in a wave of blue robes, head wrapped in white cloth, with dark sunglasses, a gold watch at his wrist, passport in hand. Not a muscle moved in his face as he approached the soldiers. He did not remove his glasses. He was solemn, poised as he spoke the greetings, "Salaam walaikoum," a show of respect, and a sign that he had been here many times before. He knew what he was doing. He was a parody, a "Lawrence of Arabia" without the conquest, but with the money. He laid two Swiss passports in the hand of the policeman. He had a beautiful boy in the car. The boy smiled, asked me for a cigarette and when I gave him one, he held it to his lips and lit it against perfect white teeth, dark sunglasses, fuchsia head-cloth.

Dakhla was full of night soldiers and music, smell of fish and salt, this last outpost filled with wind on the end of a spit of sand. The dark sea and the sands, three hundred and fifty kilometers to the Mauritanian border and 1500 back to Casablanca. There were no rooms left. But who was here? The soldiers? The tourists? I carried my bag from place to place down the sand streets and found an open café. Sand spilled across the doorway. The place was almost empty and echoed, lit by one bare fluorescent bulb. A man behind the counter was wrapping liquor bottles in bags and men came for them, concealing the bags deep in their hooded woolen *jelebas* and nylon overcoats, then left quickly. There were three European boys in the corner, their last dirham coins piled in little towers on the table, and bottles of beer.

They were Germans. They went quiet and solemn when I came in. It was the North European in them and the North American in me and we hadn't forgotten. Never trust a stranger. Funny how this feeling comes out when you are among your own kind. I worked hard against it and soon, slowly they were practicing their English and we were laughing. George was a tall Viking, with long trails of blond hair, half tied back, a beard, spectacles, rich laughter. Marcus, in the middle, was pleasant, soft-spoken, wearing Moroccan leather slippers on his bare feet that he kept losing under the table whenever he got up to buy more beer. Manfred had wild hair that looked like an afro. He was small and sour and already drunk. He lit another cigarette, played with his lighter and stared hard at me when I asked them if they were joining the convoy the next day and if I could get a lift. He was protecting this brotherhood and their initiation to the desert. They had each brought a Mercedes down from Germany. They were going to drive hard through the desert into West Africa and somewhere in Senegal or Mali, after they had spent their wildness, they would sell the cars off and go back to Europe with their stories. What did they think of me, the Canadian girl, hair wild and unbrushed, alone, awkward, a little lost? I was traveling for six months, maybe more. Where was I going, they asked. I was going to buy a horse in Senegal and ride to Mali. George smiled. Manfred said, "It will take you a long time. What is the purpose of that?" I said it was a dream of mine, for a long time.

"A crazy dream," Manfred said.

"No crazier than yours."

"No, ours is different."

George had already decided there was room for me, and Manfred did not argue. At midnight he drove us in his white Mercedes, down the long tarmac outside town to the campground.

The moon was still high and far when I got up from the clay floor of my little rented shed. Blue luminous light on the open lot, the tents and caravan cars, and cold. The bathroom was open to the sky. I stood at the sink and palmed ice water on my face and there were stars above me in the dawn.

Someone opened a camper door and a little dachshund and an old Dalmatian dog came out and sniffed the sands. A woman was sweeping the porch of her caravan, made me feel they were all holding it back, the seas of sand, and were afraid to look up and over the walls to the cliffs, the wide bays, the smooth desert beaches where no one goes because it is a place of nothing. Seas of sand and sea of seas. You could stand out there forever and nothing would ever feel or know of your presence.

I met the young boy of the green Land Rover and surfboards out on the cliffs. He came to me, charmed me for a cigarette, came too close, touched my arm. There was something in his eyes. He pretended innocence, but he knew of his own beauty. I watched him going down to swim, followed by the camp-guardian's dog. The older man appeared then off to the left, dressed in white cloth and head-wrap. They were Swiss and he was the boy's uncle. That was what I was told, but I wasn't sure. He said nothing, walked out into the wind strumming a kora, a West African harp, for the boy who swam far below him into the sea off the desert, and the white dog ran lonely along the strand.

All of this comes to me as our bus passes that same campground and I ride into Dakhla a second time. I find a room in the hotel where I could not find one before. And it is Ramadan, all of the shops are barred and dark, with nothing to eat until night. Everyone—only the men, there never seem to be any women—is surly and sleepy. Tourists, in the periphery of my eye, disappear into the maze of streets, distant and unknown. No one wants to be found.

The tourists arrive in groups or alone, having found their own ways through the length of Morocco. They come because the Algerian route has been closed for years and this is the only desert passage to West Africa. Twice a week "the convoy" leaves from Dakhla led by a Moroccan military jeep and travels 350 kilometers of dust and desolation to the Mauritanian border across the once disputed zone of the Spanish Sahara. A war went on there for years between Morocco, Spain, Mauritania, and the Sahrawi POLISARIO Front, desert rebels backed by Algeria, Libya, and Cuba, fighting for independence. But the mines are still there. How ingenious to hide them in the sands that move in waves, are never still. The same surface cannot be found twice, but the mines do not move.

That morning, years ago, I met the convoy for the first time, on the outskirts of town, not far from the campground, on the side of the highway. Thirty vehicles, Renaults, Mercedes, Land Rovers, Jeeps, a red bus, two motorbikes, all from another era, patched and repaired, and metal-worn, roof-racks roped with jerry cans, extra tires, sand-ladders. A crowd of people, mostly European, but one Japanese boy and an African man, and all the colors and styles of their clothes, a theater of army pants, desert boots, plastic sandals, stained and ripped silk shirts, camisoles, greasy t-shirts, head-wraps of black, fuchsia, orange, lime green. So many languages and accents rose from between and around the cars, and different music from sound-systems overlaid one another. Everyone was smiling, affected by the light.

I was waiting for my telex to come in from the police station in town where I had been the night before and where the Germans and I had gone to register in the morning. I was waiting to be authorized. What purpose could a telex have here on the edge of the sea of sand? I leaned against the hood of George's car and George shook his head. Officials were taking down license plates and registration numbers, noting who was in each car and searching the trunks. And in this I saw a secret language, glimpses of maps, packs of cigarettes, food being passed through the windows to the soldiers. Not a word. One soldier pocketed a bag of milk.

Over and over they did the head-count. I thought maybe they lost count each time in the blowing numbing wind. At one in the afternoon someone gave a signal—they could have fired a gun—and cars began driving onto the tarmac, one by one in a long line. Somewhere at the head of the line was the military jeep, but I couldn't see it. A soldier ran over and told me to take my bag and go to the police building behind him. Others had been pulled out, a Senegalese man from France, a French man and his bus and a Dutch couple. Was there any reason? Or was it just that we were out of time and place? I got into the Dutch couple's Land Rover, and as we turned around to go back to the campground with the red bus and a Renault behind us, the police waved us down and told us we could now all join the convoy. The Dutch woman, Lou, got out and did a dance on the highway, did it for all of us. This one great moment under the desert sky. I ran down the line of cars to find George and the white Mercedes. The police officer gave the hand signal. He smiled, "bon voyage!" and we drove off with all our colors and laden vehicles, down the tarmac and then turned off and entered the desert of rock and sand and dark sea, and cloud blue sky, all on a whim.

Everything is different now. There are too many cars, fifty or more. The lot is packed with crowds of young Europeans who do not mix with the Mauritanian, and Moroccan, travelers on the other side of the highway. It is Ramadan, the holy month of fasting for the Muslims, and while the others abstain from even a drop of water, the Europeans gorge themselves on food and beer from cold chests, chain-smoke and seem armored, unforgiving. I weave among them, looking for a ride. Everyone turns me down, they have no room and I feel I'm out of luck this time. I should not have come back. But one older French man in a white Mercedes gives in, it seems out of pity, and yet he is the only one in his car and there is more than enough room.

"How much baggage you have?"

"Just this one."

"*Pourquoi pas.*" Why not?

Again, a white Mercedes will carry me through the desert, but in a different way. The soldiers' faces are shaded by suspicion. It has become a circus. I feel nothing from these people of the convoy.

And as we begin the journey Allain says, "*Ce n'est pas comme avant, ehn? Je suis déçu, les gens sont devenus trop individus.*" It's not like it was. I'm disappointed, people have become too individualistic.

And the road is paved.

But he himself is that way, an individual, racing to get ahead. The tarmac is only wide enough for one-way traffic and held

between banks of red dirt and rock. "*Je vais doubler mainten-
ant, ehn?*" Allain says, bent over the steering wheel. He means
we are going to pass the others now. We are wavering one
wheel on the tarmac and one on the bank, Allain trying to
hold the car steady as we pass a Land Rover, a jeep, a truck,
out of control. His "special cigarettes" are hidden in a bag
behind the ashtray, to get him through. He smokes every one
in the first stretch. The road is paved now all the way to Mauritania. We go too fast. He does not notice anything at all, does
not speak except to curse the other cars. The desert floats past,
so ethereal that if you do not watch, it becomes a dream. I am
helpless, held in his world, alienated from the convoy, and I
cannot feel the desert. We are all just trying to get there.

What I remember of the desert: the open white beaches, miles
wide, dark indigo sea, periwinkle sky, wind, George and I and
our windows open, our minds, having never seen anything
like this. Always a dust blowing in veils across the tracks,
across the land, traveling in transparencies over ripple patterns and webs of thorn bush and mauve shadows. George's
music went with the land, West Africa's Salif Keita and Yous-
sou N'Dour, down the old Spanish road that was nothing but
broken rock and sand.
    "Like a mosaic," George said.
    He followed the example of others ahead of us. He did not
know the desert. It was like driving in snow and ice; you had
to go at high speeds to float across the sands and then slow in
enough time not to crack the bottom of the car on the jagged
rock. The eyes grew tired of always searching ahead. Sometimes there was a track and sometimes it disappeared. For
some reason the cars ahead would detour from what seemed a
good track and later we would see how it ended in deep sand
and craters. We thought of the mines lying under the sands
somewhere in a radius of three hundred and fifty kilometers.

I never saw the military jeep among us. Maybe they weren't
with us at all.

Once a sand dune lay across the track, an immense silent
being, and we had to go around, but then we could not find
the track again. It was just George and I, and Marcus and
Manfred in their cars with Marcus's passenger, the Japanese
boy, Mitsu. The rest of the convoy was far behind us and we
had lost the others ahead of us. Wind, sand dust in our eyes
as we climbed a hill of shale and scattered shells. We looked
through the Japanese boy's telephoto lens at the land that
seemed made of light, a herd of camels far away, like insects,
all sense of proportion gone. No track, no sign, nothing,
everything. We picked up shells. We thought of the mines
and looked at our feet. Strange how it did not frighten us.
And strange how you become when you do not know where
you are. Then far in the distance a speck, something moving
towards us, those long slow moments, one gust of wind that
carried no sound. We saw a motorbike and a red helmet glint-
ing. Mark, the Australian boy. He had already been to the first
control point and waited there with the other motorbike and
the French man and his bus. He had come to find us, and lead
us back to the track that somehow appeared again not far, a
trick of the light.

George and I drove on into night, in our own little world,
only the red taillights of the cars ahead and the long roaming
rays behind us. We were afraid to lose those lights. Often they
disappeared over a rise and George sped up, frantic until we
caught them again. We must not get lost, but we did not say
it. Our eyes strained in a darkness that had no shape. We kept
imagining shadows, could not shake off the presence of trees,
that we were moving through an endless bristling dark forest.

The caravan came to a full stop late at night in an open space
beside the track. People began setting up tents and stoves,
opening up their trunks. A cold wind, a great phosphorus

sky of stars, the small tinkling sounds of laughter and voices, lamps lit one by one. We waited for the potatoes to boil at the hatchback of Manfred's car where we had set up the Coalman stove. I had two cans of sardines that I tried to open with my army-knife. George went through his tool kit and pulled out his huge cutting pliers, bent the sardine cans in half while we laughed, oil spilling from our fingers onto the sand. We ate standing under the sky, out of pots and plastic cups, with penknives and our fingers.

Later there was instant coffee and a passing around of cigarettes. Marcus brought out his guitar, gently strumming, sitting up against his car wheel. Two Germans from another car came over, one in a giant army coat that he turned into a sleeping bag and reclined on the leeside of Manfred's car. They were businessmen, used-car salesmen occasionally, and they had been through here too many times to count. Each time they brought cars too old for Europe to sell in West Africa. "It used to be a holiday," they said. "Not anymore."

Still you come, I thought.

The Japanese boy, Mitsu had pulled on every piece of clothing he had and settled down next to Marcus, shivering. I rolled out my sleeping bag and lay beside him. We had a row of water containers against the bottom of the car to cut the ice wind. A group of Frenchmen in a van across from us were drunk, loud and laughing. A French woman sat alone in her car reading by flashlight, blowing smoke out the thin crack of her window. More laughter from somewhere among the cars, the wind ruffling the sleeping bags, the cold sifting in, the stars. Later the moon rose.

Years later, under the stars and a half-moon, I sit in this same parking lot now pressed flat and gray over time by the tracks of thousands of laden cars. There are a few concrete buildings to one side. The Mauritanians camp close to the desert, recline in their dark robes on the soft sands around their open fires, and soon the smells of grilled meat, of hot sugar and tea come on the wind. The tourists open butane stoves in the backs of their cars, bring out coolers and packages, hang gas lamps from their camper vans, and stake their bright nylon tents of red and oranges. They pull out camp chairs and pour glasses of wine.

Allain and the boys are leaning against their cars, rolling a joint, talking about that time in Algeria, or how many times they did the desert with souped-up motorbikes and junk cars, or about their equipment, what they bring, what they need for this journey of journeys, and the dangers. One man has a story about a Polish man on a motorbike who lost the convoy a year ago. Someone with a radio called the gendarmes and they sent out a search. It was a Mauritanian family traveling alone who found him when they stopped for the night to camp. The woman heard a noise over a hill like someone sleeping, snoring. He lay there half-dead and the jackals had eaten parts of his feet and lower legs. The story makes them laugh, shaking their heads with disgust. Even though it is real they keep a distance from it, but allow it to add an element of danger to their own journeys. It makes them feel stronger, wiser.

Now they are talking about bypassing Nouadhibou and going on to the capital, Nouakchott. There is a fork in the main track after the last border control and if you choose the left route it leads through the desert another 400 kilometers along the ocean. You are meant to take a government guide, but they have decided to go without one. The three of them, Allain, an older man in a Renault, and a young man on a motorbike. I wanted to go to Nouadhibou, but no one else in this convoy going there has room for me.

I know it is trouble already. I unroll my sleeping bag on the far side of Allain's car to write by flashlight, but I watch the camp instead and three Mauritanian men moving among the tourists' cars, a flow of blue robes, head-wraps floating around their necks. I watch them and they do not know even as they leave the cars and come walking back close together, talking in their language, passing the wide space where I sit. They stop and stand there a few moments and come forward. They are standing high above me in one form of blowing cloth, and then one man crouches down before me, a gentle gesture, respectful, human. He asks me why I am alone, and as I do not know how to answer, he looks at my papers and asks me what I am writing. This. I wave my hand across the camp, the land. He nods. He tells me they are enroute to Morocco to find work and make their way to Europe. And you, they ask. Where are you going? I tell them I am on my way to West Africa, to Senegal and Mali where I have traveled before and made many friends. He asks me for a cigarette and thanks me. He says they will leave me in peace, and after they walk away I find the words: something about the desert, not being able to obtain a sense of nearness, even the details at your feet. It is made for distance. Your mind cannot stay down and so you must let it go.

They come back for me, the three Mauritanians. They bring me to their fire on the edge of camp and make a space for me on their soft flannel blanket closest to the coals that glow in a pocket of sand. They have promised me tea and the small teapot is already on the coals. But they, themselves, have a bottle of wine from one of the French, a gift. Mustapha keeps the bottle close to him and they argue over it from time to time. He speaks eloquently, a poet, a man of the world. He has lived in the south of Spain, speaks fluent Spanish, French, a little German, Arabic and his own dialect, Hassaniya. Muhamed lived in Stockholm once, and has a Swedish girlfriend and child there. Their visas expired and they were told to leave, and now they will try again to get back after years of work.

I ask them: Are they not sad to leave their home, their desert?

This? they say. There is nothing in the desert.

But I am held in this moment in time, sitting in a pocket of sand surrounded forever by miles of sand and stars, with these men who are my friends who I will never see again.

The bottle drains and they turn to me. Will I not go and ask my friends for another bottle? I tell them those people are as much strangers to me as they are to them. Muhamed and the other man go off to search for themselves. Mustapha, lying on the blanket, speaks of art and beauty and the search for truth.

He says, "*Quand tout le monde sera gâté, pollué, ils vont venir au désert, ici ou c'est pur et propre.*" When the world is ruined they will come to the desert, here where it is pure and clean.

He says the scientists had said that one day the desert would be a paradise.

In the cold morning my sleeping bag is wet with dew. Over the hills above camp where I sat one morning, years ago, to warm myself and contemplate the desert of bluish light and veils of rose and white and ochre, is a garbage dump. Plastic, sardine cans, thousands of water bottles, stink of shit. The land is strewn with toilet paper and cigarette packages, as far as the eye can see.

On the first convoy we called ourselves a "mini UN": French, Senegalese, Japanese, Dutch, Belgian, German, and Canadian. We followed each other in a long wavering line and the crossing was slow. Mile after mile cars were stuck and we got out and walked through the sands, felt the burning on our skin, had a look in our eyes of being drugged or dreaming in this endless land of light. We helped each other, dug sand away from other people's wheels and pushed. The people of the Land Rovers, like the Dutch couple, Lou and Dirk, brought out their ropes and sand-ladders and became our saviors.

In these interludes there were the characters that emerged. Manfred and Marcus always stayed close to George's car and whenever we came to a stop the three of them went off to investigate, tall George in the middle, small Manfred on one side, Marcus on the other. Sour Manfred never made me forget I had intruded on his brotherhood. He ignored me, gave me dark looks, and if I spoke he always said something to put me off. Once, he lost his tailpipe in the sand. It made me smile when he came walking up to us with it in his hand and shrugging his shoulders. The Swiss boy wove among us with his sugary smiles and asked everyone for money and cigarettes, until people knew to avoid him. The French man's bus appeared against the sky like some strange moving red tower. Usually it was stuck on some horizon and needed everyone to get it out.

"I hate that bus," someone said.

"You have too much weight," others said. "Get rid of it."

He grumbled and swore at them, "What the hell am I supposed to do? Leave it all here? *Putain!*"

The military were ever hidden among us, but then they appeared in their jeep as we pulled up behind the line of cars on a high hill. People got out and walked down the line. Was this the Mauritanian border? No one knew. Far below us we saw a post and soldiers. One soldier was walking down the line counting the cars, another stood at the head of the line. The cars went forward one at a time. When it was our turn we drove down the hill and through an entrance of two posts and stopped. George and I stood before a table out in the desert. All of our passports were there in plastic bags held down by stones. The soldier rummaged through the bags and found ours. Mine blew away in the sand and his aide ran after it and caught it. They stamped the pages over and over with an inkblot that was going dry and then we officially entered Mauritania.

Farther on in the day was a place of green tattered army tents, desert men, goats, camels on the hills and a wooden hut where we picked up our passports. We climbed a steep hill of shale and from the top we saw far away the thread of sea and a lit city on a peninsula, and the sun going down, a burning red disc into gray dust. Nouadhibou.

Night fell. The Australians were worried about riding in the dark. Their motorbikes slid in the sand, toppled over. They could not see where they were going, but they had no choice. We drove on in the deep sands along the railway tracks with the dancing red lights ahead of us in the night, until we came to another open space where we were told to park. A long wait.

"Africa-five-minutes," George laughed.

We got out to stand in a crowd before a cardboard hut that smelled of milk and sheep, where we were to fill out tourist forms. People were worn, tired, sun-scorched, layered in fine dusts and grit. They were sharing their last cigarettes, looking for constellations in the stars, shivering in the wind, wrapped in their styles of desert clothes, now pale, bleached by light, dust-colored. It was the place where people parted ways or continued together in chosen little groups. George and I, we spoke in the way of travelers: "Today I know you, tomorrow we say good-bye." They would stay in town a day or so and then they would go on to Nouakchott. Did I want to come with them? I thought I wanted to go inland by train, and so soon we would part ways. Children were laughing, waving as the convoy pulled into town, past metal shop-fronts and unlit back streets, goats and dogs on the loose, wind-wrapped women, floating sunset veils, men with wrapped heads, long sky-blue cloth.

"If I ever get out alive . . ."

I can't seem to finish the sentence. This is nothing like the
first convoy. It is even more beautiful with the danger. I stare
out at the desert, pure, swept, with prints of birds and mice,
the beaded shrubs, the white shells and shale rock. It could
be a paradise, a place to walk barefoot or lie across and sift
sands through the fingers, but for the deadly sun, the burning
winds. All that is in the air, all that touches the land is fire.

Nouadhibou. It must be fifty kilometers away, but we are
not sure and we are not going there anyway. I hold down
panic, remain in the hands of these three men I do not know.
Allain, with his sad eyes, his child-like muttering and cursing,
his questioning. While we drive he always tells me what he is
doing as he learns the ways of the tracks, as if I could help him
affirm that we are okay. I am only half here, a spirit, a woman.

And Claude in the little white Renault ahead of us, with its
two long wooden planks strapped to the roof rack, his bald-
ing head, dark baked skin, tall, stooping, gaunt, always quiet.
When he speaks I hear nothing but mumbling. And Bruno
on his blue motorbike, with the words "Teneré 2000," that
he rigged up himself. Ten times in the desert, Algeria, Libya,
Niger, five times in the convoy, three times alone, first time to
Nouakchott without a guide. He is the one who leads us, with
thick silver-rimmed sun goggles, always grinning, playing the
fool. It is not that he has no fear, it is that he is laughing at the
gods.

The gods were with us on the first convoy and we arrived
safely and sanely in Nouadhibou. There was sunlight coming in everywhere at the Youth Hostel, Chet Baker played on
Jean's sound system and later Edith Piaf. The Japanese boy,
Mitsu was in the kitchen with the desert boy, preparing a feast
of lobster and fresh vegetables, a gift from the old French man,
Jean, who was pacing the sunlit hall, slowly, meditatively, listening to the music, a baseball cap on his white head, low on

his eyes. We had all spoken badly of him in the desert, the old man and his bus. Who would bring a bus into the desert?

The Germans had gone in the morning. And the others of the convoy were somewhere in town, at the other inn down the road or the campground on the edge of town. The young Swiss couple, Sarah and Udo, were doing their wash in buckets in the shower stall. Mine was already hanging on the roof terrace in the glowing afternoon sun.

Billie Holiday's voice came and Jean said, "it's too bad I didn't meet her before she died." He seemed to have known everyone.

We had a feast of fried lobster, potatoes, onions, bread, avocado salad. Jean brought out a gallon of red wine. The good thing about having a bus, he told us, was all the things you could bring. He told me stories. He lived in the south of France with his Japanese wife, his children, a dog, a cat, two pet rats. He had a bathtub out in the garden under the eucalyptus trees where he bathed even in winter, and he had tamed the magpies. They flew down from the sky when he called. But he never stayed. He went traveling. He had been through the desert too many times to count.

Hamid, the desert boy, had become Jean's guide. Jean had found him or the boy had found Jean somewhere at one of the last police posts where the gangs of guides gather to descend on the tourists. They got on each other's nerves most times, swore at each other one moment, the next moment they were laughing. They were the same, troubled, free spirits. Hamid sat at our table wreathed in smoke from the sweet rolled herb he lit, one after another. He was a street kid, had come in from the desert at some point, with long natty hair, a silver amulet around his neck. He was temperamental, seductive, burning. Every woman became his operation and I was not spared. He followed me, kept me within his periphery, put on tapes of Algerian desert music for me. I had forgotten about the war and the tribes backed by Algeria fighting for independence. I said it reminded me of Spanish guitar. He rose in a storm of anger and strode off.

From the roof terrace in the evening I could see all the rooftops of the desert port city, the antennas and the gray desert, the sea. I heard the grunting of the camels and sheep, children playing their clapping games, laughter. When you are alone in a strange place people come to you or they find you or you find them and you learn what you have to learn. The sun was going down orange into the sands, the muezzins' wailing broke from so many mosques. Later the desert boy told me his day had been like a pilgrimage.

Allain and I are stuck again. Bruno has disappeared over a hill, but Claude stops his car on the hill, unties his planks from the roof and walks down to us dragging them behind him. Bruno returns, laughing. Each time someone gets stuck he rolls another joint and they take their time smoking. He tells them what to do, smiling, teasing. I see he is strong. He could get out of here on a whim. But what about Claude, with his smoker's hack deep in the lungs, his heavy lonely look, evasive eyes, unable to accelerate the car out of the sand while we push. Bruno drives it out, gunning the engine, and then it is overheated. They fill their radiators. Bruno asks Allain how much water he has, wondering how prepared he is, questioning his capability.

"*Vingt litres*," Allain answers in defiance.

Allain, with his minimal equipment, having to borrow Claude's planks, not knowing how to place them or how high to jack the car, or that you have to lift the car on each side to get the sand under the wheels. And myself? I dig sand away from the wheels and the chassis, help to gather and lay shrubs and stones for friction under the tires.

"This is what we do in Canada, in the snow!" I tell Bruno laughing, trying to be a part of them, because there is no other way. No return. Too late. I can't walk away now with my two bottles of water.

Hours ago when we left the last border post it was pure abandon. "La vrai piste." The real track. What I remembered years ago. And then we got stuck and then it was Claude. We have been stuck eight or ten times. Bruno says we have gone no more than twenty kilometers. There were so many tracks before. Now everything is blown over with sand. We've been out here four hours.

Bruno will never say if we are lost. He is not lost, but Allain has begun to get nervous. *"Ca m'étonne on n'a pas croisé la route espanōl."* He's looking for the Spanish road, the old eaten one-lane tarmac we followed paved all the way to the Mauritanian border, and here it has all but disappeared, decayed under the sands. He says, if only we could see the train we would know where we are, the tracks that run from Nouadhibou across the desert to the phosphate mines in Zouerate.

Nothing fazes Bruno. I keep looking back across the land to see a plume of smoke, a flicker, a speck. No sign of the convoy, the train. Nothing. Space simmering in the heat. Thirst. I keep looking at these men, the surface of their faces, the red skin, bristled chins, dirt under the fingernails, old clothes grease-marked, sun-faded. Who are they?

In the stockyards of Nouadhibou the rail men were hitching the big red bus to the flatbed with cables and rope and old pieces of twisted rail ties, while we sat on a sand hill with our baggage in the shade of the boxcars. Barefoot boys played behind us, rolling their bodies down the sand slopes.

Close to evening all of us entered the French man's bus, the Australians, Mark and Daniel, the Swiss, Sarah and Udo, the Dutch, whose Land Rover was hitched behind the bus, the Japanese boy, Mitsu, Hamid, the desert boy, the French-man, Jean, and myself. The train maneuvers continued, more flatbeds and cars loaded with sacks of coal and wood careened past us on other tracks. Our own flatbed was hitched onto the engine and moved far down the tracks and left again. A CD player on the floor played Mariah Carey. The children played on the sand hills outside our windows, watching over us. The conductor came on board to look us over and tell us we did not have long to wait. He had orange tinted ski-goggles over his eyes and he seemed to be smiling insanely.

Now it was Georges Brassens, French folk music on our magic bus. How bizarre: sitting in a bus on a train on the tracks. Some of us crawled out the back door and moved along the flat bed past the rigging that held down the Land Rover and the motorbikes. We were hitched again to the engine car. We heard the conductor giving orders on the radio.

"Reculez le soulard renard!" Back up the drunken fox.

Was this the name they had given us? Because all afternoon everyone had been drinking from another of Jean's gallon bottles of rosé. Our car lurched forward again and we hung onto the motorbikes for balance. Mark grabbed an iron ring on the post of the flatbed and swung himself out over the tracks, yelling out above the drone of the engine with the wind in our ears.

We were somewhere within a one kilometer iron-ore train on its way north to the mines in Zouerate. We moved out into the desert under the night sky. The bus swung back and forth, jolted hard against the cables like a ship in strong waters. Clouds of orange dust rose from the tracks, billowing in the light of the lamp on the car ahead of us. We could not see the head of the train, nor the caboose.

We shared our food, dates, peanuts, biscuits, water. The rosé came to an end. Daniel and Mark sank down in their seats with their knees pressed against the back of the seat ahead of them. They lit their silver Mauritanian pipes and the sweetness of pure local tobacco curled around us. It had

been six months since they left Australia and began their
bike tour from Europe. They didn't know when they would
return. Daniel wondered if I missed home. He asked because
he wanted to say he had been away too long. How would
anyone at home understand him when he went back? How
could he relate again to the sedentary life? This is what we
shared: were we escaping something on our journeys? Were
we a band of exiles? Did we have a purpose? I spoke about my
intended journey by horse and they understood. To travel the
land of no fences.

Old Jean had tied himself up in his suspended bed. Once
the bus swung out too wide and snapped back with a bang.
The mattress and Jean were slowly sliding down, but Jean
didn't wake up. Mark went down and tied him up again and
he stopped snoring.

Udo and Sarah were trying to sleep. Their presence was
always quiet, subtle. They were absorbing everything but they
kept it all to themselves. Mitsu was reading. He barely spoke
a word of English, and had no French in a land where French
was the official language. The Dutch couple was sitting at
the back. Once in a while the woman, Lou came up and sat
beside me. She had drunk too much and had passed the point
of laughter. They were friends of everyone. It was how they
traveled, on their way around the world, a life journey. She
said it was the only way to live. She sat down beside me. What
she wanted to know was: what was it like to travel alone, a
woman, because she had never done it. Ah, yes, it was wonderful to be free. I told her some stories, and she told me some
more, and then everything went quiet. How it felt sometimes
to want to be free and still be held.

Nothing could be seen of the desert but the darkness in
the windows and all of us reflected there, veils of dust flashing across the small lamp of the car before us, shadows, the
glow of an ember. The desert boy, Hamid, sat in the driver's

seat smoking his weed and put the Algerian tape back into the sound system. The wailing voices and the ghostly strings. He was the guide of us all without us really knowing how or why. He was a boy, rude and childish, provoking. He said he knew the desert like his hands. There was nothing that made him afraid. Sometimes the train stopped and we leaned out the windows to the wind, but Hamid climbed out the driver's seat window and leapt down to earth and walked away, scoffing, laughing at us over his shoulder. He peed long and languidly into the sands with the stars over his head. We only came down when he was there. The need was great, but the fear of being left behind was worse, our feet on the sand on the edge of the endless dark, our feet ready to get us to the flatbed in time. Sometimes the train stood breathing for long moments, ten minutes, twenty minutes, half an hour. Other times it lurched forward violently after seconds of being still and our hearts pounded as it sped on into darkness.

It kept us from sleep, bruised and battered us. The seats were not long enough to lie down on. Mark and Daniel went to sleep on the floor. Hamid stayed in the driver's seat with his bare feet out the window. When the train slowed again and came to a stop he looked at me through the rear-view mirror. He told me they stopped to sweep the sands from the tracks, that it was true the trains sometimes left the tracks and flew. He got up from his seat.

"*Viens!*"

There were cots in the car ahead. He would take me and show me. "You can't sleep here," he said. "I'll stay," I said. He glowered at me and disappeared out the window. The train began again, shaking, shuddering, the screech of the wheels on the rusted rails beneath us, clattering, clattering on and on, our bus tilting side to side, in wider and wider waves, made me think we would go over soon, snap the cables and go free.

Allain and I are stuck again. This time the back wheels are in too deep, the bottom of the car is lying on the sand. We have tried everything. Bruno gets up from looking under the car, walks to the shade side of the car and sits down, grinning, pulls out a joint from his pocket.

"*Ah, oui, les mecs.*"

My mouth is parched. I find it hard to swallow. The sun is blinding and still, the sands are white-hot, and somewhere is a sound, a far away song.

"*Merde, c'est le train!*" Allain cries.

And as I am running up a hill to see I hear Bruno yell:

"*Les mines!*"

After all that we've done, miles off the tracks, making our own way, oblivious, it seems ridiculous to me that he thinks about the mines only now. Because the train is there in the desert, a slow tiny moving line. It tells us where we are, but we cannot move now. I carefully retrace my footprints coming down. It is then that I see the smoke and a dark spot on the empty land behind us where I have looked so many times, hoping. A car, a truck? Who is it? Brown metal, olive green, glint of sun. "*C'est les militaires,*" Claude mutters, like it is a bad joke. Is it the military? They seem to be approaching. Have they seen us? We can do nothing, but wait.

They are not following our tracks, but go around a large hill to find us. A Land Rover pulls in to our little bay in the sea of sands, two Mauritanians get out and walk towards us with their black head wraps coming undone, the cloth blowing, and the whirlwind of their language. Another man stays standing near the car. One of them is the guide Allain insulted back at the police post, hours ago. After he had negotiated with him to be our guide he drove past him, leaving him behind, and yelled out the window, "*Je m'en fou!*" To hell with you!

This man begins yelling fury at Allain and his friend declaims:

"*Ici, ce n'est pas la piste pour Nouakchott.*" This is not the road to Nouakchott.

Bruno looks him right in the eye.

"We're not in a hurry."

The man answers him, "So, it will take you a long time. Eight kilometers and already lost!"

The guide laughs outright at this as he checks underneath the Mercedes.

"*Ca c'est grave.*" This is serious.

They ask what we are doing out here. Why didn't we take a guide?

"We don't need one," Bruno states simply.

"Then you will die out here," the man answers. "Do you want us to help you?"

Bruno tells them to screw off. My heart is beating. I understand that I have now been given a choice. The guide and his friend are walking away, waving their hands angrily. Bruno is still talking, telling the men that we don't need a guide.

"We love the desert, we could live here a month or two, no problem."

The men are walking away with the harsh sounds of their language, and I find myself in this strange dream, watching them walk away, step by step across the sand, the worn leather of their sandals, the way the cloth blows at their ankles, getting to their car, opening the door.

"Wait." My voice is shaking and they turn to look at me.

"Are you going to Nouadhibou?"

"Yes."

"I want to go to Nouadhibou."

"Then you are welcome," they say.

I don't know how I take all my baggage, shoes, coat, water, food into my arms in one sweep and carry it across to their car, under the sober gaze of the Mauritanians, in the stunned silence of Allain and the others. I crawl into the back. They ask if I am comfortable. We sit there a long time. They are arguing, still angry. Finally they open their doors and I watch them walk back to the Mercedes. They get that car out of the sand in half an hour. Does anyone say anything? Allain calls out to me, darkly muttering, "*Bon voyage.*"

I drive away with the three men of the good route, I know. I want to make them understand how I feel, that the French men are crazy, that I made a mistake.

"*Oui, oui, c'est vrai,*" they say.

Maybe I'm as crazy as the rest of them, but I love these men because they have saved me. They are good and I am safe. I want to touch their hands, sitting in the back on a metal bench, watching them from behind, the way they have wrapped their long cloth round and round their heads, the way of their language, their brotherhood. There is not enough to thank them with, but maybe it is enough that I chose them.

Over the hours I look back to find a sign of the white Mercedes. Nothing. The desert, a valley of white cliffs, pinnacles. There is a black shell of a car sitting on the sand. We stop to look at it from a distance. The men speak quietly together in Hassaniya and I realize it is the story of the French man blown apart by a mine a year ago. Allain had explained it to me. Two 4x4s made a detour from the convoy. One man got stuck in the sand and the other man came to pull him out. As the one car pulled the other hit a mine. The man watched his friend explode into the sky. All that comes to rest in the desert, the old tires used as landmarks, the rail ties, the car parts broken off in passage, the garbage, the bones will remain preserved, in perfect obedience to the Lord's eye, Allah.

It is the time for tea. They welcome me into the shade of their car. They make a small coal fire, set a little silver teapot on it, take out their bag of tea and glasses from a plastic container. They give me the rest of their sweet milk, zrig in a bottle, cool, quenching. The guide, Ahmed, lies stretched out on his stomach. Moustapha, the driver sits beside me, and Ali, the owner of a tourist inn in Nouadhibou, leans against the back wheel of the car and begins the tea. The sound of the hot liquid being poured, the hiss of the coals. I take off my sandals and set my feet on the sands. The coolness, the sweet silence.

"*Le désert c'est bon?*" they ask me.

"*Oui.*"

The desert is good.

I see how it is different now. I remember.

I remember the sunrise in that bus on the iron ore train. Peach sky, ember mountains in green light, small scalloped dunes, olive green in the shadows, yellow tufts of grass, wind-blown thorn trees, a white camel and her calf moving among a dark herd. Mark woke me up to ask for a cigarette, but I thought he wanted someone to watch this with: the land revealing itself, the sand warming from cinder and ashes to ochre to salmon-orange and then becoming a plain of light.

Now the train rides ever on through the desert to Choum with the characters, the red bus, the memories. But I am not going there. I am stuck in Nouadhibou at Ali's Campement de Désert, and the tourists come and go but no one has room for me, or they do not wish to take me. There is a copy of an article up on the bulletin board about Frank Cole, a Canadian explorer and filmmaker who crossed the Sahara alone by camel from Nouakchott to Suakin, Sudan in 1989, seven thousand kilometers, and then returned to do it again and was murdered somewhere near Timbuktu. He was from my hometown. And I remember another story of a British man and his Italian wife who crossed by camel from here to Egypt. Ali and the guides say they have never heard of them. Why do we of the other world keep coming in droves to the desert? To discover our own personal odyssey? Frank Cole wrote: "I suffered continuously from fatigue and loneliness."

The tourists arrive: Frenchmen, Italians, with their laden Land Rovers and jeeps, and a Swiss man on a bicycle on the last leg of a seven-year journey around the world. Everything he has ever needed is hung in bags across the bike frame with ropes and clips and fancy knots, and all of his stories he carries in his head. He is going up through the desert and across the Gibraltar Strait to Europe, going home. Everyone wonders how he will get through the desert like that, but he wonders how he will ever get over his fear of going home.

And now the blue motorbike rolls in through the gates. "Teneré 2000." Bruno, the lunatic, of all people. He doesn't recognize me or Ali at first. He gets off his bike as if nothing has happened, expects a kiss from me and when I do not give it, sits down across from Ali, grinning, babbling, nonchalant. "Claude has broken his car," he says. Allain and Claude are waiting in the desert, not thirty kilometers away across the bay for him to bring back car parts and supplies. Allain is hoping to catch another convoy. Bruno smiles at this. "They don't know the desert," he says. He'll go back to them but in his own time. He demands a room from Ali, "*Eh, monsieur . . .*" and goes to take a shower singing, "*Ma petite douche, de douche, de douche . . .*" Ali and I exchange looks. He pulls me away to the pâtisserie next door where we sit deep on the couches in the back room with our coffees, depressed. Ali keeps muttering.

"*Dégalasse.*" Disgusting.

"They think they know Africa," he says, "but what do they know?"

"NO FEAR!" a poster exclaims on the kitchen bulletin board, a picture of one man skiing boldly down the snows of a treacherous mountain. Adrift, anonymous, free.

We left the train at Choum and rode on to Atar in the red bus, with the great burnt-purple walls of the plateau always on our left. Lou and Dirk drove on ahead in the Land Rover and the Australians came and went, and we heard the insect whine and drone of their engines, saw the smoke of sand from their skidding wheels. Hamid hung out the open bus door and watched the track and told Jean how to go. Jean cursed him and the track and chain-smoked. The track was deep sand and we were stuck time and again in places where it seemed the sea had once washed in and out and left ripples in the sands, islands, shells, great white boulders and polished stones. The cleft prints of camels told of the desert people but we never saw them. We saw the sunset on a pass between hills. It lay below us on the plains, in a swath between the high translucent sky of bottle green and the black spires of desert bush. It was a band of orange on the dark horizon and in the orange light was a play of waving light rays.

At dusk we got stuck a last time. Jean said that if we could not get out we would stay there until morning. We went look- ing for rocks and pebbles, took them from the earth without a thought for where the stinging creatures sleep. There was only one flashlight that worked and Jean needed it to find his sand ladders. The earth was humming with a side wind that came from far off over the lip of the plateau. The little sound the husk grass made, then everything hovered still with night. We dug the sands out from around the wheels, brushed the areas flat and laid our rock foundations under the wheels, hour after hour.

Udo sat in the bus and refused to come out. It annoyed us that he would not help, but I understood then that it was Hamid's temper that frightened him. The desert boy was crazy, nothing made him afraid, and he had a fire that never died. He could not stay still and would not let anyone have his peace. He ordered us, Sarah, Mitsu and me, and even Jean.

"*Allez! Allez! Non, ce n'est pas comme ca ! Putain !*"

Jean threw his wrench in the sands, swearing, raging, swung his fist and Hamid ducked. They glared at each other, eyes wild, then Hamid backed down. Jean ignored him and went to work on the bus engine. But the desert boy provoked the rest of us to burning silence, rock by rock.

A light appeared on the horizon, then disappeared again, and reappeared, the headlights of a car that took forever to arrive. We stood there waiting for it. Lou and Dirk had come back for us. Dirk brought out his ropes and hitched up the bus to the Land Rover. It roared out of the sands with Jean happily yelling obscenities. We got to Atar by midnight, to the little Hotel Adrar owned by a wealthy Sahrawi. There we found some others of the convoy we thought we had lost for good, the two German businessmen and the Swiss uncle and boy, their surfboards still tied to the roof rack in this desert land and no sea in sight. Dirk and Lou, and the Australian boys were not there, and I soon understood why. The place was full of shadowy people, guides and men of cunning. They set us up at a long table in an open shelter under a thatched roof, served us a meal of rice and meat stew, and began at once to needle us about camel tours and prices.

Daniel and Mark came while I was having coffee, sat beside me and stared at the guides. Jean with his white baseball cap seemed oblivious to the con artists, or he was in his element. The imposing Swiss man seemed to have come home. He was seen smiling, like old friends with the Sahrawi owner. The Swiss boy told us that he had found work with them. There was a war on between this inn and another one in town, and they needed to round up the tourists before the others did. Mark muttered that it was all beginning to feel like a bloody bus tour. He and Daniel whispered about the other place they had found, clean and quiet, owned by a young woman. Lou and Dirk were there.

"Nah, you don't want this bloody rat race," Mark said. "Come join us." But I stayed.

I thought everything was fine, when everyone had washed and eaten and lay content across the pillows and mattresses on

the clay floor of a cool back room. Jean and the German businessmen and the Mauritanian guides were drinking under
the shelter on the roadside. Hamid said he would take care
of the rest of us and began preparing the tea. He made us sit
around him on the pillows and listened to all we said, but said
nothing for the longest time. We were like his children. The
Swiss boy, Armond, had taken off his fuchsia scarf and his
hair was short, black and gleaming. He had a way of smiling that made it seem too delicate. He was too polite, but as I
was talking to Udo and Sarah about Europe, he broke in, saying that he was never going home. Everything bad was there.
It was a God-awful land full of hypocrites. Hamid stopped
pouring the tea and said:

"You are a traitor to your country."

Armond just smiled.

"You know what? I don't give a shit about my country."

"You are a fool," Hamid said. "Do you not know where
you come from? I know my country and I'd fight for my people any day. You are a coward."

They were fuelling each other. It was a fight between
worlds, cultures. But the Swiss boy was as fragile as a puppet.
He lost his nerve and began to roll a joint. Hamid bristled.

"You have everything in your world. Why do come? What
do you want?"

Udo and Sarah had left our circle. The silence was burning.

I saw that Hamid wouldn't go away. He was going to sleep
in our room and I knew I was afraid. There was something in
him that showed no boundaries, the desert mind, his hatred
for us, or the idea of us, and there was his knowledge of my
fear and his wanting to conquer me. I lay out my sleeping bag
on a mattress near Udo and Sarah and he came immediately,
stood over me and told me to move. It was his place. No, I said.
Yes, he said. He came closer, towering over me. I leapt to my
feet. He threw my sleeping bag off onto the floor. I grabbed it,
he yanked it back. Something broke loose in me, turbulence,

rage, driving winds. "Who the fuck do you think you are!" Dead silence. Mitsu looked away. No one said a word. I found a mattress at the farthest corner and lay down shaking. Where is shelter out in the open? Where is home? I couldn't sleep, with my arms wrapped around my body, armour, battlements, stone, walls so thick they would never let in any light.

I snuck out in the morning and found the other inn around the corner. The young woman was there, sitting at a small table on the patio. She looked like a girl, a loose orange veil floated around her small face, high cheekbones, child eyes, and she was smoking a cigarette. She was silent, mysterious, watching everything like a sage. She awoke something in me. Dirk and Lou were packing up their Land Rover in the yard. They were all going to Nouakchott. Mark and Daniel came out ruffled, still sleepy, with their knapsacks. We embraced. Mark looked long into my eyes, "Keep safe." They wheeled their bikes out of a shed. I was holding down melancholy and loneliness. I felt the end of the convoy. I held the image of the two boys riding off with their helmets and luggage strapped on the back, riding down the sand tracks, into the sun-lit open, free.

I went back to get my bags. I was going to the young woman's inn, Rebaia's place, and then I was going to find the next bush-taxi to the dunes, the oasis village of Chinguetti, there where the British man and his wife once left long ago on their odyssey across the Sahara. I wanted to know how they felt staring out at the dunes, preparing to set out across them. In their book they spoke of a world that was the beginning of time, sparse, swept, honed to a bare surface, and moving so slowly across it they were soon worn down themselves. All the layers fell away. This is what I wanted and why I wanted my own odyssey, to travel by horse in a land of no fences, slowly step by step, let it work my own inner landscape.

I met Hamid out on the street. It seemed he had been waiting for me and in his eyes I saw a truce. He was holding a

fennec, a little desert fox. He let me touch it, soft tawny fur, a
glint in the dark brown eyes, of the wilds. It was dazed, half
sleeping. He told me he had bought it from some children in
the market and was going to set it free. My eyes watering. Yes.

Five days in Nouadhibou and now I am leaving the world of
tourists behind me. Ali brings me to the market where I find
a place in a taxi-brousse with Mauritanians going to Nouakchott. I tell him I will never forget how he and his men saved
me in the desert. He says good-bye with his hand on his heart.
And I find I have placed my own hand on my heart in response.

  We follow the train tracks for hours on a bad sand track,
our little convoy of two Nissan pick-ups, the backs built up for
passengers and the roofs loaded high with baggage and sacks
of coal, grain, a few goats and chickens. It is still Ramadan.
Each time they stop to put water in the radiator, check the
engine, or push their way out, or pray, no one eats or drinks.
A few men smoke cigarettes, the apprentices or men who are
lazy in their faith. The others wonder why I don't eat. A smiling old man tells me, "*Mais, Madame, il faut manger quelque
chose. Vous faites le karem?*" You must eat. Are you practicing
the fast? And people laugh, teasing, gentle. They accept me.

  They are all "commerçants," making their living by buying
goods in one place and selling them in another. They travel to
live and they travel without comfort, especially now in Ramadan, but they make it the best they can, sharing laughter and
stories. They have stories about crossing the desert, trying to
make it to Gibraltar, the only way to Spain and the new world.
By transport truck, by camel, on foot, and all those that don't
make it. The guides betray them, or they run out of water, or
lose their way, and they are left to die in the desert. Or they make
it to the sea and the police find them and send them back. All
the way back, to start again, to find the money and the means.

  Sixteen people in a Land Rover, three beside the driver and
five in the middle seat, five of us in the back, with a baby and a

small girl. She has slipped to the floor from a young man's lap and lies there among our legs, hidden under robes and veils. Every now and then I can hear her plaintive voice and feel her pushing for space, her hand on my foot. The baby sleeps in his mother's arms, his head hard as stone weighs heavily on my arm. It will leave a bruise. The three veiled women in front of us in the middle seats take care of the young apprentice boy beside them. His hard jaded voice, his stories about the nasranis, foreigners, makes the women break into giggling fits. One woman lets him rest his head on her shoulder. From time to time she sings, "La ilaha illa 'llah . . ." There is no god but God.

We ride through towering yellow dunes, so close you can see the pleats in the soft surface where the sands have blown down the sides. Then out again in the open we see a line of cars on the horizon. Everything that travels this flatness seems to rise up like theater props. It is a convoy of Europeans, five, six cars. We pass them and a white woman with turban in one of the cars waves at us. The people ask me if I know them. No, I say. We pass a herd of camels, their front legs hobbled with green twine. They just stand there against the light, waiting.

We stop in a barren place as the sun is setting. Perfectly flat, pure sand to all horizons. The sky is larger than the land. The people wash with handfuls of sand and set out their mats and begin their prayers. They break the fast, and the happiness of eating, the relief spreads from group to group. We eat what we have. The Peul woman breast-feeds her baby and calls her small daughter who keeps running off across the sand, freed from the darkness of legs and feet, her cramped place on the truck floor. A young Malian from Kayes shares his dates with me. Everyone relaxes on the sands, feels the wind rippling across the skin. The full moon rises in the east. They pray again.

Another three hours on the tracks and we arrive in a sleeping village. It seems abandoned, empty sheds without doors, cement buildings. I can hear the sea, not far. I stand and smoke in the light. The moon is high among the stars. A young man from the other truck of our convoy climbs down from the open back where he lies with other men across the luggage and sisal nets. He unwinds his turban to reveal his rich dark kinked hair, and lays the cloth across his neck. He tells me he has been here five months as a commerçant, buying goods for Korité, the feast at the end of Ramadan. He says they ship in the sheep by train. He is from Senegal and asks, "Have you ever been there?"

"Yes, once I rode by horse across the Fouta."

"Yes?" he smiles. "Then you must know my village, Horendoldé. Our family is the one with all the goats and cattle."

"Yes, I know it." We laugh.

"Ah, Fouta," he murmurs. "Tell me all the villages you passed through, every one."

Tchile, Tarije, Njoum, Waro Jamel, Kahel, Wande, Medina Ntiabe, Fonde Gende, Tikite, Medina, Asnde Ballo, Orefonde, Thilogne, Kobila, Nabadji, Matam, Odebere, Horendolde . . .

We are waiting for the sea. Our route will continue along the beach but the tides are in, the sea is turbulent.

"*Trop agité*," he says. We can hear the rush from up here.

The wind gusts.

He says, "*Viens, on va entrer dans la baraque*."

We stand at the dark doorway of an old shed, just pieces of corrugated metal sheets, all the travelers' sandals lying on the sand. We go in slowly, stepping over and between sleeping bodies wrapped in veils and blankets. We lie down on the sand in a small space between two people. The cold wind comes in through the doorway, ruffles our clothes. People talk quietly across the room. There is an old man beside me whispering his prayers in the dark, clicking his beads in his fingers. I feel enveloped in secrecy, these places in life where time does not move. The breath of these sleeping people. The

young man lying pressed against me, warm, comforting. I can
feel his breath on my face. We fall asleep at the same moment,
I know, dreaming about the Fouta. Monayel, Bakel, Golymi,
Atofsriga, I-Gokere, Djanni, Mussola, Dialla . . .

I found Lou and Dirk again, and the Australians, Mark and
Daniel, on a beach campground in St. Louis, Senegal. It was
Christmas. We shared bottles of wine, peanuts, bread and
cheese, melon, and Mauritanian biscuits, talk of travel and
guardian angels. The crescent moon was setting and we all
went to lie on the beach.

I had changed, but who had I become? Sometimes I felt like I
was just living on the surface of my skin. And sometimes I felt
like I was transparent, just a pencil outline drawn across the
sea and the sand. The stars, the scuttling crabs. I played with
the crabs, mimicking their movements with my hands and
fingers, the game of run or stand. I always pulled away first.
There was phosphorous in the surf and one lamp of a fisherman and Mark's soft voice out of the darkness, "Do you ever
get any answers out of all this?" We were the only ones left on
the beach. I did not know. I could not move. But later, after he
left I realized I had no link to anyone. I only passed through.
Place to place, country to country, the men, the drinking and
dancing and never returning, the unresolved, the dangers, the
land and the light. The mines were there. I was a wreck, an
empty husk. The only thing that gave me courage was to go
on relentlessly in search of a new vehicle, a horse and a path,
one that taught me to retrace my tracks, uncover the darkness,
and bring me back.

Years later I sit again before the Atlantic, on the clean white
sands above the tide-line, wrapped and shivering in the winds,
while the men change the front tire of the bush taxi under the
full moon. The young man from Atar lies hidden under the

Peul woman's flannel blanket. We see lights on the horizon, glowing through the distance and the sea mist. The other truck of our small convoy has returned to find us. It pulls up in front of our car and leaves the headlights on so that they can see what they're doing.

We continue along the beach with the moon on the ocean on our right. The traveling surf sometimes reaches our wheels and the spray brushes our faces. We go around white fishing boats, through dark swirling waters and it is then I see the two jackals come running up the beach behind us. Dark shadows, swift, haunting. I think of the European man who lost his way and lay dying in the sands with the jackals. He is somewhere now, saved, alive, living his life in some city, but he will always come back with his mind to the desert, to that moment, how he lay with his eyes open, awake, staring at God. He will never forget the gift. There is always only the moment. You must never let it slip away.

The driver leans out his window to see the way. The old man beside him has his red prayer beads clicking in his fingers and the smaller man beside him is singing the prayers for us, hour after hour, in a clear loud voice holding us and as we listen it carries us through the night, in and out of sleep, over the endless waves of sand.

➤ ➤ ➤

Erika Connor is a writer, artists, and art teacher from rural Quebec, Canada. She has lived and traveled in West Africa and once traveled on a white horse through Senegal to Mali. She spent time on a nature reserve in Mongolia, observing wild Przewalksi horses, and also traveled by horse in Central Mongolia, and along the Khovsgol Lake near Siberia. She has worked with street dogs in India, and wild birds in Canada.

❧ ❧ ❧

The Land of T . M . I .

To say Korea defies expectations is an understatement.

I'm chopping this out under a violet awning on a bark patio outside of a joint called Iris. I've got a charcoal filter cigarette, some Korean brand called "This," all because the waiter said I looked like I smoked classic Marlboro—even though I don't smoke—and he swore "This" was the Korean Marlboro and that I couldn't walk away without rolling that paper torch between my fingers and drawing in that sweet and sour ocher air. So I took the free light and now it's about burned down to the final neck and I'm kind of fishing smoke in and out to the flamenco guitar rolling through my headphones while my fingers shove my thoughts through plastic keys and circuitry. And I'm trying to collect and graft all the angles of that field trip onto paper but it's all so stir-fry crazy I find myself tripping over words and words and words.

So I'll begin with something basic, something like pool water warm as rose tea, something you can ease yourself into before you step on the tacks glued to the bottom.

"Heyo, heyo, heyo."

It's a full bag vacuum cleaner voice, a hairball caught in the vent voice, a fan stuffed with too much voltage about to die kind of voice, tugging on my belt loop on the bottom stair of my apartment complex. I've got head phones in, something acoustic, I tear them out, wheel around, and find an old lady with a bag of flowers vanilla-colored shirt, a clay hewn smile, hacked teeth, grape pants, and this Tim Burton-type creep in her step with cheeks hanging like fishing nets as if she spent her entire life either laughing at corny, worn-out street jokes or drowning in Jocasta pillows thick enough to swallow all those tears from yesterday, today, and tomorrow.

I bow a tad only because I know it's polite and I have no idea what to say so I kind of string the corners of my mouth and tug them up and moon smile because she's random and old and it's awkward and I have no idea what's about to happen.

"You see Bill?"

She putters in typical Korean English, always too tonal; every letter has its own suction cup but every word slides into the next. I have to bag what she's saying and pound it into something flat, American, and understandable. I have to sift through the lingo muck, hook and pluck the consonants and vowels; I feel like a verbal Hephaestus or a special guest on "Grammar Rock."

"Bill?"

"Yeyo, yeyo, Bill, Bill."

I catch something in her eyes, a flare, filaments in a damp room, burning like a tarred tassel. It's that same look I've seen in suburban children scoping the neighborhood for their lost beagle. They come crawling up your front walk with hope as their porter until they find out you have no idea where their dog is and it's like you've just blown out the candle in their heart.

"No, sorry, I don't know any Bill."

The candle's out. Her pupils are all shadow, ink wells, a cover on a casket. She's worlds away. I don't mind when she disappears into the esophagus of the stairwell without a smile or a goodbye; it's awkward, it's random, I'm awkward, I'm random. But in a few weeks I'd find out her story. She fell in love with an American GI over fifty years ago, but one cold November day in 1951 he was rotated to the front and on that one warm April day when he was supposed to return, he didn't. Since then, she's been waiting.

"Sad, sad." The landlord would putter and turn a finger like a windmill after telling me the story in machine gun English. "She no love, she no love."

She no love . . . or she knew it too well.

I leave to work and lose myself in the dazzling wallpaper of the world. It's one of those days where the sun hangs like a Valencia orange and the sky is a kind of poncho blue you find hanging on clothes lines in rundown Madrid neighborhoods. There's enough of a breeze to catch the leaves, take their hands, and roll into a wedding dance while the daylight skips off every parked car and shop window and guttered plastic bottle on the street and it reminds me of a spotlight on a nativity scene warming up the shallow snow.

Yes, it's a good day to Bar-B-Q any American would say, it's that kind of day where you just want to lie under the trees watching all the yellow and orange and flour white drip through the branches and spines and green hands and fall like soft-pressed juice into the grass where your naked toes are buried as deep as they can go.

And I'm walking to work all through this and I see the old men in their baggy trousers and leather skin picking at old scabs on park benches and the old women with their billed caps and natty ebony hair fixing up the city gardens. I see the shopkeepers tugging up their blinds to welcome in the premature ghosts and eyes of hopeful customers and the street vendors dumping skate fish into clean tanks and peeling all the brown bag splotches off bean sprouts and yams. I see all the children with their smiles and their laughter slapping tiny soles against brick and cement and the city is as alive as it will ever be with all its faces and souls beating and breathing and huddling like mad skin down these concrete hallways under something real—the sun—and it's a beautiful day. It's a perfect day. And it makes me think of her . . .

I get to school and we're told to pack all the kids on these oriental San Fran buses with maize-colored curtains and that VW hippie van feel. I'm sitting there in a fold-out aisle seat oblivious to what's about to happen with my fingers in my ears because it's far too early to have two dozen children hollering and shouting and screaming and cheering three feet away from me.

Thirty minutes later I'm standing in the hallway of our field trip destination, Woobang Park, more confused than anyone in the entire place and wondering why there's a detailed mural of fertilization on the wall. I came here relieved, thinking—all right, this will be like a junior Smithsonian tour. A guide walks around pointing out random facts on this and that, the most traumatic thing being a Cambodian tourist washing his feet in the urinal . . .

Oh, no.

There I am standing in front of a wall with two dozen sperm burning the Roma countryside like Hannibal's army, a mob of foxes picking golden eggs in a borough, with the Dexter of the bunch homing in on the goliath egg.

It's unbelievable and it's whatever to the tour guide who collects all sixty-plus students and guides them into room one without ever bothering to comment on the Michelangelo meets the internal activity of Mommy and Daddy wall décor.

Lesson Twelve: There are two types of culture shock: culture shock and culture lightning strike.

Room One.

Titled: "The Uterus."

Strawberry red, decked out with a surround sound heartbeat, live internal footage, and a legion of pillows shaped like

sperm, hearts, and stars all over the floor. And what do I do?
What can I do? Only stand against the wall with folded arms
acting like there's nothing bent in this borderline contemporary health Salem absurdity while our tour guide stands there
for ten minutes talking in yin and yang about the nine months
of green house waylay it takes a human being to develop into
something useful enough to pop out into this clean, crayoned
world.

And then the tour guide wants us to pretend like we're in
the womb, tuck in our knees and play fetus, but I can't get
over the fact that half the six-year-olds in the room are lying
on pillows shaped like sperm because the cultivated Westerner in me is lost in translation. And then up comes Mick
with a typical shatter the glass question and those wide, innocent eyes that sell you out like Sirens sweetly singing.

"Teacher, teacher, have you baby?"

Really. Have I baby? I don't even look old enough to pay
my own taxes or play poker.

Then the tour guide with her sunflower vest and cap with
a stitched baby above the bill leads us all toward the exit into
the next room. But just when I think it can't get any worse
than the uterus room my expectations implode . . .

Lesson Thirteen: Never expect a line of what is and what is
not appropriate to exist anywhere, ever.

Never.

The exit is a birth canal. A beet-colored, ribbed and riveted, fleshy miner's tunnel, stretched like a rubber band with
sticker cutouts of giant doctor arms on the floor ready to
catch you when you slide out, reflecting the purity, backward
calamity, and beauty of blood, puke, and labor pain. Over the
chute, just as you exit into room two, is an eight by eight quilt
of Asian Adam and Asian Eve scissoring with a manila heart
for censorship and two sweet Stella Maris Sunday smiles.

No joke.

This is a cartoon version of *The Magic School Bus* meets Hugh Hefner.

Room Two.

Titled: "We were born like this . . ."

Only some of us. Chopin was certainly born like Aphrodite on the forehead of a god, Pablo Neruda with a pen in his hand, and Sean Connery with a dozen bullets in his mouth. But the rest of us around the common table—according to Korea's sexual education theme park—arrive on a precious dime-stick to the soundtrack of a few graceful "uggghhhs" our mothers' sputter as our butter-colored heads pop out like those cotton tufts you get when you blow wishes into dead dandelions.

In America it takes until late middle school for a kid to figure out on his own or over a parent pep talk session that he's not the same raspberry-drop he thought he was when his mother was twenty-six spewing out blood and chunks of Venice and that he did not simply sprout out of a tummy or fall down the chimney, compliments of a stork and FedEx.

So Room Two includes a wall with the stage of life appropriately beginning with the alphabet then a first date in the park, marriage, a queen poster-bed from a Salinger paperback, a middle-aged cliché couple with kids seated all around the dinner table, and a smiling couple with either Alzheimer's or dementia because their synthetic enjoyment of the end is all too capitalistic with their five brown bags in wrinkled arms under wrinkled smiling faces trawling through the final hours of what we might call an "appropriate reality."

Then we have the giant pregnant doll prop with one of those sonar handguns so you can find the embryo tumbling underground. But while the tour guide is pointing out the knot of skin on the x-ray screen, one of the kids is up there banging the baby detector against the mother's stomach like he's taking a sledgehammer to a sidewalk and I'm thinking it might be time to cut out all the taekwondo and "Power Ranger" films.

And that's not even the end of Room Two. We've still got the doll in the corner and her oven packed, perky nipple self, her belly bloated, her conservative smile with another-Bush-won-the-White House-again type serenity and a little baby doll that pops straight out of her chute. The doll even wails when it breaks the surface while the tour guide goes through the labor stages. In the end she has all the kids practice labor pain and moan like the world's about to be stapled to a giant ice cube and then encourages them to run around with those Kevlar pregnancy vests and maternal attire making play out of a harsh natural necessity for species survival.

I ignore it all and shove myself deeper into the wall, but the absurdity is inescapable. The labor sounds and vests—boys included—are already far too much. Then a minute later they're all oohing and awing at some picture the tour guide is pointing to of a husband death gripping his screaming wife, hollering like it's some kind of Wimbledon exhibition match, and ignoring the creepy nurse who's standing near the ball-pitch with a face like Edward Scissorhands literally yanking the child out head first with hands like those claws in those machine games with cheap wristwatches and samurai DVDs for prizes.

And here comes the cherry, the final straw, the Fat Man, little Mick with his beach ball eyes and I know what's coming and I try shimmying down the wall and acting like I have no idea he's there but—

"Teacher, teacher you pregnant before?"

Room Three.
    Titled: "Take Care of the Baby Room."
    Come Room Two and I'm done.
    But this is the room where all the kids get to play make believe. Ironic because we let children play grown up and

act like it's fun. Then when we're twenty-whatever paying taxes, we cry and wish we were twelve again with no worry in the world but what the best color is for the unicorn on page twelve of our elementary work book. If there's any one thing I could fix in the world it would be that. Let a child be a child because one day you learn Santa Claus was all a big lie and people spend more money on bombs and bullets and coke and ice cream than feeding and clothing all the poor and homeless in the world and colors run down white walls and always end up a soft charcoal black and you never get to live in that kind of Lethe state of being ever again.

So I'm standing there caught all up in these Bukowski-type thoughts when I catch the far wall covered in sepia tone shots of breastfeeding. It's all nipples, chomp, mother, child, and—

"Teacher, what that?"

Jameson is wearing the most serious face I have ever seen in my life. It is a presidential capstone look, a pallbearer look, a hybrid cross look of concern and a sincere desire to understand what is really going on.

"Uhh." I shuffle through words and try to avoid Jameson because he's going back and forth from me to the pictures and I leapfrog into the first explanatory lecture I can think of. "You know the milk you drink and put in cereal, well—"

Leapfrogging was a terrible idea. Jameson's face goes from manila to Merlot in a nanosecond. I scramble to correct.

"No, not that, no. The milk you drink and put in cereal comes from cows, the udders, you know, well women have—"

Jameson has got a solar flare for skin at this point and the situation is beyond awkward and I decide it's probably best just to chuck the woodchuck in the river and move on.

"Look, let's just go to the next room Jameson."

"Okay teacher."

He whispers and grabs my hand like I'm walking him out of a nightmare.

Room Four.

Titled: "Look at the change of the body . . ."

When I saw the English translation above the doorway I thought, my God, there's no way they're going to show the balls dropping like depth charges into plastic bags and all the hair and hair and hair sprouting like rice paddies. Oh no, was I ever more wrong. They showed them everything.

The tour guide gripped the first doll like a chalupa and unwrapped him and poked and poked and the kids let out a muse call while she muttered in Korean so I have no idea what transaction actually went down. Then she started on the girl doll and I nearly fainted . . .

Next, we get to doll set number two. Teenage years. She's got a tangerine set and he's got yams and all these kids are still too young to color in Greek mythology but, my God, cover them in all the sexual hocus pocus you can fit into a whip cream pressure bottle.

And BAM!!!

Doll set number three. She's got peach trees and open thighs and all the kids are in a rocking chair of hysteria and the guide is yanking off the wooly weevil heart boxers of her mate and his knob straight clocks out with this hazel wreathe that needs a desperate shave and I'm standing there trying not to puke and the Korean teachers are looking at me like what, what and I'm trying to explain that you can't judge the States based on "Sex and the City" because we're a prude, virgin society compared to you and your dolls and your open lingerie shops next to McDonald's play places and . . .

"Keychain, keychain."

I pop out of my color book fantasy and roll straight down a cotton candy hill into the arms of some bloated, over-the-hill Korean lady who's standing in front of my table with a rack full of cheap light up key chains. She's got a look like she just

got a pox shot in the eye and I'm left there—pen in hand like
a cutlass—wondering what the hell I'm supposed to say or do.

"Want keychain?"

I peruse them, I peruse her, and I want nothing to do with
her random, Christmas blitz colored neon key chains and her
cell phone holders so I politely shake my head and shoo her
away.

Now I need more booze. I order another beer, another
pitcher as a matter of a fact, to drown out the absurdity of this
moment, but I'm a toppling hypocrite because I drift into this
crazy idea that I should get an octopus and keep it in a rubber kiddie pool in my bathroom and feed it sardines and beer
and Skittles and call it "Spaghetti" when suddenly another
old lady stumbles through the front door and hands me a note
with butterscotch English reading:

'Help me. I live with eight blind people . . .'

Although I can't find the logic in me to swallow the supposed fact that she lives with eight blind people, I figure giving her the rest of my Won will be far better spent by her than
by me in this bar.

Lesson Fourteen: Remind yourself every morning of how
lucky you are to have the things you do.

After my charity act, I slide on rubber gloves and slip into
the wet sock of what is and what should be and try to ease
myself back into the absurd memory of this wild theme park.

Room Five.

Titled: "Pretend, pretend."

It's another grown up room where kids dress like soldiers
and shoot one another and play lawyer and exploit one another
and the dull ones with pebble scab brains have no other choice
but to cook or clean or cook and clean and pay plastic bills and
look out plastic windows and suck down plastic pills and don
plastic fashion and plastic this and plastic that.

Yet amid my cynicism, I can't help but laugh when I watch Susie and Bandit shuffle over to one of the play houses hand in hand. I'd give anything to film it and turn it into a miniseries with "Our House" as the theme song.

"Bandit, I make breakfast."

"Rice and banana?"

While the usual Korean breakfast revolves around a main dish of rice, Susie decided to get a bit exotic and shovel all the plastic eggs, toast, and bacon out of the drawers and onto the table.

"Eggs, toast, and bacon!"

While Susie is absolutely thrilled, Bandit turns spiked lemonade sour.

"I don't want it."

Lesson Fifteen: Complain to a dog. Sulk in the mirror. Holler at a cashier. Never do any of the above to the one who cooks your meals.

"You work and eat nothing."

Susie turns away, launches her nose into orbit, and stuffs her hands on her hips. Bandit lingers, mouth half-cocked and ready to do what he should and apologize, but that boy pride keeps the punch spiked and tells him to pivot and storm out the door. He makes it maybe three steps out of the house before he realizes he has no office to run to and although consciously he will never admit it, subconsciously he knows he will never win.

So poor Bandit wheels around and walks back inside the house with his shoulders slumped forward, his demeanor broken. Susie, having known this would happen, hasn't moved an inch since he left and all she has to do is stand there and wait while Bandit whispers a broken sorry in her ear and gives her a tiny hug.

Room Six.

Titled: "What is abortion?"

. . . Dead serious. The tour guide leads them in a sing-song so they can remember what abortion is all about and I've never been more happy in my life to have no idea what someone else is saying because the hand motions and dance are enough.

I'm simply left sitting there wondering if they know whether or not that aborted clot of flesh is actually a living, beating, breathing, thinking human being that one day would go to school and dream and love and feel and sit on a curb with oak eyes soaking up the moonlight as it drowns out this city.

Something also tells me there is a serious value issue in humanity when death and destruction can be put so easily into kiddie tunes like frosting on cake.

Ashes, ashes, we all fall down . . .

Room Seven.

Final Room.

Title: "Sexual Predator."

I've completely checked out by now. I'm done. I'm cashed. They've got some nut dressed up like a wolf up there pretending to be a sexual predator. It's definitely a spot on performance because everyone knows all creeps run around with coyote masks and Mr. Rogers' sweaters.

But it's not the pitiful show that grinds me this time, rather the fact that we actually have to educate our children on the caveat that comes with talking to strangers and what to do if a sexual predator comes because there are grimy, dirty, filthy, for some reason still living bone shop flesh bags that possess the nerve and perv to do that shit.

We exit the last room and break out of that sexual healthcare Chateau d'If and lead all the kids upstairs to a playground on the roof. But even with the fresh air and sparkling glue sun, my mind is still doing cartwheels from that entire experience.

"Teacher, did that scare you?"

I look down at Jameson and he's still wearing a look of grave concern and while generally I would never admit to a kid that I'm afraid I've got no other choice. What just happened was beyond terrifying.

"Yes Jameson it scared me."

I pat his head as he takes a sip of his water bottle and gives me this flat smile of envelope reassurance.

"Me too."

"More beer?"

"No, no, check please."

I pay up, close shop, and rock out of the bar. The moonlight floods the concrete like honey and milk and melting satin and I'm caught up in the faces of my neighborhood. The single father in his box hole flat behind plastic panes throwing his daughter up in the air, wearing his heart in his eyes and on his sleeve and he's far, far away from all this and all that. Then there's the old couple in their laundromat sharing a bowl of noodles with matching chopsticks and coral blue button ups watching "South Park." There's the dame on the curb out front who dreams of Broadway and tucks the dandelion necklace she got from some English boy she sold her heart to one summer long, long ago in the back pocket of her riveted jeans. And there's the middle-aged men slouching in their plastic chairs up the street, scuffing up their shoes on the pavement, tossing hanger wire vulgarity at one another between long drags and swigs of soju. There's the kid who dumped his college fund to rebuild his father's old pizza joint back up from scratch while the old man lies in bed upstairs slowly dying from cancer and the writer in me is trying not to bum himself out because we're all dying together and it's beautiful and tragic, beautiful and tragic.

Lesson Sixteen: "Even in our sleep, pain which cannot forget falls drop by drop upon the heart, until in our own despair, against our will, comes wisdom through the awful grace of God."—Aeschylus.

≫ ≫ ≫

A.E. Baer currently straddles Kabul and Washington, D.C. as a security contractor; before, he "roughed" it in Thailand, Vietnam, and Korea as a freelance writer and ESL teacher. His work has been published in Ditch, CWLJ, *and* Scars *with one act plays produced in both New York and Atlanta.*

ANGIE CHUANG

≈ ≈ ≈

Six Syllables

The gap between being an outsider and belonging
can be much narrower than we fear.

In Kabul, we napped every afternoon, a two-hour siesta
that made up for rising before dawn with the mosque
loudspeaker's first call to prayer. As with most things in
Afghanistan, naps were easy to enter, difficult to get out of.
The soft breathing of the women beside me kept time; their
headscarves lay neatly folded next to them and their black
hair tumbled over their pillows. Late-afternoon light filtered through gauzy curtains. The slide into sleep was liquid,
unknowable.

Waking was another matter. The women tried to rouse me
gently: A soft nudge on the shoulder. My name, in Pashto-
accented English, as if murmured through cotton batting. By
then the nap never felt right, like I had gotten either too little
or too much sleep. A dizzying chemical taste in my gummy
mouth reminded me that I was on malaria pills. I always forgot where I was. Was I really in Afghanistan? Or at home?
Where was "home," exactly?

In Pashto, "home" is not a single word, but four. There
is a word for home that means "house," another that means
"country," still another that means "birthplace," and a fourth

that means "homeland." No wonder that I had begun to feel—in a land that had endured invaders, occupations, war, and the displacement of its people, many times over—that feeling at home had become elusive. The dissonance between home and homeland had been written into the very language.

I had traveled here from my own home at the time, in Portland, Oregon, with members of an Afghan immigrant family I had befriended there. Just as the Shirzais had welcomed me into their own house in the fir-lined hills alongside the Willamette River, their relatives in Kabul—particularly two young women named Nafisa and Nazo—had made me feel safe and nurtured from the moment I arrived in this compound-style abode. The sisters-in-law had attended to my every need and treated me like one of their own. Nafisa had mournful brown eyes and a naturally downturned mouth—except for when her husband, Nazo's older brother, was around, in which case her face turned all coy and giggly. That, in turn, would make the unmarried Nazo roll her green eyes and tsk-tsk at her sister-in-law. Nazo had wild curly hair that was always escaping the confines of her headscarf, or *chador*. The two were inseparable and I, joining them, became one of three: We cooked together, stayed up late talking, and laughed until we couldn't catch our breath.

But outside the home's walls, I felt very different. The city was hard on the senses and psyche, a swirl of dust, diesel residue, odors from the open sewers. Amputee landmine victims and dirt-caked, sickly children begged on every street corner; widows in filthy blue burqas silently extended hands out from under the veils. High school-aged boys, giddy with post-Taliban freedom, harassed women in the streets: *Marry me, beautiful. Please marry me.* Even the catcalls still had oddly fundamentalist overtones.

The disorientation of waking from lariam-riddled naps, in a place that felt startlingly unfamiliar all over again, made me

wonder what I was doing in Afghanistan, with the Shirzais. I
wanted to be more than a hanger-on or a war tourist. I hadn't
come to Kabul to gawk at the destruction and misery of a
quarter-century of war. But why *was* I here? And why could I
not, just once, wake from a nap and know where I was?

Then one day, I did.

It was a voice, not Nafisa or Nazo's, that brought me out
of sleep that afternoon. It was faraway, male, chant-like in
cadence. It got louder, then softer, then louder again. He sang
the same six syllables over and over again. What was he singing? Why had I not noticed this voice before? It sounded
utterly new yet completely familiar at the same time.

I had forgotten to wonder where I was. It didn't matter now. Nafisa and Nazo stirred, looked at me quizzically
through sleepy eyes. Somewhere between quietly getting up,
wrapping my headscarf around my head, finding my shoes in
the pile outside the bedroom, tiptoeing across the courtyard,
and cracking the courtyard door open to sneak a peek, the
thought—*Oh, right, I'm in Kabul*—flickered across my consciousness. The voice grew louder. He was coming around the
corner. In time with the chanting, cart wheels squeaked and
strained. Something made a whipping sound, like sails in the
wind.

Then, licks of blue, gold, fuchsia, and white teased the
dusty sky and dun landscape like flames. And he was on our
street. A pushcart full of fabrics—billowing from poles, folded
in neat rows, nearly engulfing the wiry man behind it all.

"Chador au chadori . . . Chador au chadori."

He was selling *chador*, headscarves, and *chadori*, burqas.
On each corner of the cart, a post held a *chadori*, striated by
dozens and dozens of tiny pleats, billowing in saffron, snow
white, and dusky blue, the most commonly worn shade. The
veils filled with hot Kabul air to assume the ambiguous forms
of their future wearers. I studied the oval mesh face-screens at

the tops of each one, as opaque and inscrutable as they were when actual women were behind them. The borders of the screens were embroidered with repeating floral patterns, works of delicate craftsmanship. Then the wind picked up, and the hanging ghost-women evaporated as the veils became flags, horizontal in the breeze.

"*Chador au chadori . . .*"

The walnut-skinned man wore a white prayer cap. His baritone was languid, his Rs liquid, and the rising and falling notes of his tune so familiar. Had I heard him before, in my sleep? As he approached, I slipped behind the front door—a scarf and veil salesman surely would expect female modesty. But just after he passed, one more look.

"*Chador au chadori . . .*"

As he disappeared from sight, the voice faded. I *had* heard the tune before. It was not in my sleep, and not here in Afghanistan. From the time I was a child, I regularly visited my grandparents in Taoyuen, a mid-sized city in Taiwan's north. The United States was the only home I had known, but with repeat visits to Taoyuen, the city—the damp, tropical air; the people who spoke Mandarin with accents like my parents'; and the bitter scents of Chinese greens and ferric waft from organ meats at the outdoor market—had become a part of me.

For as long as I can remember, every morning in Taoyuen the same chant rang out over and over, carried by a tinny amplifier, often muffled by rainfall. The voice was female, and I can't say if it belonged to the same woman for all those years. But the words and the tune were always the same:

"*Man to bau, man to bau . . . Man to bau, man to bau*"

The woman pushed a cart full of *man to,* steamed rolls, and *bau*, stuffed breads, around the perimeter of the outdoor market. Her deep voice rose and dipped, stretching out the round vowels. The chant faded and grew as she made her way

around the neighborhood. I saw her once, a woman in a coni-
cal straw hat and a weathered face the color of weak Oolong
tea. Her cart was packed with round, stacking stainless-steel
containers full of those creamy white rolls, each as big as a fist.
The steaming dough trailed milky-sweet clouds in her wake.

"Man to bau, man to bau . . . "

"Chador au chadori . . ."

The six-syllable, rising-and-falling cadences of her cry and
his chant were echoes of each other. Different languages, different products; same song, same notes. Was it just that these
two countries, in their varying trajectories toward modernity,
still had economies that supported chanting, cart-pushing
street vendors? Perhaps. But when I heard that chant in
Afghanistan, I felt at home there for the first time.

I heard the scarf and veil salesman a few more times, always
upon waking from my nap. Once, I peered out the front door
to get another glimpse of him; the other times, I just lan-
guished, half asleep. For the rest of my time in Afghanistan, I
never again woke up feeling dislocated.

"Through metaphor," Cynthia Ozick wrote, "we strangers
imagine into the familiar hearts of strangers."

Those six syllables had rendered the differences between
the four words for home irrelevant. A week ago, this house
had been foreign to me, filled with strangers who welcomed
me with open arms and hearts. Now, I had a little bit of birthplace, country, and homeland wrapped up inside this com-
pound, with its fig trees in the courtyard and rooms lined with
pomegranate-hued rugs—and with Nafisa and Nazo.

~❧ ~❧ ~❧

*Angie Chuang is a writer and educator based in Washington, D.C.
Her work has appeared in two volumes of* The Best Women's
Travel Writing 2012 *and* 2011. *"Six Syllables" is adapted from
her book manuscript* The Four Words For Home, *about her*

post-9/11 relationship and travels with a family divided between Afghanistan and the United States. She is on the journalism faculty of American University School of Communication. Note: Names of Afghan and Afghan American family members have been changed for their protection, as some of them have been threatened for cooperating with an American journalist.

MATTHEW GAVIN FRANK

❧ ❧ ❧

Catalina

A street girl plays music you won't hear anywhere else.

This is Rock 'n' Roll, but not rock 'n' roll music. This is
some heroin addict losing a thumbnail on a G string,
Al Green on his knees, Sleepy John Estes alone beneath a
streetlight screaming, "Aaahh'm just a pris'ner!" into a Coors
Light bottleneck. This is Mick Jagger finally castrated and
Marianne Faithfull juggling his balls and a chainsaw. And
this is accordion. Just accordion played by a Zapotec girl in a
night alley that has no business being this orange.

My wife is asleep in a Oaxaca motel named for the swallows
who shit there, and I have what looks like blood on my hands;
the motel has no A/C, and a hot plate where we cooked our
dinner, and the blood on my hands is just chioggia beet and
not blood. And this is nothing like the church group accordion that the upper middle class men played (in lederhosen)
when I was a child at Strawberry Fest in Long Grove, Illinois,
when polka was still as exotic as whiskey. This is accordion
that virtuoso Guy Klucevsek can only swallow with an avant
garde sleeping pill and a Transylvanian whore.

I have to take a picture of this girl and her accordion, and
the red cup that has only one peso in it, and the kids up the
street destroying a piñata and eating its sweet organs, the

simple pleasures of balloon and lightsticks occupying the children in the Zócalo before they take their shifts behind tarps,
bearing clay burros, and yellow scarves, and wool carpets for
sale to the tourists.

My wife and I are in Oaxaca trying to find our place in the
world again, aged after a year of dealing with our sick parents.
We force ourselves to shed hesitancy and over-protectiveness,
and all manner of adult things behind food carts steaming
with pigs' heads, girls' fingers dancing over keys that were
never mother-of-pearl. My wife sleeps and I walk, stop for
this girl—motherless, pearl-less—and it's all I can do to pull
out my camera.

I'm hungry. For dinner tonight: only two passion fruits and
a cherimoya, a sautéed beet, the *chile relleno* with *salsa roja*
my wife and I split at the Mercado Benito Juarez, passing so
many stalls where intestines hang like ribbons. We've slept
little, listened to so much music. But nothing like this. This
tiny voice perched as if on a water lily, driven by some failing
engine—a horsefly with too-wet wings, food for some larger
animal with a poisonous tongue. This asthmatic accordion
scoring its attempts to fly, right itself; the instrument itself
failing, played-out after one too many cigarettes—dirty and
ugly and struggling and beautiful. There's a reason why Tom
Waits has a pathos Celine Dion never will. That reason is this
girl's accordion and its emphysema.

It's all I can do to say, "Foto?" and I feel immediately
blasphemous for doing so. You should know this: my wife is
asleep and she cried before sleeping. Something to do with the
bald old woman selling green maracas. Something to do with
her knowing, in likely dream, that her husband is interrupting a nightsong.

She doesn't stop playing, but nods, her little sister running
out of frame, standing beside me hugging my leg and the flash
explodes. Only a few months earlier, this street saw the local

teachers' strike lead to violent protests, riots, cars set aflame, rocks hurled, barking guns, military intervention. I wonder where she played then. Now, only the firing of my camera, her little sister hanging on my forearm, reaching to see the photo, her feet off the ground. I'm glad it's blurry.

On the outskirts of town the streets turn to dirt, three-wheeler moto-taxis, stray dogs and squatter camps in the valley before the mountains. The buildings here spew their exposed steel cables like industrial squid, the cisterns slanted on the roofs, holding, for now, their collected water. I begin to wonder when dark becomes too dark; what the accordion player's name is. Because I'll never know, I give her the name I've always wanted to give a daughter. This is the word I will wake my wife with.

Returning to town, the bustle has become a chug. The pushcarts of ice cream and mezcal and flan in plastic cups return home, their bells feebly ringing. At the cathedral-tops, bells more obese announce the crooked arrival of something holy: music or midnight.

She is gone, but something of her endures—something beyond music and the instrument that acts as intermediary, beyond buttons and bellows and small fingers that can only press. In this accordion is translation. A language that can stave off, just as it ignites. In it is all music—the stuff my wife snores, the shitty Laura Branigan cassettes my mom kept in her car when she was well enough to drive, when Branigan was alive and sexy and rife with the lovely strength required to belt-out crappy songs.

I head for Hotel Las Golondrinas, something of clove and orange peel in the air. Tomorrow, we are going to Santa Maria del Tule, to the church grounds there to see the Montezuma Cypress whose trunk has the greatest circumference of any tree in the world.

My wife is sleeping, so I am quiet when I enter the room. I take a long pull from the ass-pocket of mezcal on my nightstand that we bought at a market on the grounds of a different church. I need a sink, and its cold water. In the bathroom, I wash the beet from my hands, wonder what the accordion girl will have for breakfast tomorrow. I'm pulling for bananas and cream. I have no idea where she sleeps tonight, or where—if—she wakes up. Because I know there will be a fence around the trunk of that giant tree, because I'll never know, I knife her name into the bathroom door.

Matthew Gavin Frank is the author of Pot Farm, Barolo, Warranty in Zulu, The Morrow Plots, Sagittarius Agitprop, *and the chapbooks* Four Hours to Mpumalanga, *and* Aardvark. *Recent work appears in* The New Republic, The Huffington Post, Field, Epoch, AGNI, The Iowa Review, Seneca Review, Crazyhorse, Indiana Review, North American Review, Pleiades, Crab Orchard Review, The Best Food Writing, The Best Travel Writing, Creative Nonfiction, Prairie Schooner, Hotel Amerika, Gastronomica, *and others. He was born and raised in Illinois, and currently teaches Creative Writing in the MFA Program at Northern Michigan University, where he is the nonfiction editor of* Passages North. *This winter, he prepared his first batch of whitefish-thimbleberry ice cream.*

CONNER GORRY

❧ ❧ ❧

Caribbean Two~Step

Life goes on in all its glory, humor, and misery.

1. WHERE THE SIDEWALK ENDS

I've known plenty of men like Paco. At the far side of forty and still devilishly handsome, his fading sexuality combines with his big mouth to expose him for the tropical satyr he is. A catty, almost vicious gossip, Paco laces acidic barbs with details of Cuba's minor celebrities. Not insignificantly, he's also an out gay man who will tell you to go to hell if you have a problem with that.

Paco is my hairdresser.

Getting a decent haircut in Havana—where the mullet remains popular—can be a challenge. Big Hair is still in here, along with Kenny G and spandex, as if 1980s tacky landed on Cuban shores, sticking like spilled oil on a duck.

So imagine my relief when I was introduced to Paco, a hairdresser for the national film institute. He lives in a three-flight walk-up in Centro Habana and runs his private salon from his dining room. Paco is talented, experienced, and good at taking direction if he likes you, a prickly bitch if he doesn't. Lifelong fag hag that I am, Paco and I get along all right and I turn up at his door every once in a while for my five dollar 'do.

Today is one of those days, with my hair a mess of split ends like the splayed bristles of an old toothbrush.

It's one of those hot and sunny Havana May mornings and I'm performing a mitzvah by introducing my sister-in-law Flor to Paco. Like hooking up with a reliable, on-demand pot dealer in the United States, personal introduction is the preferred way to connect with the best entrepreneurs in Cuba.

We alight from our begged ride on the uphill side of the university. It's leafy and cool up there and we chit-chat about friends and colleagues—who's working where, who's staying abroad—as we make our way around the walled campus into Paco's barrio. A blast of sun assaults us once we turn the corner onto L Street at the bottom of the hill, where the trees end as abruptly as an ocean pier. An apathetic crowd is assembled in the bright light of the shadeless concrete plaza, waiting for a bus.

"What was her thesis about?" I ask Flor, shifting my bag to the other shoulder as we pass the wide, steep steps leading up to the university.

"Equity in disaster management, but that wasn't the problem."

"Oh, really?" I'm intrigued. The juiciest part is coming and I'm heartened that Flor is finally taking me into her confidence—even if it is just neighborhood gossip. The sun is beating down on my face and neck and I start opening my umbrella for some shade. "What was the problem?" I'm about to ask, but can't.

Everything has instantly gone dark. My eyes are open, but not working, like a sticky shutter on an old camera. In those seconds, my words and thoughts and breath are sucked away. The umbrella is laying half open on the ground.

"I must have dropped it," I think, before the shutter becomes unstuck and I realize it's me that has dropped—hard and fast into a deep hole in the middle of the sidewalk. My breath comes back in a sharp, high-pitched inhale that peters to a hiss as the pain shoots from body to brain.

"Conner! Oh my God! Are you okay?" I hear Flor asking, but she sounds muffled and far off, like she's calling from across a lake.

My heart is beating fast. I feel Flor's hand on my arm and become aware of the crowd watching from the bus stop. I worry about my pants, the capris with the pink and yellow flowers my husband brought me from Brazil. "I hope they're not ripped," I think vainly. "My ass looks so good in them."

Next thing I know, Flor is hauling me out of the hole. I was in it to my waist, the entire lower half of my body suddenly below ground. She collects the umbrella and helps me hobble to the bottom step of the university's famous staircase. I squeeze the first tears away, but my chagrin is not so easily vanquished. I imagine the bus passengers laughing at the sight of a gringa in tight pants swallowed by a sidewalk and start laughing a bit myself (which keeps me from crying—a tried and true Cuban survival strategy). Concerned bystanders begin coming to our aid and I wish I could disappear, though I love how strangers always jump to the rescue here in Havana.

A homely woman in a cotton dress identifies herself as a doctor and cups my purpling foot in her palm. She tells me to move it this way and that, which I do with surprising agility.

"It's not broken," she says in Spanish, looking at Flor instead of me, assuming I need translation.

Just then a young man pulls up in a Coco Taxi—one of the three-wheeled buggies Cubans call *huevitos* because they're the color of egg yolk—and idles at the curb, offering me a ride to the nearest clinic. His fare in back looks at me with concern. A tourist squats down to my level.

"Are you all right?" she asks in a nice, but shrill way that implies I might need backup; that maybe these Cubans surrounding me aren't properly equipped to help.

"I'm fine." I repeat twice, saying it a thi
for anyone with doubts.

"It's just . . . I have to get home," I spit

"C'mon, let's go," Flor says grabbing
and steering me towards the Coco Taxi.

"No, that's okay. It's not broken. I just need to get home
and put it up." I'm embarrassed and in pain. I don't want to be
a burden—to be dependent—on top of it. I'm also concerned
that Flor should get a good haircut.

"Call me later," I tell her, before begging my second ride of
the day and sending her off to meet Paco alone.

Bracing myself between stairway wall and banister, I hop up
five flights on my good left foot which now hurts as much as
the banged up right. It's a slow, laborious ascent that leaves me
covered in a gritty sweat. Wincing, I try not to make any sound
as I fumble with my keys: I have to get inside before my neighbor comes out and takes pity. Basest coin in the realm, that.

Hopping inside, I collapse on the red pleather (that's plastic
leather, the upholstery of choice here) loveseat near the door.
More than an hour has passed since I fell in the hole. It will
be a lost cause if I don't ice it soon. I hop over to the Russian
refrigerator older than me. It opens apathetically, the spent
gasket giving way with a sigh as if to say: "Retire me already."

There's no ice I discover upon removing the bent, soggy,
cardboard that substitutes for a freezer door. And no drinking
water either. I hop three steps to the stove and grab our pot for
boiling water. Encrusted with years of boiled minerals, the pot
weighs a bit even empty and it takes some tricky maneuvering
to fill it with tap water and get it back on the stove. I'm sweating again and my foot has turned a ghoulish color. I pop a trio
of Cuban ibuprofen, hop to the bedroom, and lower myself
into bed.

When I come to, I smell the "get well" soup my husband
so artfully whips up on occasions such as these. (The man

many faults, but at attending my witchy, bitchy sick self ⁄ith grace and aplomb, he's peerless). "It's early for him to be home," I think as I swing my feet clumsily to the floor and lunge at the termite-infested bureau, hoping this isn't the moment it crumbles once and for all. Working with just one foot, it becomes clear, is awkward and loud, like a gang of bored teens searching for meaningful experiences—or at least something Tweet-worthy.

The little pot-bellied Buddha I bought because it reminded me of my husband clatters to the floor and rolls away, followed by an incense burner that once belonged to my dead brother. I'm looking down at it dumbly, wanting to pick it up fast in case big brother is watching (he had some eerie extra-sensory powers while alive which I have reason to believe linger in the terrestrial ether), when my husband appears.

He's wearing his favorite apron, which always makes me smile and a little bit horny in that post-feminist, "fuck machismo" kind of way that has taken on new meaning since moving to Cuba and marrying a *Cubano*.

"You're awake! How do you feel? I'm making soup," he says, gathering me in his arms.

Already I feel better, but dread what comes next.

"We have to go to the clinic," he commands, encircling my waist and helping me to the couch. "You need to see the doctor and will probably need a cast."

In the States (from where I'm self-exiled for a lot of reasons, including the dynamic that puts quality health care out of reach of the poor), a sprained ankle is usually treated at home using the RICE method: Rest, Ice, Compression, and Elevate. But not in Cuba where health care is free and there's a doctor on nearly every block.

Even after so many years here, I'm still not used to health care as a right and on demand. Part of it is due to my hand-to-mouth upbringing and what amounted to the Christian

Scientist's approach to health care with which I grew up (i.e. suck it up, you'll get better some day, some way). So I'm neither used to going to the doctor, nor do I like it. But how can I say no to a man in an apron who's tending me *and* a pot of soup?

We're summoned fairly quickly at our community clinic and attended in an examination room lit by a bare bulb over a wobbly desk. Doctora Yenly is young and thorough—declaring it a bad sprain without ordering X-rays, instead performing a clinical exam at which Cuban family doctors excel (not entirely by choice: X-rays and lab tests are expensive and use scarce resources, so are usually left as a last resort). Dra. Yenly prescribes ibuprofen and rest, plus I'm told to keep all weight off the bad foot for two weeks.

"You'll have to find a pair of mulattas," she says, escorting us out of the examination room. With that parting piece of medical advice, she gives us each a kiss on the cheek and sends us hobbling on our way.

Once we're out of earshot, I turn to my husband. "What was that about the mulattas?"

My question is met with that same stumped pause that overcomes parents when their kids ask what holds up the sky? or why is the ocean blue? Suddenly he bursts out laughing.

"Not *mulatas*, *mi vida*," annunciating slowly and clearly as if he were speaking to a six-year-old asking about the sky and ocean. "*Muletas*, you need a pair of *muletas*." Only when he mimes tottering around propped up by something do I understand my mistake: I don't need two hot chicks of mixed race, but simply a pair of crutches.

Like so many times before and since, Cuba succeeds in making me feel like that six-year-old, pointing up such silly, laughable mistakes. But rest assured, I'll never forget the

word for crutches—I just hope I won't have cause to use it
again any time soon.

2. ANVIL

It's dark still, but I can't sleep. The drone and clank of earth-
moving equipment through the long night, the acrid burning
garbage fumes pressing down, and chirping cell phones con-
spire me awake. But above all, I'm roused today, like all days,
by the "gringo alarm clock"—incessantly crowing cocks. It's
astounding, the number of roosters, hens, and chicks running
around our tent camp at the defunct military hospital in central Port-au-Prince.

I've never understood how folks keep track of their free-
running fowl in the developing world. How do they know
which of the chicks pecking at the hard, packed earth is
theirs? How come they aren't stolen? Why don't they make a
run for it, the dumb birds? Here, just a month after the earthquake that cursed Haiti even further, I'm doubly baffled by
chicken behavior—how can they run around willy nilly with
so many hungry people about?

When I emerge from my blue igloo, a speck in the sea of
tents belonging to the Cuban medical team, the sun is just
rising, and with it another day of hunger, amputations, and
crookedly knit bones for Haiti. Already I'm sweating like
swine. The heat here—suffocating and foul-smelling—is like
only one other I've known: New York City subway cars in the
old days, before they had air conditioning. In this pre-dawn
moment, as the sun and soldiers begin to stir, an ominous
light hovers above the clearing where clothes lines are strung.
Walking towards the wrinkled bras, t-shirts, and jeans hanging as listlessly as the girl I saw dying of malaria yesterday, I'm
convinced the metallic, cold light is being thrown by fluores-
cents. But it's just an odd, eerie light hanging over the piles of
dried almond leaves littering the ground.

I'm startled by loud voices, what sounds like a squabble but is just how Haitians communicate, everything passionate, everything a possible argument. It's coming from the spontaneous refugee settlement abutting our camp, a few families trying to make it one more day. The women and children fill their buckets at our spigot, struggling to protect the liquid gold from sloshing as they pass our tents. Since many Cubans share genetic similarities with Haitians, it's hard to know who is who. I cover all bases with the smiling fellow sweeping up the almond leaves, starting with *bonjour* followed by a quick *buenos días*.

Good day? Let's hope so.

Hope is as scarce here as ice: that small refugee settlement adjacent to our camp? It was razed while we were vaccinating all comers in the sprawling tent city across from the Presidential Palace. The freshly cleared land, now free of chickens and trash, is being prepared for the new Ministry of Public Health. So they say, but rumors are a staple in the disaster realm. I worry for the families, our neighbors, who were surviving there. What will they do? Where will they go? For now, they're squeezed into a narrow strip of no-man's-land with their few belongings—a plastic tub, a cook pot, some clothes—piled outside their tent flap. All day, bulldozers mound detritus closer and closer to the makeshift kitchen the families cobbled together, the women and children doing most of the work.

Later that day it starts raining and doesn't stop. As night falls and deepens, through those long, dark hours and at daybreak, it's still raining.

"How did you sleep?" I ask my neighbor, a doctor from Guantánamo who had been serving in Haiti a year already when the quake hit and treats her patients in capable Creole.

"OK, but I wake up tired."

We all do. Sleep is elusive, especially when it's raining. With each drop you think of a different patient or person—the malnourished four-month-old; the young girl caring for a trio of smaller siblings; and the twelve-year-old boy who is now the head of his household, made fast a man on that Tuesday. No matter how much good the world is doing Haiti, regardless of the size and sincerity of the tender outpouring, no one can control our most pressing problem: the rain. Perhaps more than any other place on earth, in Haiti circa March 2010, you don't need a weatherman to know which way the wind blows.

Leaving the Cuban camp, we make our way to the primary care post set up in one of Port-au-Prince's hardest hit areas. Toxic dust fills our eyes and noses and mouths if we're not careful. There are people living in cars and tents are pitched in the middle of rubble-fringed streets. Even folks whose homes are intact prefer to sleep in tents in the driveway or family courtyard. The earthquake is too fresh in their minds, the massive aftershocks fresher still. Signs on the outside of partially crushed homes read: "Help us! We need water and food," in three (or more) languages.

Flies swarm over garbage, shit, people. Four-story buildings are flattened like millefeuille pastries—thinking about what lies between the layers is ill-advised. Other buildings dangle concrete-encrusted rebar from skewed balconies like Christmas lights or strings of rock candy. People are starving to death, yet there are mounds of food for sale: fried chicken, grilled hotdogs, and corn on the cob, fresh fruits, vegetables, bread, and rice.

And I thought Cuba was surreal.

Inside the camps, conditions are not fit for cattle, but you wouldn't know it looking at the children. Smiling and laughing and dancing in spite of it all, no matter that they're barefoot and bare-bottomed. They're adorable and wide eyed, playing alongside garbage heaps shouting *"blan! blan!"*

(whitey! whitey!) with affection as I walk by. I flash them the peace and thumbs up sign and dance to music only we can hear. It's my only way to communicate beyond my high school French. I make them smile, just for this one moment; Patch Adams I am not.

To be honest, the scene here is depressing and some days even all those smiling, jigging kids can't help me shake it. The stench of shit, piss, and garbage envelops us, unavoidable and constant and the visuals are assaulting: by day, little boys and grown men lather up naked in the street while U.S. soldiers look on through dark shades, guns slung casually by their sides; by night, young girls sleep in doorways hunched beneath pink, threadbare blankets.

It's fair to say that every last person in Port-au-Prince is sleep deprived these days. There is so much to keep us awake at night—the rain, thoughts of the homeless families, widows with AIDS, TB, anemia, and scabies—but it is the terrible, horrific tales of rape that terrorize my waking moments. What protection can a single mother in an overcrowded, pestilent refugee camp provide her teenage daughter from the men who enter in the predawn to beat and rape innocent children? From the reports we're getting and the patients we're seeing, none, it seems.

The rubble, of course, remains. Some motions are made to clear it—in buildings prioritized by the U.S. high command or their private subcontractors (one never can tell) and by men salvaging rebar. It's part of the permanent landscape it seems, these piles of pulverized rocks and crumbled facades. We just step over and through it every day, on every street. This capacity to move on and around is how Haitians cope—with death squads, foreign occupation, and natural disaster, too.

As for us, we share almost-cold Cokes and Colt 45s sold by Wilfred, a Haitian who set up a small commissary in our camp. Prestige, the local beer, is in high demand and runs out fast. One Cuban nurse, who has been in Haiti for more than two years, takes a long pull on his beer and tells me: "Best to stay anaesthetized." Beer and moonshine: effective weapons here in the arsenal of cope, including ours.

"Thanks to God, you're better," my Haitian friend Madsen tells me when I catch him up on my now-cured explosive diarrhea.

God is very much on the tip of the tongues of the folks I meet here. Jesus is ubiquitous and more popular (but only slightly) than the NY Lotto numbers—a serious vice in Haiti. Alongside the daily numbers—on buses, in barber shops, taped to tents, tagged on partially fallen walls—the Word of God is found everywhere.

Descending the steep hillside upon which is perched a large, makeshift orphanage where the Cuban team is providing free health services, I see a garage door that proclaims: "God loves us. He saved us." That's some heavy food for thought and doesn't help lift the anvil that's been pressing on my heart ever since I huffed up that hill to where 347 orphans are ill, thirsty, hungry, and too alone.

I wasn't expecting this unwavering faith. None of my pre-trip research prepared me for the Jesus craze that grips Haiti. Casual conversations peppered with holy references and the massive Sunday migrations through the dust-choked streets by young and old alike, Bibles tucked close, catch me unawares. Heathen though I am, I'm grateful these beleaguered people have something to hold on to. From Tribeca to Cite Soleil, when disaster strikes, believers find succor in their faith. Indeed, I remember something like envy overtaking me as I walked downtown on September 12, 2001, passing full to overflowing churches.

"You're just cheap. You should give your salary to the church," a Haitian medical student teases a Cuban surgeon in the emergency room.

My ears prick up at this playful culture clash unfolding. Turns out the medical student gives 75% of her salary to her church and she is trying to convince the surgeon to follow suit. Her beauty and killer smile don't win him over to the light and when he asks why she would do that, she explains the church is where she finds love and happiness and so is entitled to her earnings. More dense food for thought.

After a particularly terrible sleepless night, I'm assaulted by this godliness. Seems someone in the massive tent city up the block thought it a good idea to blast religious pop on a powerful sound system starting at 6 a.m. sharp. In my mind, food, potable water, and safe shelter would be more appropriate for the thousands now getting an earful of "Merci, Jesus." Thank you, Jesus? For what I wonder? Later that day, I see a sign and point it out to my doctor buddies: "God is the chef of this house?!" Everyone has a good laugh at my bad French: clearly God is the *boss* of this house, not the chef. But while He might be the boss of those houses still standing, I'm dubious.

To my God-fearing friend Madsen, whose younger sister just died of anemia, I tell it like I see it.

"No, friend. It wasn't God that cured my dysentery. It was the Cuban doctors and the almighty power of antibiotics."

Madsen nods. "You know, we Haitians have a saying here in the countryside: 'After God, the Cuban doctors.'"

And Lotto.

Who says Haiti's godforsaken?

❧ ❧ ❧

Havana-based journalist and author Conner Gorry covers Cuban health and medicine for MEDICC Review, *a privileged gig that has sent her to post-quake scenarios in Pakistan and Haiti with Cuban disaster relief teams, as well as deep inside the island's health system. She has written a dozen guidebooks and maintains "Here is Havana," a blog about life on the "wrong" side of the Straits, on heinously slow dial-up while smoking her daily five cent cigar. Researching and updating her app, "Havana Good Time," keeps her (mostly) out of trouble.*

KATE McCAHILL

❧ ❧ ❧

Notes on My Father

She takes an anthropological view of a parent.

There aren't any seats left in the Calcutta domestic terminal, so my father and I sit on our packs. We lean against the grimy wall and pass a bag of nuts back and forth, nuts that have come as far as we have—all the way from Lake Placid, New York. We left for India two days ago, and now, five flights and two airport breakfasts later, we are propped up against these gray airport walls watching the display as it ticks away the names of this nation's cities. People line up and shuffle out the big main door towards their planes. While they wait to exit through that door, women breastfeed their babies and grandmothers nap. Ladies adjust their veils, lengths of translucent emerald and saffron and turquoise fabric. Fathers buy sandwiches and fat samosas from the snack stand near the bathrooms. My father takes it all in, his latest book unopened in his hands, his khakis creased from all this time wearing them. He is taller than everyone else in this room, but people have grown tired of looking over at us, and so now we're just being ignored. We've accepted that we'll never get a seat while we wait; speedy grandmothers hover over the emptying ones, poised to rush in and occupy.

Our flight is finally called, and by the time we're seated on that plane, we're asleep. When we land in Bagdogra an hour later, we stumble outside into the humid afternoon and blink into the sun that beats off the flattened grass and the distant, snow-capped mountains. The sky, streaked with filmy haze, presses onto us. We hire a taxi for twenty dollars and then ride for four hours, first through mad Bagdogra and its crazed neighbor Siliguri, with the men who stitch mattresses together on the side of the road and those big, unfinished plaster hotels. Bicycles and cows and trucks clot the road, and then finally the city dwindles into fields of tea and corn. The route rises and winds and finally pitches up into jungle, and then we are in the Himalayan foothills. The views are so incredible that I feel guilty sleeping, but I can't keep my eyes open and neither can my father. While our young driver navigates the curves and blasts American dance music, our heads loll in the backseat and the sky grows dark.

We close our eyes on our first night in India to the sound of the rain on the Dekeling Hotel's tin roof. When we wake twelve hours later, we look out over the clouds to the distant hills, swathed in green bushes of tea. We eat breakfast and write an email to my mother, who decided she'd be okay with never setting foot on the subcontinent and so stayed home with our cat and dog and my brother. And then we leave Darjeeling, because we aren't here for the cities. We want to be in those mountains, those Himalayas we can see from our hotel room window, the ones my father has always dreamed about. So on that first morning we drive with the guide we hired weeks ago over email to a tiny checkpoint town three hours from Darjeeling. We print our names and passport numbers in a dusty ledger at the offices of the border control, and then, just as the rain is tapering off, we start hiking.

We climb a rocky road that starts out wide, with gentle curves, but quickly grows steep and narrow and studded with ruts. We stop often for tea, for pictures, and to enter tiny monasteries dotted along the route. For the whole of this five-day trek, we will straddle India and Nepal, crossing into one country and then into the other as the trail dictates. We pass men who herd goats and cows who herd themselves, and miles and miles of prayer flags, long faded by the rain and wind but still flapping in tatters. These are the Himalayan foothills, we remind ourselves, breathless.

"Have you ever been anywhere cooler than this?" my father asks me once as we amble past a herd of billy goats. I shake my head, no, but in truth it doesn't matter whether I've been anywhere cooler than this or not. What matters to me is that my father, from the tone of his question, has told me that he has not.

On the second day of our trek, we pass an Indian man in a neon green poncho and a white baseball cap, the visor still flat as the day it was purchased. He stops when he notices my father, puts his hands on his hips and blocks our way, not unkindly. He draws a handkerchief from his pocket and wipes his brow, taking a moment to catch his breath, and then, "Where you are from?" he asks. He doesn't look at me; he is watching my father. It is perhaps the twentieth time so far that Dad has been asked this, but he still replies enthusiastically: "We're from the States!"

The man pauses, considering. He wags his head, once to the left and once to the right, a slight and particular movement that you see all over India. He reaches into his pocket and draws from it a package of gum, pulls out three sticks and hands two to my father, who passes one to me. We unwrap our gum, put the sticks in our mouths, and then the man crumples up his wrapper and tosses it on the ground. My father and I put ours in our pockets.

"Thank you," my father tells the man. We chew for a minute. "It's nice gum."

"Welcome to India," the man replies, smiling to reveal white teeth. All around us, the land sings with crickets, and the clouds are passing fast over our heads. A fresh wind rolls up the Nepalese side of the ridge and down the Indian one. The gum-man reaches out to shake my father's hand, then turns from us and trudges on down the hill. Our gum tastes slightly of lemon. We watch the man pick his way down the rocky trail, until he turns the bend and disappears. Ahead of us, we can see where someone has strung two strands of prayer flags, stretched between boulders at the ridge's edge.

Outside, it's pouring rain, and my father is vigilantly watching the sky. This is our third morning in India. It has been dark and wet like this every day so far, with just a few blessed patches of bright light. My father woke up this morning before five and went outside, his hiking boots unlaced, and saw that miles away, at the edge of the horizon, there was sunshine peeking through the cloud cover. He had rushed into our room to get the camera, his binoculars, and his book, to wait outside for the rain to stop and the clouds to break up so he would finally get to see the snow-capped peaks. We'd come all this way, after all.

But the mountains hadn't revealed themselves; the clouds only thickened, and he'd finally come inside again. And yet he was not dissuaded.

"Morning clouds," he'd declared, while I pulled the pillow over my head to cling to sleep. He stuffed his clothes and his sleeping bag into his pack and, ignoring my grumpy silence, spoke with a grin in his voice. "I think we're in God's pocket, now."

Now he has finished packing, has glanced again out the window, and has picked up his book but hasn't opened it. He sits down on the bed and crosses one leg over the other to wait. "After the rain is when the sun comes out," he says. "So we'll be ready." He peers out the window, searching for the light that he swears lies just beyond those clouds, and as if the gods have decided to give him a gift, a slant of sun enters, suddenly, to fill the window's four chipped panes.

My father tells me that he is too old to learn new words. It gets harder every year, he tells me. *Namaste,* that Hindu greeting used everywhere here, is a phrase I have heard a thousand times in the course of a decade of yoga classes, three years of Cambridge bumper stickers, and four months in India after college. It is, however, a word that my father just cannot remember. "Hello," he always says pleasantly as we walk past Indian families, or boys with big bales of sticks on their backs, or old men leading donkeys down the road. "Dad," I always whisper afterwards, "say na*ma*ste."

"Na*ma*ste," he repeats, putting the emphasis on the *ma* in the center of the word. But each time we pass someone new, my father gives them a jolly *hello*. For this he receives gruff nods.

The other word we most often use is *dhanyavad*, the Hindi word for thank you. My father can't get that one right, either.

"Danyabob," he tells the man who takes our picture on the trail.

"Danyabob," he tells the women who bring us our chai at the hill stations. I have given up on correcting him, and anyway, for *danyabob* we always receive a smile.

As the track rises up and up, through the clouds and then above them, my father notices that the plants resemble more and more the ones he finds at home.

"See this?" he asks no one in particular. "That's sedge." He leans down and smells.

"Sedge," I repeat, peering at the scruffy, sage colored brush.

"Sedge," says our guide, Satjin, a twenty-one-year-old Nepali guy with gel in his hair and a tiny backpack with all his clothes tucked inside. He smokes cigarettes when he thinks we aren't watching, coming out from behind trees and boulders, stinking of smoke.

My father runs a finger along the length of the plants' slender leaves.

"It looks like grass, but it's not," he tells Satjin and me. "It's a high-elevation plant." He turns to look at me. We're both dotted with raindrops, but we've long grown used to the constant water that trickles from the sky onto our packs, our shoulders, the napes of our necks. "This is what we have on Algonquin."

Maybe Algonquin is my father's favorite Adirondack peak; I forget. I wonder whether he even has a favorite; he knows them all so well, has climbed each one so many times. Algonquin he's summitted in summer and winter both, at least twice a year for many years, and so I figure that this sedge must come as a comfort, like meeting an old friend on the other side of the world. As we continue along, he points out monk's hood, bachelor buttons, stubby pines like the ones that grew at the deepest points of his mother's garden path, back before she had to sell the house and move into a nursing home.

He points out many times a spiky plant with tiny green leaves and red berries. I guess that it's holly; he's certain it's not.

"Satjin," he calls, and Satjin turns around and slips his phone in his pocket and walks back to where my father has stopped walking. He is a chronic text-messager, Satjin, and is adept at walking and texting in sync. To be polite, he puts the phone away when he talks to my father.

"Yes, sir?" he asks delicately.

"I don't know what this plant is called," my father says. He leans into the leaves and draws one close to his face. "But we have it at home. What is it, Satjin? What's it called?" Satjin peers down.

"My mother had this in her garden at home," my father tells him. "Every year I'd have to go there in springtime and clip it."

"I'm not sure what it is, sir," Satjin finally says. Together they continue to examine. Satjin, I suspect, knows he will get a better tip if he shares my father's interest in the fauna.

"Yup, we have this at home," my father declares, straightening up. "All the way in Lake Placid, New York." Just then, the rain lets up a little and a little slant of sun shines down onto us. My father notices and looks up into the sky. From where we stand, we can hear the light clanging of cowbells; the unseen cows are eating the sedge, and when night begins to fall, they will head back down into the valleys. Satjin told us this. The sky opens a little more and the sun pours onto us, all of a sudden, and so much like a gift that we have to blink our eyes in surprise.

"Looks like we're in God's pocket now," my father says, and takes off his glasses to clean them on his shirt.

We sit in our room as the sky darkens, and we wait for the rain to stop. We've opened the windows to let the cool night air in, because the mildew is making my father cough. We wait for the clouds to bleed from the sky and the stars to appear; we wait for the wind to empty of its flecks of rain. There is no sunset, only the lengthening shadow of night. We check the windows every few minutes, wiping the condensation from the glass with our fingers to peer out, but the mountains remain ghosts, shrouded in the incessant fog.

On the last morning of our trek, I wake up to my father saying my name. I pull my pillow over my head, but I can still hear him talking.

"You gotta see this," he says, and by the tone of his voice I know I won't be getting any more sleep this morning. This is the voice he uses when he wants my mother to come out and look at something in the sky—Jupiter, or the full moon, round and bright and illuminating the road and fields around our house. He used this voice the day he spotted a bear, a black momma bear with her two cubs, in the backyard of our house eating apples from the stubby crabapple at the edge of our property. "Pearl," he had said to my mother in a hushed, frantic whisper that morning. "You gotta see this!"

He says it with me now, and so I push the pillow off my face. He is standing by the door, his hat pulled down over his ears, his green puffy jacket unzipped, and he is pulling on gloves. He has tugged on his hiking boots without tying the laces and his socks have been hurriedly yanked on so that they stand at uneven heights on his shins.

"It's about to turn pink!" he tells me, and then he dashes out of the room, leaving the door wide open.

What is about to turn pink, I grumble to myself as I pull on thick socks, my fleece, my gloves, my hat. Even with the sunlight coming in, it's freezing in here, and I can see my breath. God, I hate being cold. I slide my glasses on last and then I stumble outside, cupping my hands to my face and blowing on them. But when I make it out the hotel's front door and see what he sees, what the clouds have concealed for days, I forget my numb fingers and the way my breath looks in the cold air.

The mountains are turning pink, that's what he meant. Past where he stands, at the lip of the ridge, I see the jagged edges of the Himalayas. We are closer to them than we've ever been in our lives. *Oh, God,* I say, because it's the closest thing to a prayer I can think of. And then I am crying. I can see the outline of my father's body before me, standing there, gazing at the mountains he has waited his whole life to see. He has imagined how they would look so many times, but all the hours he's spent studying maps, pictures, reading *National Geographic* and the chronicles of Sir Edmund Hillary and Jon Krakauer—none of that has prepared him for this. Mount Everest has never looked this way to him before.

They glisten in the sun, those mountains, and the morning is so very still, so perfectly clear. *Oh, my God,* I say again, my voice high and tight with emotion. When he turns, finally, to me, my father takes off his glasses and wipes them on his pants and I see that there are tears in his eyes, too. I can't remember ever seeing my father weep. He blinks and looks back and we just stand there, dazed, watching as the coat of pink rises up over the jagged peaks of silver.

Before we left for India, my father told me that the Himalayas were a Mecca for mountaineers like he. His home is in the mountains, the high peaks, the ranges that stretch all over New York State and Canada, breaking across the middle of North America and then starting up again in the west, running down the length of British Colombia and Montana, Colorado and Utah. These are the places, I think, that my father is most free. They are his church, they are where his God resides.

As the morning continues to swell open, continues to wash the earth in gold, my father and I search for a better place to watch the peaks. The clouds are already rising; soon they will sock us in, and so this could be our only chance. Not far from the lodge rises a short, steep pitch without a trail, and we scramble up it, passing our cameras to each other, glancing over our shoulders every few minutes to make sure the mountains haven't disappeared in the clouds. They are growing redder and redder with the movement of the sun.

We reach the top of the mound and discover that its knobby summit is swathed in prayer flags; they flap from every rock, every crag, every stubby bush. We have to push them out of our way at times to get to the top. When we look down either side of the ridge, we can see that the flags trail deep into the valley, curved lines of alternating red and white, blue and green, bright yellow squares. Satjin told us what the flags represented: blue is the sky, white is the wind, red is fire, green is the water, and yellow is the earth. From where we sit, we can look at those flags and feel all of the things that they mean, smell all of the elements in the wind. I want to tell my father how full I feel, how rich, sitting on that ridge beside him, but I don't. We have never really been that kind of family.

My father has lost his book. "I just had it," he says, more to himself than to me. I don't look up from my own novel; he will find it, I assume. He's always putting things down and then forgetting where. He's already in bed, in his sleeping bag, so he doesn't stand up, just looks in all the places he can reach: under the bed, beneath strewn-about clothes, on the nightstand. He rummages through his backpack, grumbling. But this seated search comes to no avail, and so he must stand.

He doesn't climb out of the sleeping bag; he just stands up in it and holds it up around his waist like he's competing in a sack race. I imagine that he does this because it is too cold to step out of the sleeping bag and onto the cold floor. He is barefoot; for as long as I can remember, my father has slept in the white JC Penny briefs my mom buys him. He hops around the room, sack in one hand, while with the other he moves things around, in search of the book.

"It's bright red," he remarks, opening the tall wardrobe at the other end of the room, a wardrobe he hasn't opened until that moment. "You'd think it would be obvious, where it is." Next, he jerks open the little drawer of a tiny dresser in the corner. This drawer, too, we haven't yet opened. I can't think why the book would be inside, and only now, when I laugh out loud, does he notice that I'm watching him. He looks at me, grinning, and shrugs his shoulders, holds his free hand out in front of him, palm up. He has done this motion for as long as I remember; it can mean many things—maybe he is mad at my brother, maybe he is tired of his administrator at work—but today it means that he is baffled, and he is willing to laugh at himself. I could get up and help him, but he looks so silly, his sleeping bag in hand, and so I lean back and watch.

"Did I bring it in here?" he asks himself, checking the bathroom. Of course he did not; all that's in there are our bottles of shampoo and conditioner and our tube of toothpaste. There isn't even a real shower in there, just a tap and a bucket and a toilet and a drain in the middle of the floor.

"I *just* had it," he mutters again, befuddled. He checks the wardrobe again, his backpack again, the bathroom again. He is looking in the funniest of places. He lifts the cushion by the window seat and checks there; he gets down on his knees, the sack still around him, and peers under the bed. Finally, he sits down on the bed, defeated.

"I don't know where it is," he says, and does that thing with his hand again, holding it out in front of him, palm outstretched. "I just don't know."

"I might have something else for you to read," I tell him, and reach into my pack for one of the books that I've already finished. While I'm digging, he fluffs his pillow, flips it, and finds the red book underneath.

Ridges covered in tea bushes; women under umbrellas, plucking the leaves. The smell of wet earth, wet clay, chai when we pass the smoky hut. The smell of the constant rain. The sugary smoke of fruit trees burning, an open fire, and the sweet hint of a jasmine branch that hangs over the road. Banana trees, their wide leaves bent and dripping. Gutters overflowing with brown water; a girl washing her hair in the street. She returns our driver's smile, her head still bent over, her hair to her knees. Wild orchids growing off the trunks of trees. Cardamom, corn. A toothbrush and toothpaste placed for safekeeping in the crack of a stone wall. Rain, rain, and a patch of blue sky. Rice paddies in layers; cardamom, corn. This is our drive to Sikkim.

In Yuksom, one of Sikkim's tiny hill towns, you can hike to a monastery at the top of the nearest mountain. The path is paved the whole way, a narrow, winding track with steep, even stairs, but you have to be careful, because the abundant rain of this region makes the going slick. The green moss is beautiful, though: emerald-soft. It's humid in this jungle, and we stop often to drink water.

But when we break out onto the ridgetop, the thick vegetation is replaced by a crisp and sudden wind, and there is the monastery, recently whitewashed and surrounded by neatly cropped grass. Both sides of the roof curve slightly to a point, upon which a big, brass bell is perched. There's no one around except a small, white cat who sits with her tail wrapped around her on the steps of the temple.

"A holy cat," my father says.

We have been to so many monasteries so far that we know just what to do—you can see a lot of monasteries in three days in Sikkim. First we walk all around the outside of the temple, admiring the carvings on the wooden columns and the luminous paint, rosy pink and pale blue, seafoam green. We can see that the monks take care with that careful paint, the manicured grass, the even hedge, but there aren't any here, not today, just the holy cat so far.

After we've circled the monastery, we take off our shoes and set them on the step, beside the heavy front door. It's been freshly painted red, a deep color like bricks, and the wood gleams in the afternoon sun. The door has been propped half-open, and we slip inside. Every monastery feels this way: dark on the inside, cool and silent. Each one has a smooth floor like this one, the boards wide and stained almost black. Every interior has this scent of old documents, of mildew, of the incense and candles that burn all the time, that are burning now, flickering and fragrant.

We circle the inside of the monastery, examining, as we have at each one before this, the stacked scrolls and the rich

embroidery of the tapestries, colored like jewels, that hang
everywhere. Every surface is adorned: framed photographs
of the Dalai Lama, artificial flowers, white silk scarves,
chunky candles. We clasp our hands behind our backs and
walk slowly around, and when we come to the tall red door
again, my father takes a bill from his pocket and slips it into
the offerings box. He has done this at every monastery; it has
become part of our viewing ritual.

When we step out of the monastery and into the sun, we
are surprised, as we always are, at how bright it is, how crisp
the wind feels. The holy white cat is cleaning her feet; she
freezes, watches us for a moment with big, blue eyes, and then
resumes washing. We sit on the step and lace our shoes. Two
small boys wander over; one squats a few feet away from us
and sets three marbles down in front of him. He arranges
them in a perfect line. The other one, the littler of the two, is
not wearing any pants or shoes, just an old T-shirt that's too
big for him. They watch us the way the cat does, perfectly still
and with eyes open wide.

"Namaste," I say to them.

"Na*ma*ste," my father says; he still cannot get it right. But
the boys think this is funny, and they glance at each other and
giggle. The littler one sits down on the grass. They both look
expectantly at my father. We finish lacing our shoes, and then
my father removes one of his hearing aids and holds it out to
the little boys.

"See?" he says to them, although I'm sure they can't understand. "It's for my ears." He taps his ear, empty of the aid, with
his index finger. He turns a tiny knob on the hearing aid so it
makes a tiny, high-pitched whine. The boys inch forward and
peer at it. My father sticks it back into his ear.

"Much better," he tells them, nodding and grinning. They
are entranced. The littlest boy's mouth is slightly open.

"Much better," my father says again.

For our last two days in India, I have convinced my father to splurge for a fancy hotel in Calcutta. I tell him that we'll need a comfortable place in order to survive the city.

"We need to see Calcutta, Dad," I told him, "otherwise we won't have really seen India." Of course that wasn't really true; I don't add that even if we visit every large Indian city, we will never, ever *really* see India; in ten years you couldn't see it all. In a lifetime you couldn't, because India has far too many faces to ever be known. But my faulty argument worked; my father agreed on the fancy hotel.

When we land in Calcutta, we are dusty and dirty, our packs stuffed with white scarves— gifts from the monks— and boxes and boxes of tea. At first we think we are in trouble when a tall man in a suit, a typed badge around his neck, approaches us at the baggage claim. He says my father's name, a question, and for a moment we both stare at this neat-looking man who knows us.

The man is telling my father that he has come from the hotel.

"Your ride is waiting," he informs us, then steps towards where I am standing, pressed up against the claim's revolving belt.

"Madam," he says to me, "let me get those for you. Please indicate to me which ones are yours." *Indicate to me which ones,* I say to myself, tucking that away. You don't hear words used like that every day. But I do, I indicate which ones, and my father and I are led in amazement to a white limousine that is waiting outside, as shiny as that red monastery door up in Yuksom. The driver lifts his hat for us; he is wearing a white suit and white shoes and when we climb into the car he offers us water and cool, scented towels. We ride the thirty minutes from the airport to the hotel in air-conditioned silence, marveling at the unexpected luxury a hotel reservation in India can bring, marveling too at the India that still clamors outside, the carts and rickshaws and cows and cars all sweating, all roiling, all moving to the pace of this hot afternoon.

"I wish your mother was here," my father says, once we've checked in and gone to our room and shut the heavy door. He has said this outside of the sky-blue temple in Sikkim, on the windy ridge on the first day of our trek, and on the morning we saw Mount Everest. "She'd kill us, if she knew we were here," my dad adds as we take in the plush pillows, the balcony with the marble floor, the luxurious bathroom with its deep, clean tub and its rose in a vase on the sink. We've peered inside the minibar at the bottles of expensive liquors, and in the closet, where wood hangers sit silently in a row, waiting to bear our unworthy garments.

"She would have loved this whole trip, don't you think?" he says, looking out at the pool. We cannot leave the door to the balcony open or else all the air conditioning will get sucked out, but my father stares down at the pool just the same, and for a moment I think that he leaves me. I think he goes to be with my mother, who is thousands of miles away across the ocean, waiting for us to come home.

The waiter at breakfast suggests we visit the flower market while we are in Calcutta. Immaculately polite, he brings us a map and draws out the route we must take to reach the market, which sits right on the shores of the River Hooghly. He speaks in perfect English: "You will love it there, madam," he assures me, refilling my coffee cup.

So my father and I pack water and money, our camera and the map with the delineated route, and we set out after breakfast towards the river. We pass the Royal Palace, the Botanical Gardens and the Central Park. We walk up and down the streets, whose sidewalks alternate between being very wide and almost nonexistent. We push past shoe shiners, juice makers, makeup sellers, potters. Men who fix watches; men who fix cars; men who sell saris. There is no time to talk, for all of the looking. At one point we have to hold hands as we push through a sidewalk market, cramming past bangles stacked on wooden poles, so as not to lose each other. When we finally reach the Hooghly, a wide, muddy strip, we can barely see to the other side because the smoke in the air is so thick.

We follow the waiter's map along the river; we move from a park, where lovers sit beneath trees or on benches, their arms around each other as they stare at us, to a slum, which reeks of urine and rotting vegetables and old, dead cars. Skinny, shirtless men without shoes walk past us, barely glancing at us, huge bales balanced on their heads. On either side of us, we can see into homes, shelters erected out of scrap metal and tarp and cardboard; we see tiny children and cooking fires that burn right on the floor.

This has to be right—that nice waiter wouldn't lie—but I'm suddenly scared, though I don't tell my father. This is not like the park, even with those uncomfortable stares from the lovers, and it is certainly not like our lush hotel, with its deep, blue pool and the tall, waving palms. It is not like the ridge that straddles India and Nepal; it is not like the planes, the airports, the taxis. It is like this: the roads that we drove past but didn't go down, the alleys we hurried by as we walked down the main streets. The big, black eyes of the little girls who squatted on the stoops of their huts and stared at us as we hiked past, drove past, rode past without stopping. I wonder what could happen to us here, my father and me, with our backpack jammed full. I want to hold his hand the way I did in the bangle market, or the way I did when I was just a little girl.

But when I glance at him, he does not seem scared; he is calm, his mouth relaxed and not set in that tense line, his hands in his pockets. And so I relax, and we walk, and we breathe. Eventually, of course, for that waiter knows his city, we begin to see piles of flowers for sale, big baskets of marigolds and roses, daisy petals, big stacks of leaves tied together, and pails of lilies. Irises, birds of paradise, and always those marigolds, yellow and orange like little suns. I want to take a picture.

"Give that guy some rupees," I tell my father, and while I gesture to my camera, point to the man's huge pile of marigold heads, my father passes over a ten. Another guy sees the exchange; he says something to my father, shaking his finger at us and grinning. I know that he is teasing my father—*I have flowers too!* I guess that he's telling us. *Take pictures of those!* After I snap the shot, both men slap my father on the back and waggle their heads and then watch us go, their hands on their hips, while we walk towards the bridge through the rest of the market.

Next, I take a picture of my father; he has his camera around his neck, and he is wearing a shirt he got twenty years ago in a running race. *Whiteface Mountain Annual Uphill*, it reads. Sponsored by Coca Cola. The rain has just begun; drops fleck onto his glasses as the market churns behind him. This is my father, tall and thin and grinning, a marigold petal on his sleeve. He has bent before monasteries to drop money into donation boxes, and he has stood on a ridge and looked out at Mount Everest, surrounded by flapping prayer flags, his hand shading his eyes. He has tasted the street food of Calcutta; he has sniffed the sedge on a wind-swept trail; he has walked through this market, flowers around him, and he has closed his eyes to the scent of it, taking it in.

≈≈ ≈≈ ≈≈

Kate McCahill is a writer, reacher, and visual artist. She recently returned from a year of riding buses through Latin America, and now lives with her cat, Pants, in Santa Fe, New Mexico.

PAT RYAN

≈ ≈ ≈

Where Things Happen

The "third" in "third world" can be an existential
multiplier, not a mark of poverty.

*One recent winter I spent five months wandering around East
Africa. I flew into Nairobi, Kenya, and flew back from Cape
Town, South Africa. In between I had many interesting adventures. I climbed Mt. Kilimanjaro and Mt. Kenya, went on safaris
and visited semi-forgotten ancient ruins. For the first month or so,
I traveled with a Polish guy named Marius I met during a layover
in London. He's a short, stocky punk rocker with a shaved head,
lots of tattoos, and a fondness for camouflage. I'm tall and gangly
with crazy long hippie hair, so you might appreciate the image
of our traveling partnership. Indeed, the amount of laughter we
seemed to cause everywhere was enough to make the entire journey worthwhile . . . but then this other stuff happened too.*

We arrive in the town of Tanga on the coast of
Tanzania shortly after finishing our safari in the
Ngorongoro Crater. Our original plan is to go directly to the
island of Zanzibar for some rest and relaxation on the world
famous beaches. But when we learn that it is possible to take a
ferry to the smaller island of Pemba from where we can connect to another ferry for Zanzibar, we decide to take a small
detour. Unfortunately, the ferry from Tanga only runs on

Tuesdays and we arrive on a Saturday so we have to wait for a few days. No matter, we buy ourselves a nice bag of local weed, get a room with a balcony overlooking the ocean and proceed to amuse ourselves by socializing with the good citizens of Tanga.

When Tuesday arrives, we ditch the marijuana before catching the ferry because there is supposed to be a customs inspection on Zanzibar. Hopefully, we'll be able to get more after arrival. The boat trip across the ocean takes about five hours. Docking the boat on the island, however, takes another three hours because there is no jetty or dock and it's low tide. We end up having to slog through ankle deep mud in order to reach the shore. Customs inspection is minimal. A single officer in a plain wooden shack has to process all hundred or so people who disembark from the ferry. He looks at my passport and waives me through without searching me at all. Nevertheless, I'm still glad I got rid of the contraband before the process. Formalities complete, we follow the crowd up a steep path and into the town of Wete on the north side of the island.

Wete is a Muslim place . . . a very Muslim place. All the women wear a dark black covering over their whole bodies except the tiny slits for their eyes and all the men wear long pants and long sleeve shirts even though the temperature is around 100 degrees. The Koran teaches that both men and women should be modest in dress and these people take their religion very seriously. Wandering around in shorts and a t-shirt while looking for a place to stay, I feel like I am half naked. Nevertheless, the people don't seem offended by my attire. To the contrary, they seem amused by my strangeness and they all greet me with smiles and nods. Ultimately, we find a nice but inexpensive place to stay where we are welcomed by a very friendly older man. He's not the kind of guy to ask about marijuana though so instead we ask about swimming. He gives us directions to a nearby spot and that's where we go after dropping our backpacks in the room.

But the swimming hole is a shithole that no sane person would immerse himself in. No doubt the local kids are taking the plunge but I am not the least bit tempted even though the temperature hovers around a hundred. It's just a tiny opening between the mangroves with lots of floating plastic bags and bottles.

That's the thing about Pemba which separates it from Zanzibar. Zanzibar has perfect blue waters, endless white sand beaches and an almost infinite number of tourist hotels to choose from. Pemba is covered with overgrown mangroves so it has almost no beaches and therefore no tourists. It's a totally different universe. Pemba is also 99 percent Muslim and alcohol is not a part of their culture so finding beer here is nearly impossible. So we are on an island but there are no beaches, no grass, no booze and the women are covered from head to toe. What in the hell can we possibly do for fun here?

In the evening, the hotel owner informs us that there is indeed a beach on Pemba. It's called Vumawimbi beach but it's very hard to get to. There's no public transport; it's 25 kilometers away and the road is very very rough. We can rent bicycles if we want but the journey will be extremely difficult. I, however, disagree with the assessment of difficulty. Fifty kilometers round trip on a bicycle should be easy. That's only 30 miles. I do that almost every day back home. So we agree to rent the bikes and plan the excursion for the following morning.

Fifty kilometers in one day is no problem on my nice 20 speed expensive American made bike on well-paved roads in comfortable temperatures in upstate New York. Fifty kilometers round trip on a one speed, very old, half broken, very small, Chinese bicycle with a basket on the front on the worst roads on the planet in hundred degree temperatures is a whole different transportation reality. Visualize the absurdity: A peaceful African village on an island in the middle of nowhere calmly going about its day- to-day activities when all of a sudden, two crazy *muzungus* (Swahili for white guy) come pedaling through on shitty old bicycles that are way, way too small for them. In the first hour or so, we pass through four such villages and the following conversation takes place no less than 100 times.

Local man: "*Jambo!*" (hello in Swahili).

Pat and Marius: "*Jambo!*"

Local man: "Mambo vipee?" (how are you?)

Pat and Marius: "*Poa.*" (good or fine).

Local man: "*Karibu sana.*" (very welcome).

Pat and Marius: "Asante." (thank you).

Admittedly, the conversations are extremely short because my knowledge of Swahili is limited and I am speeding by on a bicycle (well, O.K., not exactly speeding). But just imagine having literally hundreds of people welcome you to their island. Real welcomes too; not just words, but smiles and gestures with honest enthusiasm. In addition to the remarkably friendly adults, there are the kids. They all shout "Muzungu! Muzungu!" or "Hello, hello," or "Good morning." Oh what a bizarre sight Marius and I must be. But they have no fear whatsoever. Nothing but openness and welcome. I can't help but think of my own country. What would happen if two black Muslim guys came riding through a suburban neighborhood on bicycles. How would they be received?

About an hour or so into the ride, tragedy strikes. Marius gets a flat tire. Now what? We have no spare and no pump. We are stuck. We have to walk the bicycles. But we manage to make it to the next tiny village. I am not exaggerating in the least when I say that the entire village comes out to help Marius fix his flat. They all gather around us to shake our hands and welcome us . . . "No problem the bicycle. We can fix."

About ten of them actually work to take the tire off and patch the leak while the rest just gather around and smile and pat our backs and shake our hands. "Look. How cool? There's *muzungus* in our village." Eventually, they fix our tire and we continue on our way. After several more hours of very hard riding we come to a forest. The trail goes through the forest and past several more villages. The farther and farther we go, the more primitive the villages become. By the time we get close to the beach, the villages are nothing but houses made of reeds and lots of half-naked children running around. But still, it is the same. "Look at those crazy *muzungus*. What are they doing here? Welcome strangers. Welcome strangers."

When we finally get to the beach, it's downright amazing. It's several kilometers long with gorgeous white sand backed by palm trees and forest with absolutely nobody on it. The water is shallow so we have to walk a ways out on a sandbar to swim. I can hardly believe that a beach of this size is absolutely empty . . . Yeah, that's right, life is very very good. Why haven't the Western developers taken over this place and spoiled it with big fancy hotels yet? I don't' know. But I hope they never do.

The journey back from the beach is more of the same except that I am absolutely worn out and somewhat overwhelmed with heat exhaustion. The crazy Muzungu thing takes on a whole new dimension as I start to hallucinate. Who needs marijuana? Just push the body to absurd extremes in torturous heat; wow, what a buzz. . . . *Muzungu! Muzungu!* Welcome! Welcome! Smiling happy faces jumping up and down. Is this really the planet Earth? I didn't think people could have so much fun. And these people have nothing by our standards, absolutely nothing . . . no electricity, no television, no indoor plumbing, no computers, no iPods, no iPads. They do have food; plenty of it I think: fish and fruit and rice.

But they have nothing else. Yet they seem so damn happy? How is it possible?

Somehow, we make it back to the guesthouse and I don't die from the effort. I have a good meal and then lie on my back in the room under the ceiling fan. A day like today makes me think. I'm not one who idolizes the primitive, subsistence lifestyle. I don't exactly believe that we should abandon all Western luxuries and live simple lives. And I do realize that people in these villages have hard lives and they suffer and they die and it's not paradise. But still, there's something about it; something pure, something beautiful; something that I'm having a difficult time expressing. I guess it's this: In the Western world, we are taught by the media and the government and the religious institutions that we are supposed to pity and feel sorry for the suffering in the Third World. Theoretically, the rest of the world needs the First World to help them progress and develop. But the reality I experienced explicitly contradicts this notion. Honestly, I see more happy smiling kids in one day on Pemba than I have seen in the U.S. in the last forty years. If the purpose of our constitution and government is truly to help citizens pursue happiness, then maybe, just maybe, we have as much to learn from the Third World as they have to learn from us.

The next morning, we leave Wete and travel by very crowded mini-bus (dalla dalla) to the town of Chake Chake in the middle of the island. Once again, it's a Muslim place so there is no beer or weed anywhere to be found. What the heck can we do? The guidebook recommends some stone ruins on the end of Mkumba peninsula as a good destination. It's only 40 kilometers round trip but the road is really bad and there is no public transport. Should we rent bicycles again? If only we could get some decent ones. Surprise, surprise; we meet a guy who says he can get us mountain bikes, real mountain bikes.

All right then, that'll be easy; only 40 kilometers round trip is no problem on a mountain bike.

Rather remarkably, the guy is true to his word and shows up at our hotel with decent mountain bikes. So once again, for the second time in three days, we set out on a long bicycle journey through the villages of Pemba. I don't think it's possible but the road on the second journey is even worse than the first. Imagine the most difficult mountain bike course possible with steep down-hills, jumps, sand traps, potholes, mud holes, rocks and everything else. Then throw in some hundred degree African heat and you pretty much have the scenario. Not only that, this time, the villages we go through are even more and more remote. The farther we get from Chake Chake, the less and less they seem to have. I mean; these people have nothing. Nothing but straw houses and food and hot sun. But shit, they sure can smile. And they can shout *muzungu* very loudly. And they all wave and jump up and down. A crazy *muzungu* on a bicycle riding through their remote villages is an uncommon and very exciting occurrence.

But it seems like a lot longer distance than twenty kilometers from Chake Chake to the ruins. It feels like the peninsula points out into the ocean forever and ever. "This has to be the last village." "No, there's another one up ahead." And then another one and another one. On and on we pedal, through the heat, the intense unbearable heat. I sure hope there's a place to swim near the ruins or I will never be able to make the return trip.

Finally, we reach the last village and people in the village point towards a path that leads to the Ras Mkumba ruins. As we head towards the path, two teenagers follow us. We keep on going as they run along beside us. After a while, the trail splits into two trails and the teenagers have to show us the way. We keep on pedaling. Again, the path diverges and the two chasing teenagers show us the way. After what seems an eternity, we reach the spot. Truthfully, the ruins aren't much, just a couple of fallen down stone walls. I like ruins and all, but this is pretty mediocre. Nicely though, there is a small but perfect beach right next to the ruins. So we go for a swim and relax as the two teenagers try to make conversation with us. They don't speak English and we don't speak Swahili so the conversation is rather limited. Mostly they just point and laugh as crazy Marius goes through his karate routine in the sand. After an hour or so, it's time to head back. And that's when the miracle happens.

Marius has the idea so he deserves the credit. As we head back the way we came with the teenagers running along beside again, he stops his bike and offers one of the teenagers a ride on the crossbar. Accordingly, I offer a ride to the other one. Have you ever experienced a spontaneous eruption of pure joy? You know what I mean: A baby is born, you discover love, you sink the winning shot in the championship game . . . Something happens that is so wonderful, so terrific, so fantastic the good feeling bubbles forth and expands until it seems to take over the entire universe. When we ride into the village with the two teenagers on our bicycles it is truly one of the most amazing experiences of my entire life. It's like a parade or carnival and we are the stars of the show. The entire village comes running out of their huts. They are all jumping up and down and laughing and smiling and God . . . I can't explain it. I've never seen anything like it. I feel like a hero coming home after victory. Joy . . . happiness . . . glory . . . Can the world really be this wonderful? They shout out the names of the teenagers. They shout out "*Muzungu! Muzungu!*" The old people are laughing, the adults are laughing, the young people are laughing. It's like some kind of miracle and that's all I have to say.

Sure enough though, all that goodness, something is bound to go wrong afterwards. After we leave the village behind, we still have a long ways to go. We are descending a steep, bumpy hill when the accident occurs. Truthfully, I'm not really sure how it happens, but a complex thought runs through my head as I fly head first over the handlebars . . . fuck . . . it's a long goddamn ways to a hospital if I break a leg. The bicycle flips over on top of me and the gears slam into my shin as I crash more or less head first onto the ground. The pain is intense and I think for a second that it might be broken . . . oh shit oh shit . . . very bad place for a broken bone. . . . But it's nothing; just a flesh wound. I have a nice big gash below the knee and the blood looks rather gruesome as it drips down my leg but nothing is broken. Yeah sure, I spilled a little blood on African soil . . . but at least it didn't kill me.

So the last 15 kilometers of the ride back are quite a challenge. If I was a crazy *muzungu* riding through the villages before, just imagine how much more crazy I look as blood drips down my leg. But we make it back. And the gods reward us for our efforts with some double bonus points. As we return the mountain bikes to the guy, thank him and express our surprise at the quality of the bicycles in such a remote place, he responds, "No problem. You want mountain bikes. I get mountain bikes. This my island. I born here. Anything you want or need, I can find."

"Anything?" I say, thinking about the fact that we have been marijuana and alcohol free since we arrived on Pemba four days ago.

"Anything!" he replies with a knowing smile.

It sure is a beautiful universe. God damn I love this island . . .

⋇ ⋇ ⋇

Pat Ryan works seasonally in upstate New York doing landscape stonework. Because of the snow and ice that comes in the New York winter, he works only from early April until early November. In the winter months, he goes traveling for four or five months a year. In the last thirteen years, he's been to forty countries on five continents. Visit his website www.patryantravels.com.

≈ ≈ ≈

Negrita

It's more than just paint on a Saigon wall.

More than half a century ago, sometime in the 1950s, a small triangle of vacant land lay at the confluence of Tran Hung Dao and Nguyen Cu Trinh Streets. Its address today is 148 Tran Hung Dao, on the way west to Cho Lon. Sometime back in those olden days, it might even have been in the waning days of French rule, a billboard size advertisement was painted on the eastern wall of the adjacent building. The ad was for Negrita Rum, a very popular tipple here from earliest French days to Reunification in 1975 when it pretty much disappeared. But until that time it was the drink of choice for many Foreign Legion soldiers, their heirs the American G.I.s, and who knows how many hard drinking journalists. The ad features Chinese script, which is appropriate to one's destination should you see it driving westward down the street.

Negrita Rum (the French spell it "rhum") was first blended and labeled in 1847 by the Bardinet Company of France. And Bardinet still produces it. It's the most popular rum in Spain and high on the list in other European countries. It's a blended rum, being made in distilleries on Reunion, Guadeloupe, and Martinique islands. It's the Martinique element that gives Negrita its distinctive taste. Rums of Martinique are "agricole" rums. They are made from sugar cane juice, not molasses, a by-product of the refining process.

The painted ad on Tran Hung Dao (in the French time known as Rue Marine, or Sailor Street) would have beckoned thousands of soldiers and sailors as they headed into Cho Lon for nights of debauchery at the House of 500 girls. It would have stimulated the thirst of gamblers flocking to Le Grande Monde. The dark lady on the label might have winked at Graham Greene as he scoured the steamy streets for atmo to spice up *The Quiet American*. She was part of a neighborhood and a city whose former character is now almost entirely gone. But she has been (temporarily) preserved. In 1960 the Metropole hotel was built on that triangle of land, hard against the adjacent building, sealing up the commercial art as a time capsule. Through all the subsequent decades of war, upheaval, high times and low, change, change and hyper change, the painted Negrita slept.

She had not been seen for fifty years, until December, 2010. With yet another tower in mind, developers demolished the Metropole, revealing that shrouded bit of bibulous history. I stopped in my tracks when I saw her. I must have stood and contemplated her for ten minutes, imagining all the people and events that she had witnessed, and those she had slept through. I resolved to have a drink of Negrita. I had to have a sip of Saigon history. But where to find something that disappeared decades ago?

I called my bibulous buddies. Michael Kloster, formerly of Black Cat fame and now with The Vine Group wine merchants; Linh Phanroy of Gringo's Bar; and Charlie Wong the Hot Dog King of Saigon: all went to work and did their best. But the search seemed to be in vain. Kloster managed to locate a bottle in Phnom Penh and was standing by to have it "transferred." Phanroy promised to invent a dedicatory cocktail for it upon arrival. But King Charlie's network of informants and operatives proved unmatched. As we sat despondently one night nursing our suds at the Drunken Duck, a dusty and battered old *xe om* arrived at the door. Both driver and vehicle looked hard-ridden. A barman was dispatched to meet him. A fat wad of cash changed hands. A bottle of Negrita rum was set before me. It was a thing of beauty.

We four repaired to my quarters. With due ceremony I cracked the bottle. I poured four measures. We toasted Old Saigon. We tasted. How was it? Well may you ask. "She weren't a goer," as an Aussie might say. But she weren't bad, neither. I didn't care. I tasted Old Saigon, and that was more than enough for me. Phanroy made good on his promise. He combined equal measures of café sua da, Kalua and Negrita. He calls it the Negringa.

I plan to make that bottle last until the Negrita ad is once more consigned to darkness, no doubt for good this time. I pass by that echo of Old Saigon every day on my way home. And every day in my mind I drink a silent toast to her. And she replies, "I just came back to say goodbye."

≈≈ ≈≈ ≈≈

Richard Sterling is the author and editor of many books, including a travel memoir The Fire Never Dies, *the Lowell Thomas award-winning anthology* Food: A Taste of the Road, How to Eat Around the World, *and numerous Lonely Planet guides. He served in the United States Navy for seven years during the Vietnam War, and now lives in Saigon. (Editors' note: The Negrita ad has since been covered up again, but you can see it here: http://www.panoramio.com/photo/46830955.)*

JESSICA WILSON

⚜ ⚜ ⚜

What the Trees Try to Tell Us We Are

Injuries. Mountains. Love.

... Arranging by chance
To meet as far this morning
From the world as agreeing
With it, you and I
Are suddenly what the trees try
To tell us we are:
That their merely being there
Means something; that soon
We may touch, love, explain ...

—JOHN ASHBERY, "SOME TREES"

It started in the White Mountains. I don't mean the tumor—that came later, or at least I found out about it later. I mean the rest of it. My myth of disunion.

It was summer camp and we were eleven and there were twelve of us, and two counselors, and one overnight trip. Does it matter where we were? It wasn't about specificity, we didn't know about wildlife, we couldn't name plants. But we threw ourselves into the rocks and the dirt and the green, we gasped our way down southern slides stone-strewn and northern ones steep and bald. We loped along summit ridges and watched our skin grow dust-matted, turning the precise copper-brown of the duff beneath our feet, and then streak with beaded and rolling sweat. The loping and gasping brought the pleasure of novelty, carried out by limbs grown gangly so that every step was to some degree an experiment. We carped at each other for picking the chocolate chips out of the trail mix; we dangled our feet red and swollen into icy streams; we exulted at every peak. Green, green, green. Light on the glittering lakes below.

A week later my knees looked like water bladders filled to bursting. If you want to prevent muscle strain, my counselor had said, lock your knees. She demonstrated. I practiced. So I had spent those three days, up and down peaks, popping my knees violently in and out of lock with every step. Assiduous like only a sixth-grade overachiever can be. The advice, my doctor told me afterwards, was the worst advice I could have taken. There wasn't any way of knowing what I'd done to my cartilage. I hobbled around for another ten days, and eventually the swelling went down. Ever since: the specter of knee pain, hovering ready, sharp and gummy. Ever since: dreams of the mountains. Fevered dreams, subtle dreams. Dreams that lie in wait. We are wearing each other down, the mountains and me.

As for the tumor, it started on a train platform, fifteen years later. I mean the awareness. I had just left the orthopedist with a backpack full of knee braces and an appointment for an orthotics fitting. This after three years of pain on city streets. Foot pain, this time, but that story comes later. I wanted to go back to the mountains so badly the only way I could say it was offhandedly. It was that or cry. Too girly. On this particular day, though, I wanted to celebrate. The braces, the orthotics: the scallop shell of my Camino, the rising hope.

While I wait for a train back into the city, my phone buzzes with a restricted number, and when I answer it, the physician's assistant is on the other end. "The X-ray we took," he says. "Of your knee. The radiologist looked at it. Your knee is fine."

"Oh that's great," I say.

"But," he says.

But? I think.

"But the X-ray turned up a bone lesion," he says. "In the left tibia."

"A lesion," I repeat. "In the left tibia. I—what? What does that mean?" I ask. (*The tibia*, I am thinking, and trying to remember back to seventh grade anatomy. *That's the shin?*)

"It's a small tumor," he answers. "A bone tumor. We call this an incidental finding. We'd like you to get an MRI."

I have a tumor?

I have to write this down, I think, but I don't have a pencil so I am patting my pockets with my free hand as we speak, trying to find one; and when my pockets yield nothing I start patting the rest of my body, like I think I might find a pencil hidden in my ear, on the top of my head, like there must be something in arm's reach to hold onto. A train car rumbles by on the other side of the tracks, so now I am yelling into the phone and my coat is whipping across my thighs.

With my phone hand I am pressing the cellphone into my cheek. It will leave a mark. He is talking. I am patting my nose, my shoulders. This tumor. It's in the bone, a permanent brand. Two centimeters by one and I don't know how thick. A spot, a smear. A warped dime, or a torn-off bit of gaff tape, littering the canals of my shinbone. I want it to erode. An MRI, he says again, there are any number of reasons for such a lesion, something something better to be sure, small chance of malignancy. The probability, he says, is slim.

Possibility, that's a wide word. A spread-your-arms-in-the-sunlight word. Probability, though—probability's just waiting to fuck you.

Bodies. Landscapes. Stories we invent thereof. I was twenty years old and I left college and I went back to New Hampshire, back to my mountains. Nine years since summer camp but I'd returned most summers, kayaked in the broads of Lake Winnipesaukee and picked blueberries from the squat bushes running over the grey granite tops of Mounts Welch and Dickey. But then I got older, I took summer jobs, got distracted with School and My Future, and the mountains fell away. Two years into college I was sick of theories. I wanted something I could touch. I wanted the woods again. I moved to a state park and spent a year as a service volunteer, living in a cabin with no electricity and eighteen other volunteers. We chopped wood, served soup, taught school, built trails.

Again I fell in love, and first it surprised me, the suddenness, the absoluteness. Then it surprised me that it surprised me. It was the most inevitable thing I knew, this love. I was in love with the workings of rock, slow leverages. With wind on my face and arms growing strong and trails opening below our picks and mattocks. With the deep silence of white snow on white pines under midwinter moonlight. In love with the gaudy, baptismal chartreuse of the first leaves of April. We were building a turnpike in the park, embedding flat stones alongside a muddy trail to hold in a gravel fill that would raise the tread above the water running below; and my friend Josh, who was on the same trail crew, brandished a rock bar in the direction of the spring woods all around us and flung his arms open. *This is my job!* he yelled, and it echoed *job ob ob* through the wooded and reverberate hills, and then we were all whooping, stomping in circles around our worksite, dancing a berserk sort of spring dance in our work shirts and yellow hard hats, waving a scattershot assortment of unwieldy hand tools like offerings to the spirits of the place, the odd pair of safety goggles flying off into the baby oaks.

I was careful with my knees, but twisted my foot that summer one week up on Mount Monadnock; it swelled so each morning I could hardly flex my toes. An hour into the day, I could walk around, gathering stones for drainage and cutting timber waterbars, but by evening I would be lame again. I had to ease it into my workboots the rest of the season. It took a good two years to heal completely, long after I'd rolled up my sleeping bag and gone back to college.

The climbing of mountains is a love that shows itself in motion. Every step whisks a fine layer of earth away, even as the ground presses upward, grinding my joints into one another. There is no love that does not damage us both at least a little bit, no matter the clattering joy of scree tumbling down the mountainside, no matter any catalyzed desire to watch over and protect the land. Meanwhile peaks crumple upwards where plates collide, bubble in magma where they separate. This is the mountains' own motion, a metamorphosis too grand and slow for human eyes to see. Still, we are both moving. Perhaps all it takes to become like a mountain is to live long enough. Arthritics become tectonics. Tumors become tremors. The world shakes, and the world shakes. But it's been over two hundred years since the last great earthquake in New England. The only fault lines are my own.

In proper tales things happen in threes. What choice did I have but to go back to the land? Three years after I left that New Hampshire park, by the time my foot had healed, I flew to Georgia and started walking north on the Appalachian Trail. Of all the reasons I had for going the simplest was this: I wanted, again, to be whooping and berserk and head over heels.

And I was.

The Trail winds some 2200 miles up the Appalachian range, Georgia to Maine; every year a couple thousand hikers aim to do the whole thing in a season. At best fifteen percent of them make it the whole way. I thought I'd be among the lucky. Doesn't everyone?

It wasn't my knees that undid me, though it could have been. Four days and thirty miles in, my knees were launching a full-scale rebellion and I was picking my way painfully down every slope, popping Advil six at a time. But a fellow hiker, a Marine Corps vet who went by the name Weatherman, said he had a pair of high-end orthopedic knee braces he didn't need anymore and did I want them? He could have his wife bring them with her to the next town up the trail. When they came I eyed them askance. They were massive things, hinged titanium, stretching from mid-calf to mid-thigh. Wearing them I looked like a cyborg. People who passed me hiking looked appalled, like: what is a cripple doing all the way out here, and with a pack that big? I didn't care. The braces worked. They kept me walking.

And yet, it turned out, to minister to one kind of harm was not enough to prevent others, nor to encourage me to pause, to think, to try to gently separate them, love and destruction. This spirit, this body, and all of these mountains: too tangled too tell top from talus. And so I pushed too hard and too far. I decided it would be a good idea to walk twenty-plus miles for days in a row, without stopping between to rest. Somewhere in there I twisted the same foot I'd injured years before; and then something tore; and then it was worse and worse and finally, eleven hundred miles in, I knew that if I did not stop walking I might not walk again.

The doctor said it wasn't broken. Just battered and torn and strained.

"What do I do," I said.

"Wait," he said. "You wait."

The clouds were hazy and heavy the day I went home. The doors were locked and I had no key so I climbed in a window, and not thirty seconds later the first thunderclap sounded, and the rain sheeted down. It was a closed parenthesis, and a pathos so obvious I felt absurd. But later I went for walks in my neighborhood, frowned at the concrete, wandered into the woods, stood on the verge of the valley and looked out over the summer trees. I thought about my season in the mountains, about my battered body, about how with every mile it had seemed that a story was unfolding, that it, and I, were becoming something vast and new. And I thought about how I'd been afraid that when I came back I'd decide the story wasn't worth telling. And for a moment—for as long as the moment lasted—I wanted to tell a story as big as the sky.

Instead I took a job at an outfitters' where one state route crossed another; when they put me on the front cash registers, I watched from where I stood as the headlights grew brighter and the sun dimmed. I had a manager so enamored of corporate-speak he offered me 'an exciting opportunity to interact with product as it enters the store!' when what he wanted me to do was unload the truck.

And here we are three years later. When they X-rayed my knees they said: Is there any chance you might be pregnant? I said no. That was true then. I don't know whether it's still true. What I mean is: my period is late.

So: maybe a baby. If there is a baby it is Jonathan's. I flew to San Francisco two weeks ago. Right after the phone call on the train platform. We are apart, we are together, we cannot figure how or whether to do this thing. I got a diaphragm. I didn't want to go on the pill; I was afraid it would make me fat and crazy.

I am afraid of what might in me be growing. I am afraid of what is shaking loose.

A year earlier, when we still lived so close I could see his door from my window, before he left for a postdoc on the

West Coast, before we broke up and slid back together in a joining with no clarity but some desperation, before all that:

We lay together lazily. His hair tufted and twisted beneath my fingers. Skin to skin.

"If we were Maasai," he said, "I would pay many cows for you."

"If I were Margaret Thatcher," I said, "and you were a republican prisoner in the IRA, I'd grant you political status in a heartbeat."

"If we were Yamomami," he said, "I would start a war with a neighboring village to make you mine."

"If I were Rosie the Riveter," I said, "and you survived the war, I'd let you have your job back. But I would probably still wear pants a lot of the time."

We kissed each other's eyelids and slept in spoons. Now he is so much rocky terrain away. I am sitting in my room, reading through snarky e-cards online to keep myself from Googling bone cancer or thinking about fetuses. *If you were pregnant*, reads one card, *I'd MapQuest directions to the abortion clinic for you.* A wry smile. Unfunny.

I cannot be pregnant and cancerous at once. The thing is too ridiculous. Ionesco in my living room, a rhinoceros in my uterus. Is a pregnancy panic a luxury? I'm twenty-six, after all. I'm no knocked-up sixteen year old. I sound like an aging rocker in denial, that empty protestation, *too young*. But what if I did and what if I didn't and what if there isn't and what if there is—

Jaime comes over at the end of a Saturday in which I meant to do a thousand things and instead barely managed to get out of my pajamas. "I spent six hours today," I say, "reading a medical blog."

I don't tell her about my period being late. I don't tell anyone, except Jonathan, and I toss it off casually to him: "How are you," he asks, and I say I'm okay, will be glad when this MRI nonsense is over, would be better if my period would come, but you know, not bad. "It's late?" he says, and I hear the perking concern.

"Oh, well, not *very* late," I say. "I'm sure it'll come in the next few days. No need to panic."

"Okay," he says, and even though I cannot see him I know exactly how his brow is smoothing.

The strongest longing comes from a distance. See also: *absence,* and *heart; grass, greener; wanting,* and *what you don't have.* I have been living in the city for three years. It is likely that I'm being ungrateful. The Charles is beautiful; I walk the bank in loopy miles, lulled by the grassless voice of the river, willing my foot to stop aching. Still, I feel hemmed in by the buildings, by the cars, by the noise that never abates.

I find myself resisting my own claustrophobia. I love the Common, the dogs and babies and geese and grass of it all, the toddlers squatting over brass ducklings and the wedding parades. Why shouldn't it be enough? I am inclined, on glum days, to see it as a moral failure, or at least a failure of imagination. I'm a shitty naturalist so it's not like I even have that as an excuse. I wouldn't know bloodroot if they sold it at Whole Foods.

In the meantime I am *still* limping, and that's on paved roads and carrying nothing. Probably, I think, I ought to forget about the mountains. I ought to stay away. Because how else can you build a life in which you can stand to be elsewhere? You cannot be always in the mountains.

I do not know what to do with this most material longing. I try to talk around it, to think it into behaving. That is the sort of thing I do. But that does not stop it organically rising. I might as well try and theorize breathing. Now there is this fear that I have waited too long to go back to the mountains, that this my only body will never carry me there. That there will be no children. I am young but no longer quite so young. It all runs together. The rich brown of duff, the million shades of earth. A sunset. One. Many. *Here is what I know:* if you thump a sapling with your palm, its leaves will shudder like rain. And spiders with bellies the colors of pumpkins, and fallen crumbs a stone an ant a world—

Two weeks later the waiting room is lit patchily in fluorescent pools. The lights in the hospital corridors aren't on yet, so the few offices that are open are small scattered islands of half-light, and everything is shot with dim. It is too early and I am so tired and the other woman in the waiting room, who in a rumpled sweatshirt looks frail and scared for all that she must be sixty and three times heavier than me, is trying to get answers from the desk attendant, who is terse and brusque with her. Probably the attendant, who has circles under her eyes, is as tired as the rest of us, but still I hear her snapping at the older woman—telling her she can't have the MRI yet, she has to get approval or pretesting from somebody-or-other, and the older woman saying, But I'm supposed to get a breast biopsy in four hours, and they need the MRI in order to do it, and the attendant saying, Well you'll just have to reschedule the biopsy then, and the older woman with confusion in her eyes saying But—and I ache in a way I cannot pinpoint, part anger and part grief and part fear. The older woman's head and shoulders have rolled forward, slowly, by a bare few degrees, as if pressed by a great heaviness, and suddenly I see my grandmother and her sister and my three aunts who have all had breast cancer in the last ten years and then I think about the bracelet I am wearing, which was my grandmother's grandmother's once. It is large and metal and I should never have worn it here, I was dressing for work, I have to go to work after the scan is over, they told me no jewelry, what was I thinking? I take off the bracelet, and take off my earrings, find a pocket in my bag, zip them up, tuck them away.

Twenty minutes later I am still sitting there. I let fall my copy of *Under the Devil's Thumb,* which I've been pretending to read. I can't read. But Gessner is distracting, which I am and am not thankful for. My eyes drop back down to my lap.

Fall on a paragraph. Being outdoors, he says. *It does more than it has any reasonable right to,* or something thereabouts.

That landscape. I think of my New England and I think of walking through Virginia, those last weeks before the pain got bad. I think of it because it was beautiful, and because I was happy, and because it was before I tore apart my foot, before three years of undiagnosed plantar fasciitis, before the doctors who didn't disbelieve me when I said my knees wouldn't take pounding but suggested maybe I should come back in after abusing them again for a little while, before the German-accented orthopedist who barked "CHUMP! CHUMP! You're fine!" like some kind of orthofascist as I hopped and flailed about his office with my quick-dry pants hiked up, before the bone tumor edged its way in on the knee X-ray like it wanted to join the party. But mostly I think of Virginia because that whole time was haloed with the conviction of walking home. The scree on the mountain, the sun over the broads, some kind of immanent holiness, God help me. Fall on your knees. Don't mind if I do.

When they call my name at last they ask me if I've ever been around welding. "No," I say, "unless you count some soldering in eighth grade jewelry-making." They ignore this. They do not ask me if I'm pregnant. I do not think they ask me if I'm pregnant. I don't think I'd lie, and I don't think I'd forget having to say—maybe. But I do not remember their asking, even though later, when I carry out a post-facto internet search, I will learn that it's a standard question. Instead they make me take off my bra so that the underwire won't go flying toward the magnet. I change into a flimsy paper gown and walk the hallway to the scanning room with a paper-filled fist clenched shut at my lower back. On the way I make eye contact with the older woman, who in the meantime has changed into her own ridiculous gown. She must have talked the attendant into letting her have the scan after all. We look at each other, in our twin Kleenex caftans, and I recognize her rueful expression, like she realizes it is a lost cause to try to look dignified wearing one of these things, but one must keep up appearances.

Afterwards the tech tells me he "uh, hopes it'll be nothing." By the way I have "really intense musculature." Am I "an athlete or something?" Or something, I tell him, and again I am thinking of the mountains.

They say mountains breathe. Daily, in long slow exhalations, in curling lifts of mist after a night's airy intakes. I never noticed this myself. But on this morning, in this particular held breath, here is what I want: take me farther, farther, onward, backward, elseways, someplace, any place, no place, to the place where even the mountains are moved.

The tumor ends in the airport parking lot. The Pennsylvania hills rise bluely in the distance. The day is misty and clammy and slate-grey. I've come off a plane. And the phone buzzes in my pocket, and I answer it, and again I'm fumbling for a pen, trying to solidify the words coming disembodied into my ear while the cars drive by, while my feet stand still. It is not so much that there is a delay over the phone lines as it is that there is a delay in my comprehension: words like *solitary,* words like *benign.* "We'll keep an eye on it," he says; "get a follow-up X-ray in a year," he says. "To be sure."

So it is benign. A nothing on the wind. I am so deeply relieved a sort of strangled half-laugh bursts out from my throat, sounding for all the world like a sob. The taxi drivers look at me sideways. For a moment I turn my head and close my eyes fiercely into the wind, where the pricking behind my lids turns into the mizzling air. For the space of a breath I am embarrassed, too: like I should have known all along, like the worry that's been pulsing through my days has been the grossest self-indulgence. *I knew it* though mixes with a very peculiar *I did not know it at all*; and like the mountain there is this beating-heart *could have been, could have been, could have been.*

The laws of large numbers tell me never to put too much faith in chance. But for now I am holding fast to gratitude, to grace.

Four days later my period comes, and I am, I estimate, ninety-six percent thankful.

That summer I go West. I visit Jonathan. I drag him camping with me, out at King's Canyon. He gets altitude sickness and we get lost for a good portion of the afternoon when we wander off-trail and mistake one lake for another. It seems, for a couple of hours, like we may be stranded out there, without our packs or food or shelter and night coming on fast at ten thousand feet. We find our way back, though. At the top of a mountain pass, here in these western mountains where I have never been, we set up camp, the brown stark bowls of snow-tipped peaks rising all around us.

That night he sleeps. The moon casts crosshatched concentric rings through the netting of the tent door. The night is colder and windier than the night before. Still, I think—later, I'd like to look at the stars. A litany of private blessings. My foot does ache, a little. I worry about this. Like clockwork, the ache. But it's mild yet. Protesting precisely as much as is called for and no more.

I look at Jonathan. I watch his breath rise and fall. I'll be damned if I think we've made any sense of whether we make any sense. Probably, I think, we don't. But what the hell.

~≈ ~≈ ~≈

Jessica Wilson is a native Northeasterner currently living in the Midwest while scheming ways to travel to the opposite side of the globe. She holds an MFA in nonfiction from the University of Iowa, and is working on a memoir about landscape, performance, and long-distance walking trails. Her work has appeared in Alligator Juniper, *the* Daily Palette, Glimpse Magazine, *the* Seneca Review Online, *and* New Fairy Tales.

Acknowledgme

"The Offer that Refused Me" by Marcia DeSanctis published with permission from the author. Copyright © 2012 by Marcia DeSanctis.

"Rabies" by John Calderazzo published with permission from the author. Copyright © 2012 by John Calderazzo.

"Vanishing Vienna" by Peter Wortsman first appeared in *Grand Tour, The Journal of Travel Literature*, Summer 1997, and thereafter in abridged form for his E-book *The Urban Nomad - Vienna*, published by New Word City 2011. Published with permission from the author. Copyright © 2011 by Peter Wortsman.

"Mysterious Fast Mumble" by Bruce Beger published with permission from the author. Copyright © 2012 by Bruce Berger.

"Spirals: Memoir of a Celtic Soul" by Erin Byrne published with permission from the author. Copyright © 2012 by Erin Byrne.

"Chip off the Old Bloc" by David Farley first appeared in *AFAR Magazine*, May/June 2011. Published with permission from the author. Copyright © 2011 by David Farley.

"Seal Seeking" by Anna Wexler published with permission from the author. Copyright © 2012 by Anna Wexler.

"Precious Metal: Me and My Nobel" by Tom Miller published with permission from the author. Copyright © 2012 by Tom Miller.

"The Babushkas of Chernobyl" by Holly Morris, originally published as "A Country of Women" in *MORE Magazine*, published with permission from the author. Copyright © 2012 by Holly Morris.

"How I Got My Oh-la-la" by Colette O'Connor published with permission from the author. Copyright © 2012 by Colette O'Connor.

"The Ghost of Alamos" by Lavinia Spalding published with permission from the author. Copyright © 2012 by Lavinia Spalding.

"Engagement Ceremony" by Carol Severino published with permission from the author. Copyright © 2012 by Carol Severino.

"My Black Boots" by Juliet Eastland published with permission from the author. Copyright © 2012 by Juliet Eastland.

About the Editors

James O'Reilly, publisher of Travelers' Tales, was born in Oxford, England, and raised in San Francisco. He's visited fifty countries and lived in four, along the way meditating with monks in Tibet, participating in West African voodoo rituals, rafting the Zambezi, and hanging out with nuns in Florence and penguins in Antarctica. He travels whenever he can with his wife and their three daughters. They live in Palo Alto, California, where they also publish art games, books, and apps for children at Birdcage Press (birdcagepress.com).

Larry Habegger, executive editor of Travelers' Tales, has visited almost fifty countries and six of the seven continents, traveling from the Arctic to equatorial rainforests, the Himalayas to the Dead Sea. In the 1980s he co-authored mystery serials for the *San Francisco Examiner* with James O'Reilly, and since 1985 has written a syndicated column, "World Travel Watch" (WorldTravelWatch.com). Habegger regularly teaches travel writing at workshops and writers' conferences, is a principal of the Prose Doctors (prosedoctors.com), and editor-in-chief of Triporati.com, a destination discovery site. He lives with his family on Telegraph Hill in San Francisco.

Sean O'Reilly is editor-at-large for Travelers' Tales. He is a former seminarian, stockbroker, and prison instructor who lives in Virginia with his wife and their six children. He's had a lifelong interest in philosophy and theology, and is the author of *How to Manage Your DICK: Redirect Sexual Energy* *and Discover Your More Spiritually Enlightened, Evolved Self* (dickmanagement.com). His travels of late have taken him through China, Southeast Asia, and the South Pacific; his most recent non-travel project is redbrazil.com, a bookselling site.